What Do We Owe Other Animals?

Philosophers Bob Fischer and Anja Jauernig agree that human society often treats animals in indefensible ways and that all animals morally matter; they disagree on whether humans and animals morally matter equally. In *What Do We Owe Other Animals?: A Debate*, Fischer and Jauernig square off over this central question in animal ethics. Jauernig defends the view that all living beings morally matter equally and are owed compassion, on account of which we are also obligated to adopt a vegan diet. Fischer denies that we have an obligation to become vegans, and argues for the position that humans morally matter more than all other living creatures.

The two authors each offer a clear, well-developed opening statement, a direct response to the other's statement, and then a response to the other's response. Along the way, they explore central questions, like: What kind of beings matter morally? What kind of obligations do we have towards other animals? How demanding can we reasonably expect these obligations to be? Do our individual consumer choices, such as the choice to purchase factory-farmed animal products, make a difference to the wellbeing of animals? The debate is helpfully framed by introductions and conclusions to each of the major parts and by smaller introductions to each of the sub-sections. A Foreword by Dustin Crummett sets the context for the debate within a larger discussion of sentience, moral standing, reason-guided compassion, and the larger field of animal ethics.

Key Features

- Showcases the presentation and defense of two points of view on the moral worth of non-human animals
- Provides frequent summaries of previously covered material
- Includes a topically-organized list of Further Readings and a Glossary of all specialized vocabulary

Anja Jauernig is Professor of Philosophy at New York University, working in the history of European modern philosophy (seventeenth to nineteenth century), aesthetics, and animal ethics. Her book on Immanuel Kant's theoretical philosophy, *The World According to Kant—Appearances and Things in Themselves in Kant's Critical Idealism* (Oxford University Press), was published in 2021.

Bob Fischer is Associate Professor of Philosophy at Texas State University, a Research Manager for Rethink Priorities, and Director of the Society for the Study of Ethics and Animals. He has written and edited several books about animal ethics, including, *Animal Ethics—A Contemporary Introduction* (Routledge, 2021).

Little Debates About Big Questions

About the series:

Philosophy asks questions about the fundamental nature of reality, our place in the world, and what we should do. Some of these questions are perennial: for example, *Do we have free will? What is morality?* Some are much newer: for example, *How far should free speech on campus extend? Are race, sex and gender social constructs?* But all of these are among the big questions in philosophy and they remain controversial.

Each book in the *Little Debates About Big Questions* series features two professors on opposite sides of a big question. Each author presents their own side, and the authors then exchange objections and replies. Short, lively, and accessible, these debates showcase diverse and deep answers. Pedagogical features include standard form arguments, section summaries, bolded key terms and principles, glossaries, and annotated reading lists.

The debate format is an ideal way to learn about controversial topics. Whereas the usual essay or book risks overlooking objections against its own proposition or misrepresenting the opposite side, in a debate each side can make their case at equal length, and then present objections the other side must consider. Debates have a more conversational and fun style too, and we selected particularly talented philosophers—in substance and style—for these kinds of encounters.

Debates can be combative—sometimes even descending into anger and animosity. But debates can also be cooperative. While our authors disagree strongly, they work together to help each other and the reader get clearer on the ideas, arguments, and objections.

This is intellectual progress, and a much-needed model for civil and constructive disagreement.

The substance and style of the debates will captivate interested readers new to the questions. But there's enough to interest experts too. The debates will be especially useful for courses in philosophy and related subjects—whether as primary or secondary readings—and a few debates can be combined to make up the reading for an entire course.

We thank the authors for their help in constructing this series. We are honored to showcase their work. They are all preeminent scholars or rising-stars in their fields, and through these debates they share what's been discovered with a wider audience. This is a paradigm for public philosophy, and will impress upon students, scholars, and other interested readers the enduring importance of debating the big questions.

Tyron Goldschmidt, Fellow of the Rutgers Center for Philosophy of Religion, USA
Dustin Crummett, University of Washington, Tacoma, USA

For more information about this series, please visit:
https://www.routledge.com/Little-Debates-about-Big-Questions/book-series/LDABQ

What Do We Owe Other Animals?

A Debate

Anja Jauernig and
Bob Fischer

Routledge
Taylor & Francis Group

NEW YORK AND LONDON

Designed cover image: © Getty Images

First published 2024
by Routledge
605 Third Avenue, New York, NY 10158

and by Routledge
4 Park Square, Milton Park, Abingdon, Oxon, OX14 4RN

*Routledge is an imprint of the Taylor & Francis Group, an
informa business*

ISBN: 978-1-032-57958-0 (hbk)
ISBN: 978-1-032-57957-3 (pbk)
ISBN: 978-1-003-44182-3 (ebk)

DOI: 10.4324/9781003441823

Typeset in Sabon
by KnowledgeWorks Global Ltd.

Contents

6. **Second Reply to Anja Jauernig**   **214**
    BOB FISCHER

Foreword

Dustin Crummett

The authors of this book *agree* that humans treat animals in morally indefensible ways. So do nearly all ethicists who study this topic, including me. That's notable: philosophers aren't exactly known for agreeing on much. Further, it's not just that our treatment of animals is indefensible only in isolated cases, like when someone is arrested for animal cruelty. It's indefensible in a systematic way. This book talks mostly about factory farms. Factory farming is the form of mistreatment of animals to which you, the reader, are most likely to be intimately related. You probably consume the products of factory-farmed animals multiple times every day. And factory farming may also be the single worst way that anyone has ever mistreated animals. Many of the things done to animals on factory farms as standard procedure would literally be considered torture, if they were done to human beings. And *tens of billions* of animals are factory-farmed every year, a figure many times the number of human beings in the world. (Unfortunately, chickens are both treated the worst and raised in by far the greatest numbers in this system. If you want to do something about all this but are not ready to become a complete vegan, giving up chicken and eggs might be the best place to start, followed by fish and shrimp.) All this, Anja Jauernig and Bob Fischer and I and nearly all ethicists agree, has to stop.

But this book is supposed to contain a *debate*. What are the authors debating, if they both agree that human society treats animals in indefensible ways? What they're debating is exactly *how* bad our treatment of animals is, and *what you need to do about it*. Here, they take positions which are radically different from one another, and from most animal ethicists.

Their differences follow, in part, from differing philosophical methods. Anja Jauernig has relatively little faith in our ordinary, commonsense beliefs about animal ethics. Maybe they are biased or poorly thought-through, and it is suspiciously convenient for us that we are typically inclined to think we are the most morally important beings in the world. (We *would* think that, wouldn't we?) So if her philosophical arguments have conclusions which radically contradict what we ordinarily think, Jauernig is not too bothered by this. Bob Fischer, on the other hand, begins with concrete, commonsense claims about what we should do. He is willing to hold onto these, even if they turn out to be puzzling in light of philosophical reflection. For Fischer, abstract philosophical principles which conflict too strongly with these concrete judgments are likely to be wrong.

These approaches lead Jauernig to a position which is *more* radical than that of most animal ethicists, while leading Fischer to a position which is *less* radical than that of most animal ethicists. I will describe what I take the dominant position in animal ethics to be, and then describe how Jauernig and Fischer each depart from it. I am myself sympathetic to something in the neighborhood of this dominant position (which is not to say that I agree with every bit of it).

We can begin discussing the dominant position by considering the question of *moral standing*. Roughly, having moral standing means that you count morally, that we have moral reasons to do things *for your sake*. (I should not hit you. This is at least partly because of the harm it would do to you. I should not hit you *for your sake*. It may be that I should not hit some rock, if the rock is important to you for some reason. But it's not true that I shouldn't hit the rock for *its* sake. I shouldn't hit it for *your* sake. You have moral standing; the rock doesn't.) It seems obvious to most of us that at least some non-human animals have moral standing: you wrong a dog if you torture it, say.

Most animal ethicists are sympathetic to the idea that *sentience* is what grants moral standing. Sentience is defined as the ability to experience pleasure and pain, or sometimes more broadly as the ability to have conscious experiences of any sort. We are sentient; dogs are sentient; there's controversy about insects; plants almost definitely aren't. So on this view, we, dogs, and maybe insects, but not plants, have moral standing. I think sentience is the right cutoff. I say the ability to have conscious experiences, the possession of a first-person perspective on the world, is what makes you some*one*, rather than some*thing*. I say that's what makes it possible to wrong you or the dog or (maybe) the insect, but not the rock.

We can next discuss moral *status*. Among the beings with moral standing, moral status concerns *how* morally important an individual is. Most people think that both humans and dogs have moral standing, but that the human has a *higher* moral status than the dog. The human, somehow, is inherently more important morally. But ethicists have long known that it is very difficult to find any kind of credible explanation for how this could be the case. The most commonly-raised problem is that it's very difficult to find a property to serve as the explanation which is (i) possessed by all and only humans, and (ii) also seems like it could affect moral status. For instance, some people think humans are more morally important because we are *rational*. But it isn't clear that all humans *are* rational: there are babies, for instance. So many animal ethicists endorse *status egalitarianism*, the view that all individuals with moral standing have the same moral status.

This does *not* mean they think that if, say, a person and a dog are drowning and there is room for only one in the lifeboat, then you should just flip a coin. Rather, they generally think there are other differences that explain why you should save the human. For instance, it may be that humans generally lose more from death than dogs do. We live longer than dogs, have richer experiences, have many plans about the future which will be frustrated by death, etc. If the interests of humans and dogs are, all else equal, equally important, it may still be that we have a *stronger* interest in being saved than the dog does. That might justify saving us.

Still: if animals have anything above an *incredibly trivial* degree of moral status, as they seem to, then our treatment of animals is incredibly bad. Perhaps (as Jauernig thinks) it is one of the worst things humans have ever done, up there with the great historical atrocities. Most ethicists think you have an obligation not to partake in this treatment. They think, for instance, that at least if you can do so while still meeting your needs, as most of us can, then you should refrain from consuming factory-farmed products, and perhaps should eat a vegan or a mostly vegan diet more broadly.

Jauernig's position is more radical. First, it goes further than the sentience criterion. She thinks that *all* living things have a good of their own. For instance, a flower could be helped, in the morally relevant way, by getting water, or harmed by not getting enough. And she thinks this is sufficient for moral standing. Accordingly, she thinks that not *only* animals have moral standing, but also, say, plants and bacteria. And she endorses status egalitarianism, so that we, dogs, plants, and bacteria all have the *same* moral status.

Further, Jauernig rejects the usual case for saving the human over the dog. Among other things, Jauernig is skeptical of our ability to make wellbeing comparisons between species, and so to say that humans are really better-off than dogs. She thinks it may be that we should save the human because we have some special relationship with our fellow humans (just like, say, maybe you should save your own child over someone else's child, even though objectively they are equally important). But she also thinks it may be that we *don't* have decisive reason to save the human over the dog. Perhaps, she thinks, that is a mere prejudice on our part.

Ultimately, Jauernig believes that the moral equality of all living things entails that we should behave towards them with "reason-guided compassion" which seeks to help and not harm them. It is easy to see how this might rule out factory farming. However, we may worry that it rules out *too* much, and Jauernig considers whether her position is too "demanding." If plants are equal in moral status to us, then even vegans are not in the clear. She suggests that we might attempt to sustain ourselves in ways that cause minimal harm even to plants, such as by eating fruit. But she also worries that it may really turn out that we are morally obligated to starve ourselves. We may not be very *blameworthy* for doing what we need to do to survive: it's perfectly *understandable*. But still, she thinks, it may be wrong.

My own view—and I think most animal ethicists will agree with me here—is that the idea that we might be morally obligated to starve ourselves to avoid harming plants is *so* implausible that it shows that something must have gone wrong with the reasoning that led to it. From that point of view, what I've called the dominant view looks better. The sentience criterion implies that we do not need to worry about plants at all, since they have no experiences or feelings. Some animals are harmed even in the process of making vegan foods (e.g., they are caught by harvesting machines). But while you should *minimize* this harm, harming some animals is okay if necessary to stay alive, since your interest in continued life is so much stronger. Of course, Jauernig, with her low view of commonsense intuitions, will not be moved by appeals to the intuitive implausibility of her conclusion. So that returns us to the question of philosophical methodology.

Bob Fischer, meanwhile, defends a very different position. He accepts that all sentient beings have moral standing, and even accepts that animals have a decent degree of moral status. Accordingly, he accepts that factory farming is very bad, and tells us he would end it if he could. However, he does not think you are obligated to go vegan, or even to refrain from buying factory-farmed products. It is *good* if you do, he thinks, but you don't *have* to if you don't want to.

Here's why. Fischer thinks the burden of proof is on the person who claims something is morally forbidden. If someone tells you you're not allowed to do something, it's their responsibility to give a convincing argument as to why. But Fischer is not convinced by the two main arguments for the conclusion that buying factory-farmed products is wrong. One of these arguments claims that you seriously harm animals by buying these products—harm them far more than you benefit from the purchase. But Fischer doubts this is true, since he doubts that your purchase actually affects how many animals are factory-farmed. Production quotas on factory farms are set with an eye towards large-scale trends, and Fischer thinks it is incredibly unlikely that any one individual's decision will make any difference. (This is called the "causal impotence problem.")

The other argument claims that it is wrong to be complicit in "especially heinous wrongdoing." For instance, it might be wrong to join the Mafia, even if they would commit all the same crimes without you. But Fischer does not think this argument works, either. We are complicit in *many* unjust practices when we buy things, from unjust labor practices to environmental harm to … It is good, of course, to avoid this when we easily can, but demanding that we avoid any complicity with unjust harms is just asking too much. We would have to withdraw from society altogether. And while there may be some sorts of very direct complicity—like working for the Mafia—which we should avoid, Fischer thinks the kind of complicity involved in purchasing factory-farmed products is not quite like that, for various reasons he provides.

Still: if factory farming is among the worst things humans have ever done, you might think there has to be *some* compelling argument against supporting it. And Fischer agrees that, if status egalitarianism is true, factory farming is among the worst things humans have ever done. However, Fischer thinks status egalitarianism is false. He does not offer any *explanation* of what makes human interests more important than those of animals. In fact, Fischer *agrees* with Jauernig that we have no plausible explanation. However, he thinks status egalitarianism has such radical implications (e.g., maybe we'd need to grant animals citizenship) that *something* has to be wrong with it. Here we can see methodological differences arising again. Where Jauernig is willing to overturn commonsense beliefs about what we should do when they conflict with what she takes to be our best philosophical theories, Fischer holds onto these beliefs despite having no theoretical explanation of how they could be correct.

And here is another important methodological point. Fischer supposes that the burden of proof is on the person who thinks you are obligated to refrain from buying factory-farmed products. But I would be inclined to instead suppose that, if you want to do something that *could* be extremely wrong, and if there are no strong moral reasons *to* do it, the burden of proof is instead on *you* to show that doing it is sufficiently unlikely to be wrong. (This is a version of what is sometimes called the "precautionary principle," which Jauernig also defends.) E.g., if we're demolishing a building and we haven't checked whether anyone is inside, and you want to go ahead and blow it up so you can get home for dinner, it seems to me that the burden is on you to show that it's sufficiently unlikely that anyone is inside.

Supporting factory farming could be extremely wrong, and for those of us who can survive without it, there is no moral reason to support it of anywhere near comparable strength. So perhaps the burden is on Fischer to show that the arguments for an obligation to abstain from factory-farmed products *definitely* fail. And I'm not at all sure they do. The causal impotence problem is hotly debated by philosophers and economists; there is some reason to think you really do make a causal difference to how much factory farming happens. And even someone sympathetic to Fischer's arguments against status egalitarianism might be worried by our inability, even after much searching, to find a plausible explanation of what gives humans a higher moral status. So it seems to me that we should err on the side of avoiding factory-farmed products, and this makes me skeptical of Fischer's conclusion.

In any event, both of these methodological issues are discussed by the authors in their replies to each other. Speaking of which: so far, I have only described the opening statements, and I have simplified many things even in those. Much more happens, but that's what the rest of the book is for. Suffice to say that both authors defend bold proposals, ones which condemn ordinary practices while also differing from one another and from most ethicists, and that the differences between these authors flow partly from what might otherwise seem to be sterile and abstract differences about how to do philosophy. I hope that readers will gain important tools to think both about animal ethics and about philosophical questions more broadly.

Factory Farming

Things to Know Before We Start

Our task here is to have a debate about what we owe other animals, not to review how badly animals are treated by humans. But animals are treated badly indeed—especially in so-called "concentrated animal feeding operations" (CAFOs), better known as factory farms. Of course, animals are mistreated elsewhere too: in laboratories, zoos, circuses, fur farms, and puppy mills, to mention only a few other places. But factory farms deserve special attention both because of their enormous scale, involving billions of animals each year, and because this book includes, among other things, an exchange about the permissibility of purchasing factory-farmed products.

Here are three examples of standard practices on these farms:

- Producers castrate male cattle (bulls) for several reasons: for the sake of the taste of the meat, to reduce aggression, and to prevent mating, as cattle are not separated by sex. Most producers do not use any anesthetics to relieve the pain that this involves. There are two main methods of castration: the Burdizzo clamp and the band method. With the Burdizzo, producers crush the spermatic cords one at a time, cutting off the blood supply. This method causes less pain in the long run, but also requires more training to employ correctly, which means that errors can be particularly painful for the animals. Even when

DOI: 10.4324/9781003441823-1

things go well, there are signs of stress and discomfort for more than two months post-procedure. The band method slows the blood supply rather than cutting it off entirely, but eventually causes the testes to die as well. However, it causes more lasting pain, as evinced by signs of stress and discomfort for nearly three months. Other than slaughter, being castrated is probably among the most painful events in a male cattle's life.

- For the last 50 years, most female pigs (sows) in the US have spent their pregnancies in gestation stalls. Gestation stalls are metal pens just wider and longer than the bodies of the animals they house; so, pigs are unable to turn around for that entire period. Producers use stalls because they improve reproductive performance: they get more pregnancies per barn (because it is easier to ensure conception) and more piglets surviving per litter (because sows cannot roll over on them). Stalls also make life much easier for producers, as the orderly rows make it convenient to feed and monitor the animals. However, their use means that the pigs spend the bulk of their lives in intense confinement. Pigs are highly social, like to root, and have a strong desire to build nests during their pregnancies. All those impulses are entirely thwarted in stalls.

- Producers want chickens to reach slaughter weight as quickly as possible. So, they breed chickens for fast growth and structure the environment to maximize weight gain. Breeding for fast growth makes chickens subject to a host of welfare problems. For instance, their large muscle mass and short legs compromise their ability to walk. Instead of recognizing this as a serious problem, the National Chicken Council (NCC), an industry trade group, has lowered its welfare standards accordingly. In the guidelines it uses for audits, producers get the best score on chickens' gait if the chickens can walk five feet, with no requirement that the gait be normal. The environment is also designed to get chickens to eat as much as they can. Chickens eat more, and so grow faster, when it is light. So, producers are incentivized to keep the lights on all the time, even though this is stressful for the birds. Chicken houses are supposed to provide darkness for four hours a day, but this darkness may be provided in one-hour increments. Chickens' eyes probably do not develop normally in such environments, and compromised vision may explain why some birds die long before they reach slaughter weight: they simply were not able to find food.

These examples only begin to illustrate the many ways in which factory farming harms animals. We could list many other equally unsettling examples. Moreover, we have chosen familiar "barnyard" animals—cattle, pigs, and chickens—but humans raise plenty of other animals for food, including carp, salmon, shrimp, goats, sheep, turkeys, and geese. It is important to have a working knowledge of standard farming practices to understand what is at stake in our debate, and to join in. So, if you are not familiar with these practices yet, please fill this gap in your education right now. In this context, a picture truly says more than a thousand words, and so one way for you to get better informed is to watch some of the following videos (listed in the order of ascending length):

- Farm to Fridge (2011), directed by Lee Iovino, commissioned by Mercy for Animals, 12 mins.
- Food Inc. (2009), directed by Robert Kenner, 93 mins.
- Dominion (2018), directed by Chris Delforceutes, 119 mins.

These videos are not for the faint of heart. If you prefer a less graphic account, please check out some of the following sources:

- Beauchamp, Tom L., Orlans, Barbara F., Dresser, Rebecca, Morton, David B., and Gluck, John P. *The Human Use of Animals* (New York/Oxford, Oxford University Press, 2008, 2nd edition).
- Kirby, David. *Animal Factory* (New York, St. Martin's Press, 2010).
- Fischer, Bob. *Animal Ethics—A Contemporary Introduction* (New York, Routledge, 2021), Chapter 6 ("Animal Agriculture and Aquaculture").

Opening Statements

Chapter 1

Opening Statement

Anja Jauernig

Contents

1 Introduction

1.1 *Why Our Debate Question Matters*

The history of our species is not an unqualified success story. Humans have committed uncountable moral crimes throughout their existence on this planet: expansionist wars; colonialism; genocide; oppression, exploitation, and discrimination of their fellow

DOI: 10.4324/9781003441823-3

humans on grounds of gender, race, religion, sexual orientation, and socio-economic class; and the list goes on. Given this historical evidence, one could be excused for concluding that we are a lost cause, morally speaking.

On the other hand, there have also been some glimmers of hope that the incurable optimists among us might want to count as signs of overall moral progress. In the age of Enlightenment, ideas of equality, personal liberty, and religious toleration started to gain wider currency. This is reflected in the famous line in the US Declaration of Independence that the undersigned "hold these truths to be self-evident, that all men are created equal, that they are endowed by their Creator with certain unalienable Rights, that among these are Life, Liberty and the pursuit of Happiness." Ever since the Enlightenment, activists of various kinds have been fighting for the realization of these ideas. These efforts coagulated in several mass movements in the nineteenth and early twentieth century, including the political upheavals that swept through Europe in 1848, the abolitionist movement, the labor movement, and the first wave of the women's rights movement. These movements gained several important victories, such as the abolition of slavery and the right for women to vote in many countries all over the world. The fight for equality continued into the later parts of the twentieth century in the form of the civil rights movement in the 1950s and 1960s, the second wave of the women's rights movement in the 1960s and 1970s, and the LGBT rights movement in the 1960s, 1970s, and 1980s. And further victories were won too, such as the passing of the Civil Rights Act in the US. So, I think it is fair to say that, at least in certain respects, there has been moral progress.

To be sure, a lot of work remains to be done to achieve a situation in which our practices and institutions fully reflect the truths that struck the US founding fathers as self-evident. The battle for equality of all people continues to the present day, as evidenced in more recent movements such as #MeToo and Black Lives Matter. Also, arguably, some ideologies that grew out of further developments of Enlightenment ideas can hardly be entered into the annals of moral progress. This includes the ideology embodied in unchecked free-market capitalism with its single-minded focus on the maximization of productivity, efficiency, and consumption, an ideology that played a significant role in leading us to the brink of an impending climate catastrophe and to the torture of millions of animals in the food industry. But despite these later disfigurations, the Enlightenment produced some unquestionably salutary ideas, the idea of equality chief among them. And although equality among people is by no means fully realized yet in our political and social institutions, at least the issue is on our collective moral radar screen, so to speak. There is broad consensus among all reasonable members of our society that all of us ought to be regarded as equal and as having the same basic moral rights.

Assuming that we can somehow turn this ship around and escape self-wrought annihilation through climate change, my hope is that the next big step in our moral progress will be a transformation in how we think about our relations with and how we treat non-human animals. (In the following, I will use "animals" as short for "non-human animals.") More specifically, my hope is that we will further expand the circle of equality to include all animals at least in the minimal sense of acknowledging that their claims to life, liberty, and the pursuit of happiness have moral force. This is my hope mainly for the sake of the animals but also for the sake of humanity, for the sake of our souls, as it were. What we, in the industrialized so-called first world, are currently doing to animals—in factory farms, laboratories, entertainment establishments, and other exploitative arrangements—adds up to a moral wrong of mind-boggling proportions. It ranks very high in the worst-moral-evils-of-all-times list. Billions of animals suffer unspeakable terrors at our hands every year, day in and day out. When I imagine future generations or members of possible advanced alien civilizations—or God for that matter, if there is one—surveying these kinds of practices and judging us for them, I feel deeply ashamed of belonging to the human species in this particular period of its history.

The shame is exacerbated by the fact that many of the practices I have in mind—such as factory farming, frivolous invasive experimentation on animals without any medical benefits, and species-inappropriate treatment and confinement as well as trauma-inducing training for purposes of human entertainment—are obviously morally wrong, or so it seems to me. For ease of communication, I will call the practices on this list "atrocities against animals." There are many moral issues in life that are quite tricky and about which reasonable, well-meaning people can disagree. Moral progress with respect to these kinds of issues can be expected to be slow and halting. Atrocities against animals are not among these issues. To pick the most egregious example, factory farming, I find it hard to believe that anybody who is emotionally healthy, minimally reasonable, and not in the grip of some prejudice or seriously misguided theory, and who takes the trouble to really look at what is happening in these places of horror could disagree with the assessment that factory farming is an utter moral disgrace. Moral progress with respect to our treatment of non-human animals is urgently needed and long overdue and, in theory, should be within our grasp given how clearly wrong many of our animal-involving practices are.

There are likely many different reasons why this progress has not happened yet. But one reason that strikes me as central is that our treatment of animals is not on everybody's moral radar screen yet, to stay with the metaphor introduced above. Despite the fact that most people would agree that, say, torturing a kitten for amusement is morally wrong, it seems that many people have not accepted yet that our treatment of animals in general is liable to and calls for moral evaluation. The question whether we owe something to animals, let alone what we owe them, is not a live question to many people—to repurpose William James's useful notion of a live hypothesis.[1] That is, it is not a question that they regard as having relevance for their lives, as something that they need to come to grips with. This makes it easy for people to compartmentalize their relations to animals, treating their pets as family members and cooing over adorable kitten videos on the internet, while not giving a second thought to what happened to the center piece of their dinner before it ended up on their plate. We must change that—if kittens matter morally, so do pigs, cows, and chickens—and, hopefully, this book will make a contribution to this task, however small.

Ignorance is no excuse. One minimal obligation that we all have as responsible consumers is to know where and how the things that we consume have been produced. Do you eat meat, eggs, or dairy products? If you do, and if you purchase these items in ordinary supermarkets or restaurants, you are most likely consuming animal products that originated in factory farms. Anybody who is in that situation ought to know

---

1. See James 1896, 14–15.

what factory farms are and how they operate. Do you know the story behind your breakfast, lunch, and dinner? If the answer is no or not really, you have some homework to do. (And if you think it cannot be that bad, you have no idea.) Suggestions for what to read or watch to remedy your ignorance can be found in the text box "Things to know before we start" at the beginning of this book.

The examples of factory farming and the other mentioned atrocities against animals illustrate that our debate question of what we owe other animals is not merely academic. It is an urgent question with real-life implications that everybody who lives in an industrialized country must face up to. To be sure, many questions in applied ethics have weighty real-life implications, as for example, questions about the permissibility of abortion or physician-assisted suicide. But, apart from the problem of climate change, there is no other serious problem in applied ethics today in which each one of us is as personally, inevitably, and inextricably implicated as in the problems of factory farming and some of the other atrocious practices indicated above. Whether to have an abortion or whether to help somebody end their life with dignity in the face of a terrible illness are questions that arise in extraordinary circumstances, circumstances that many of us hope we will never have to confront. But we all make decisions every day about what to eat, drink, and wear, which toiletries and cosmetics to use, what kind of entertainment to consume, and which companies and industries to support. There is no hiding from the question of what we owe other animals.

1.2 What Exactly Does Our Debate Question Mean?

Different ways of presenting our debate question would be to ask what our moral obligations or duties are *to* other animals or what moral claims or rights other animals have against us. It is important to distinguish the former question from the related but distinct question of what moral obligations we have with *respect to* animals. Beings to whom we owe something are beings who not only can be treated in ways that are morally wrong, but also can be wronged. For example, if I were to trash your bicycle for fun without your permission, I would have acted wrongly, but I would not

have wronged your bicycle. I would have wronged you. I have a
moral obligation with respect to the bicycle, qua your property, but
you are the person to whom I am obligated.

> Saying that we **ought to** do a certain action is another way
> of saying that an action is **morally obligatory** or **morally
> required**, which, in turn, is another way of saying that not
> doing the action is **morally wrong** or **morally impermissible**.
> This also means that an action is **morally permissible** if, and
> only if, it is not morally obligatory not to do the action. Many
> people take the determination of what kind of actions are
> morally obligatory to be one of the central tasks of normative
> ethics.

Some philosophers who hold that we can act in morally wrong
ways with respect to animals deny that we can wrong them. Such
philosophers might agree, say, that setting a dog on fire for fun is
morally wrong but disagree with the claim that doing so amounts
to wronging the dog. For instance, Immanuel Kant famously holds
that we have moral duties only to rational beings. The relevant kind
of rationality that Kant has in mind here is quite sophisticated. It is
a form of practical rationality or **autonomy**, which centrally includes
the capacity to set ends for oneself and act on the basis of reasons.
Since, in Kant's assessment, animals are not autonomous, he concludes that we have no duties to them or, as he also puts it, that we
have no direct duties concerning them.[2] Nevertheless, Kant also
emphasizes that animal cruelty is wrong. The reason for the wrongness, roughly put, is that people who are cruel to animals will
become desensitized to cruelty in general. And being desensitized to
cruelty in general, in turn, will make them more likely to be cruel to
other people, which would be a violation of a direct duty.[3] So, we
can say that we have duties with respect to animals or indirect
duties concerning animals, on Kant's view, but we do not have
duties to them or direct duties concerning them. Our duty not to be

2. See Kant 1785, 4:428.
3. See Kant 1797, 6:443; *Lectures on Ethics*, 27:459, 210.

cruel to animals is a duty to ourselves. Despite his opposition to animal cruelty, Kant's answer to our debate question—what do we owe other animals?—is thus a brief and sobering "nothing."

Immanuel Kant (1724–1804) was a German Enlightenment philosopher with enormous influence in many different areas of philosophy. In ethics, he advocates a reason-based deontological normative ethical theory, that is, a theory that describes what we ought to do in terms of a system of duties that are derived from the nature of rational agency. Kantianism is one of the dominant positions in ethics today.

1.3 Outline of This Opening Statement

In light of these considerations, a first useful step toward answering our debate question is to determine whether animals do belong in the class of beings to whom we owe things and who can be wronged. This question is closely related to the question, perennially popular in the animal ethics literature, whether animals have what is called moral standing or moral considerability, a question that can also be expressed by asking whether animals matter morally.

> **Moral standing (moral considerability):** X has moral standing (is morally considerable) if, and only if, all **moral agents**, that is, all beings who are morally responsible for their actions, (a) have moral obligations to X or (b) are morally obligated to take X's interests into consideration in their moral deliberations.[4]

I address these questions in section 2 and argue that, in virtue of being creatures who have a good for which they strive (in a sense to be spelled out), all animals have moral standing and do belong in the class of beings to whom we owe things.

Once it is settled that all animals have moral standing, a second useful question to address is whether all beings who have moral standing have the same moral status, as one might put it. That is, do

---

4. The reason for the disjunctive formulation of this definition will become clear in section 2.3.

all of them matter equally, morally speaking, or are some of them more equal than others, to use Orwell's memorable formulation, in the sense of mattering more? If it were the case that, although all animals have moral standing, humans have a vastly higher moral status than all other animals, the answer to our debate question, of what we owe other animals, might still turn out to be "practically nothing" or "not much."

The questions whether there is a difference in moral status between humans and animals and, relatedly, whether human lives are more valuable than animal lives are considered in section 3. I defend the position that there is no hierarchy of moral considerability among beings with moral standing, and voice doubts about the meaningful comparability of the values of the lives of members of different species. All beings with moral standing are equal in the sense of morally mattering equally, including humans and animals, and it makes no sense, strictly speaking, to say that human lives are more valuable than the lives of animals.

Taking the arguments from sections 2 and 3 together, I thus arrive at the view that, at the fundamental level, we owe other animals exactly what we owe other humans. What it is that we owe them, is the main question of section 4. My answer is that we owe all beings with moral standing compassion, which entails, minimally, that we appreciate and are moved by two basic moral reasons involving them, namely, the reason not to harm them and the reason to help them in need. I conclude by (a) addressing what I take to be the main objection to this answer, namely, that the moral obligations entailed by it are overdemanding, and (b) briefly spelling out some concrete practical consequences for our treatment of animals implied by it.

One important concrete practical upshot of the proposed account of what we owe other animals is that factory farming and the other noted atrocities against them morally wrong them and thus ought to be terminated. We owe it to the animals to end these practices. I stand by my earlier prediction that the moral wrongness of factory farming will be obvious to any sane person who is not in the grip of some prejudice or misguided theory as soon as she takes an honest look at what is happening in these facilities. Unfortunately, not all sane people are prejudice-free or will voluntarily subject themselves to the tribulations of a fact-finding mission in a factory farm. So, it would be very useful indeed if we also had an argument for the moral wrongness of factory farming up our sleeves that we can present to those who still remain to be convinced. Moreover, as reflective beings and especially as philosophers, we do not only want to know which practices and actions are morally wrong but also understand *why*. This opening statement, *via* its discussion of foundational issues surrounding the question of what we owe other animals, provides the desired argument for and explanation of the moral wrongness of factory farming and similar atrocities against animals.

It is worth noting that the case against factory farming is overdetermined. Its contribution to climate change by way of its significant greenhouse gas emissions also counts strongly against it. For the present discussion, however, I will set this consideration aside. For it may be classified as a prudential rather than moral consideration and at any rate does not support the claim that we owe it to the animals to shut down these industrialized farming operations, which, however, is the claim I want to establish and elucidate.

Our subsequent debate will be partly about some of the foundational issues that are the focus of this opening statement, which Bob also addresses in the second part of his opening statement, in particular the question of whether humans morally matter more than animals, and partly about the practical question of what each one of us is obligated to do individually in the face of the moral wrongness of factory farming, a question on which Bob focuses in the first part of his opening statement.

2 To Whom Do We Owe Something?

2.1 Human Centrism

Who has moral standing or, equivalently, what beings matter morally? For a long time, the default answer to this question, in philosophical circles and society at large, was that all and only humans have moral standing. I will call this view "human centrism."

> **Human centrism:** X has moral standing if, and only if, X is a member of the human species.

Even nowadays, many people still feel allegiance to human centrism and in philosophical discussions it is often designated as the commonsense view.

In my judgment, human centrism is clearly false and perniciously so. Just spend five minutes interacting with a dog and you will agree with this assessment on the strength of the tail-wagging counterexample before you who is trying to entice you to play a game of fetch. But everybody deserves a fair hearing, so let us take a look at how human centrists try to justify or could try to justify their position.

2.1.1 An Intuition-Based Justification of Human Centrism?

Many human centrists, in particular those of a less reflective bend of mind, will be inclined to respond to the justification challenge by saying that it is simply intuitively obvious to them that all and only humans have moral standing. To me, it may seem obvious that my neighbor's dog has moral standing; to them, it is obvious that only humans have moral standing.

I will come back to the dog in a minute, but, before I do, I want to comment on the envisioned strategy of the human centrists to rely on their pre-theoretic intuitions to support their position. The general question of the legitimacy of using intuitions as justificatory grounds in philosophical theorizing is much debated. But I think it is fair to say that, at least with respect to the specific issue at hand (to determine who has moral standing), the intuition-based strategy of the human centrists is highly problematic. While intuitions can be useful as heuristic devices, exclusive reliance on them comes with a serious risk of importing prejudices and biases into one's position, be it one's own personal biases or the biases of one's culture, society, or social group. More specifically, it seems hard to dispute that the following kind of situation should raise a red flag: a great good is to be given to members of some select group, the people who determine who will enjoy the great good belong to group G, they rely on their intuitions for this determination, and the content of these intuitions is that only members of group G are to receive the great good. A situation like that should make us feel very uncomfortable. Think about white males in the eighteenth and nineteenth century relying on their intuitions to determine who can vote in political elections, intuitions to the effect—surprise, surprise—that only white males are to have that privilege. These men did not have to think about it; it was simply inconceivable to them and struck them as obviously ridiculous to allow women or non-white people to participate in a political election. We do not want to make the same mistake as those misguided white guys when deciding who morally matters.

But, you may wonder, did I not also just invite you to rely on your intuitions about dogs to support my view that human centrism is false? Actually, no, I did not. I invited you to *interact* with a dog. For I am confident that, if you are a normally functioning human who is not in the grip of a seriously misguided theory, based on your direct experience with him you will come to see that he matters morally. So, am I suggesting that we all have some mysterious quasi-perceptual capacity that detects moral standing? In some sense, I am suggesting that, except that the capacity is not all that mysterious; it is called "empathy." By empathizing with the dog, we come to appreciate him as a being with interests that can be realized or frustrated, which, in turn, prompts and warrants the judgment that he morally matters. But I am getting ahead of myself. For now, I just want to stress that arriving at the judgment that a particular being has moral standing based on one's personal interactions with it is a very different kettle of fish from arriving at the summary judgment that a whole group of beings do not have moral standing based on nothing but one's potentially biased pre-theoretic intuitions.

2.1.2 The Speciesism Objection to Human Centrism

In order to justify their position, human centrists need to do more than invoke their intuitions. One of the things they need to do, in particular, is answer the speciesism objection that is often launched against them.[5] There are different ways of formulating the speciesism objection, depending on how exactly speciesism is characterized.

Speciesism: Speciesism is discrimination directed against a being or a group of beings on the basis of their species.

The speciesism objection to human centrism:

1. Racism and sexism are morally wrong.

2. Speciesism is just like racism and sexism in all relevant respects.

3. Speciesism is morally wrong. (Intermediate conclusion; from 1 and 2.)

4. Human centrism is a form of speciesism.

5. Human centrism is morally wrong. (From 3 and 4.)

---

5. The *locus classicus* of a version of the speciesism objection is Singer 1975, chapter 1.

Since race and gender are morally irrelevant, discriminating against people on the basis of their race or gender is an expression of a mere prejudice and morally objectionable. Similarly, since species membership is morally irrelevant, discriminating against beings on the basis of their species is an expression of a mere prejudice and morally objectionable. The denial of human centrists that non-human creatures have moral standing is a form of discriminating against them on the basis of their species. Human centrism is thus morally wrong.

2.1.2.1 Reply I: Moral Standing as Grounded in Sophisticated Psychological Capacities

A popular general strategy for replying to the speciesism objection on behalf of human centrism is based on the proposal that moral standing is grounded in the possession of certain sophisticated psychological capacities.[6] There are two variants of this kind of reply. Proponents of the first variant target the intermediate conclusion that speciesism is morally wrong by arguing that the second premise of the objection is false. Speciesism is not just like racism and sexism in all relevant respects. Unlike race or gender, species membership is morally relevant, and discriminating against beings on the basis of their species is neither an expression of a mere prejudice nor morally objectionable, so the reply goes, because all and only humans have the psychological capacities that ground moral standing. Proponents of the second variant admit that speciesism is morally wrong but argue that the premise in line four of the speciesism objection is false. Human centrism is not a form of speciesism, so the reply goes, because, by denying moral standing to non-human creatures, human centrists discriminate against these creatures, not on the basis of their species, but on the basis of their lack of the special psychological capacities that ground moral standing. On either variant of the reply, the speciesism objection fails.

For our purposes, there is no need to try to adjudicate which variant of the reply is preferable. Regardless of which variant they favor, in order to flesh out their reply and make it convincing,

---

6. A prominent example of such a capacities-based view is the Kantian account mentioned in the introduction, to which we will return at various places throughout our discussion.

human centrists must complete the following three tasks: they must
(1) specify what psychological capacities they are talking about,
(2) make the case that these capacities indeed ground moral standing such that all and only beings who have them matter morally,
and (3) show that the capacities in question are indeed possessed by
all and only humans. But this challenge proves to be unmeetable for
human centrists, as we will see in the following.

2.1.2.1.1   WHICH PSYCHOLOGICAL CAPACITIES?

Regarding the first task of specifying the relevant psychological
capacities, the most popular choice of human centrists by far is to
say that moral standing is grounded in the possession of a demanding form of practical rationality, **autonomy**, which is understood
to comprise a host of other sophisticated cognitive capacities such
as theoretical rationality, instrumental rationality (i.e., means-end
rationality), self-consciousness over time, having propositional
attitudes such as beliefs, valuing, setting ends or goals for oneself,
acting in accordance with self-given rules, recognizing other selves,
and communicating, to name but a few.

> **Autonomy criterion for moral standing:** X has moral standing
> if, and only if, X has autonomy.

Autonomy is not the only possible sophisticated psychological
capacity one could cite in this context, but because of its over-
whelming popularity in the literature I will focus on it and treat it
as paradigm example in the following discussion.

2.1.2.1.2   ESTABLISHING A CONNECTION TO MORALITY

The second task, of justifying the claim that the relevant psychological capacities ground moral standing, is the most challenging
one from a philosophical point of view. The challenge is to establish
what these capacities have to do with morality in the first place.
How is autonomy morally relevant? Why is being autonomous special from a moral point of view, while being white or male or having
the ability to fly are not?

In order to provide the desired justification, human centrists
must rely on certain assumptions about the nature and purpose of
morality, if not a specific normative theory. One such assumption,

on which a popular justification strategy is based, is that morality essentially includes a certain reciprocity condition. If morality demands of me to accord moral consideration to you, then morality also demands of you to accord moral consideration to me and *vice versa*.

> **Reciprocity condition of morality:** (i) A has moral obligations to B if, and only if, B has moral obligations to A; and (ii) A is morally obligated to take B's interests into consideration in her moral deliberations if, and only if, B is obligated to take A's interests into consideration in his moral deliberations.

The justification strategy comprises two steps. In the first step, based on the reciprocity condition, it is inferred that all and only moral agents, i.e., beings who are morally responsible for their actions, have moral standing. As noted, a being has moral standing if, and only if, all moral agents have moral obligations to it or are morally obligated to take its interests into consideration in their moral deliberations. The reciprocity condition implies that such a being itself has moral obligations to all moral agents or is morally obligated to take the interests of all moral agents into account. But this means that such a being is itself a moral agent. For only beings who are morally responsible for their actions have moral obligations. In the second step, based on the assumption that all and only beings with autonomy are moral agents—which we will grant for the sake of the argument—it is then concluded that all and only beings with autonomy have moral standing.

Whether this strategy is ultimately successful crucially depends on what can be said in defense of the reciprocity condition. One might try to justify it by appeal to general fairness considerations. If the laws of morality constrain me in what I can do to you, it is only fair that they also constrain you in what you can do to me. Since no lion who wants to kill me would refrain from doing so on moral grounds, it would be an unfair burden on me to expect me to refrain from killing lions on moral grounds if I want to kill them.

One also can find the suggestion in the literature that a certain kind of meta-ethical theory has reciprocity built into it, as it were. This kind of theory includes various forms of Kantianism and **contractarianism**. On this kind of theory, moral laws are understood to be jointly legislated by free rational agents in such a way that they thereby bind themselves to these laws. The basic idea is that moral laws are created through a mutual agreement, convention, or contract among free rational agents, which they enter under certain specific conditions and for particular reasons. The suggested conditions include, for example, (a) a state of nature where everybody is at war with everybody else and life is "nasty, brutish, and short," as on Thomas Hobbes's view, (b) a "kingdom of ends," as on Kant's view, where every member is committed to treating every other as an "end in itself," that is, roughly put, only in ways to which the other would consent if they expressed a view, or (c) an "original position" behind a veil of ignorance where nobody knows what sort of person he is or what place in the resulting society she will occupy, as on John Rawls's view. The reasons for the agreement that have been identified include, for example, (i) self-interest, as on Hobbes's view, which, the parties to the contract reckon, can be realized in an overall better way if they all cooperate in a society, or (ii) the nature of or respect for rational agency, which entails that rational agents treat other rational agents only in accord with principles that can be justified to all of them, as on Kant's and Rawls's view.[7] The suggestion is that, on a theory like this, all parties to the agreement, and only parties to the agreement, are bound by the jointly legislated laws, and all parties to the agreement, and only parties to the agreement, can make claims against each other on the basis of these laws. By adopting one of these theories, one thus gets a justification of the reciprocity condition for free, so to speak, or so the argument claims.

Thomas Hobbes (1588–1679) was an Early Modern English philosopher who is best known for his political philosophy, in particular his social contract theory, and for his defense of materialism, that is, the view that all there is in the world is material, including the mind.

John Rawls (1921–2002) was the most important American political philosopher of the twentieth century. His theory of political liberalism has been immensely influential.

---

7. See Hobbes 1651, esp. chapters 13 and 17; Kant 1785, esp. 4:433–436; and Rawls 1971, esp. chapter 3.

2.1.2.1.3   DO ALL AND ONLY HUMANS POSSESS THE RELEVANT CAPACITIES?

It is not necessary for us to look at any further possible strategies that human centrists might adopt to justify their claim that autonomy or some other psychological capacity grounds moral standing. This is unnecessary, not because the justification strategy just considered is irrefutable (it is not), but because, whatever the chosen capacities and whatever the defense, human centrists will inevitably shipwreck on their third task of having to show that the relevant capacities are possessed by all and only humans.

The problem is that there are *no* psychological capacities at all that are possessed by all and only humans, let alone psychological capacities that are plausible candidates to serve as the grounds for moral standing. There are many humans, as for example, babies and people with severe cognitive impairments, be it due to a genetic or developmental disability, an injury, or some kind of illness, who have no psychological capacities that are not also possessed by various kinds of animals such as dolphins, apes, dogs, or pigs. Indeed, even the weaker claim that membership in the human species is sufficient (but not necessary) for moral standing on account of the fact that being human entails the possession of certain psychological capacities that are sufficient for moral standing, is not defensible. For some humans do not seem to have any psychological capacities whose possession might be proposed as a possible sufficient condition for moral standing, for example, anencephalic human babies (that is, babies who were born lacking parts of the skull and brain).

Note that, apart from causing trouble for human centrism in general, young children and severely cognitively impaired humans also provide a counterexample to the autonomy criterion for moral standing. We regard all of these humans as having moral standing, but they lack autonomy.

2.1.2.1.4   RECIPROCITY RECONSIDERED

Young children and severely cognitively impaired humans also serve as counterexamples to the reciprocity condition and thus cast doubt on the two attempts to justify it sketched above. None of these humans are moral agents. But we do take ourselves to have moral obligations to them and do so without regarding this situation as in any way unfair. Granted, in a case where Karl and Franz are both morally responsible for their actions, it would be unfair if morality made demands on Karl with respect to his treatment of Franz but not on Franz with respect to his treatment of Karl. But if Franz is a young child or a senior with Alzheimer's, while Karl is an unimpaired human adult, we would think that there is something seriously wrong with Karl if he complained about unfairness because he has to treat Franz with moral consideration while not receiving the same consideration in return. The situation is similar to what we find in a legal context: there are many laws that provide protections and benefits to beings who are not themselves legally responsible, including children, cognitively impaired people, and animals.

It is also worth noting that, initial appearances to the contrary notwithstanding, the reciprocity condition is actually not an inevitable consequence of all versions of the contractarian or Kantian kind of meta-ethical theory sketched above. It is correct to say that it follows from the conception of the laws of morality as due to the joint legislation of a group of legislators who thereby bind themselves to the laws that it is the legislators, and the legislators alone, who are subject to these laws. But this conception per se does not imply that the group of beings who receive protection or other benefits on the basis of the legislated laws is necessarily restricted to the legislators.[8] For purposes of illustration, if the sisters Mary and Jane make a pact that whenever one of them gets her hands on some candy, she will share it equitably with their baby brother, the baby brother has legitimate grounds for complaint whenever the sharing does not happen even though he was not party to the agreement and could not have been party to the agreement (given that he is still a baby).

Whether, on a given contractarian or Kantian theory, other beings apart from the legislators enjoy the protection and benefits of at least some laws of morality depends on how the hypothetical situation is characterized in which the contractual agreement happens and what the nature of the legislators and the reasons for the contract are assumed to be. Crucially, we need not accept that in setting up the agreement the prospective legislators are exclusively motivated by self-interest, as Hobbes thinks, or by self-interest and respect for autonomous agents, as on the Kantian and Rawlsian view. An alternative assumption would be that people care not only about their own interests but also about the interests of others, including the interests of children, the disabled, the mentally ill, and

---

8. This point is exploited, to great effect, in Christine Korsgaard's 2018 book, *Fellow Creatures*, in which she defends a largely Kantian account, on which animals have moral standing, despite not being among the legislators.

animals. On this assumption, a more plausible contractarian gene-
alogy of morality would be to think that people banded together
because they understood that, if they formed a society, life would
be better for them *and* the other beings whom they care about and,
accordingly, jointly legislated laws that protect and benefit not only
themselves but also these other beings. Similarly, if one takes respect
for sentience or life as the underlying reason for the joint legislation and characterizes the original position as involving ignorance
about what kind of sentient or living being one is, it stands to reason to expect that the resulting laws will include laws that protect
and benefit all sentient or living beings, not just the ones who are
endowed with autonomy. This is all to say that philosophers who
find the general contractarian or Kantian meta-ethical approach
attractive are not forced to accept the decidedly unattractive reciprocity condition into the bargain.

2.1.2.1.5   POTENTIAL CAPACITIES AND TYPICAL CAPACITIES

At this the point in the dialectic, human centrists who want to defend
themselves against the speciesism objection by endorsing a capacities-
based account of moral standing tend to resort to one of two moves.
The first move is to claim that moral standing extends not only to
beings who actually have the relevant psychological capacities but
also to beings who potentially have them or who have potential versions of them. While it may be true that there are no psychological
capacities that all humans but no animals actually have, there are
psychological capacities that all humans potentially have but no animal actually or potentially has. Case in point: autonomy.

Many people are highly skeptical about this kind of move, and
so am I. First, there is the problem of specifying what exactly it
means to potentially have a capacity or to have a potential capacity.
One suggestion would be to understand the contrast of actual ver-
sus potential as one between present and future. Human babies are
not autonomous at present but they are potentially autonomous or
have potential autonomy, in the sense that, unless a tragic accident
occurs that interferes with their natural development, they will be
autonomous in the future.[9]

---

9. This kind of view underwrites Don Marquis's account of the wrongness of abortion as consisting in that it deprives the fetus of a "future like ours." See Marquis
   1989.

But this suggestion is of no help in the case of severely cognitively disabled humans who neither are, nor ever will be, autonomous. To cover them, it is often suggested to understand potential capacities not as future but possible capacities.[10] The challenge for this suggestion is to pin down the appropriate sense of possibility. One might propose that severely cognitively disabled humans are not actually autonomous but could be autonomous in the sense that they would be autonomous if whatever interfered with their development and caused their impairment had not happened. But that proposal is not going to work for the case of severely cognitively disabled humans whose impairment is not developmental but genetic. Making the relevant sense of possibility even more permissive to include these genetically disabled humans runs the risk of rendering the account useless for human centrists by letting various animals back in the door as well. For example, arguably, a pig could be autonomous in the sense that it would be autonomous if it had been enhanced with some suitable cybernetic brain implants, at least if we assume that this kind of enhancement is identity preserving (that is, that the enhanced pig would still be the same pig, albeit enhanced, as opposed to a distinct, new super-pig).

In this context, an additional challenge and source of considerable awkwardness stems from the fact that many scholars who defend human centrism do not want to extend moral standing to human embryos and early fetuses in order to allow for the permissibility of abortion without having to resort to the argument that the right to life of the fetus is trumped by the right of the mother to withhold gestation assistance.[11] The challenge for these scholars is to identify a sense in which severely cognitively disabled babies have the potential for autonomy but embryos and early fetuses do not. That is a very thin needle to thread.

A second general problem for the move to potential capacities is that it seems to be purely *ad hoc*. The only recommendation in its favor is that it allows human centrists to hang on to their preferred

---

10. Different versions of this kind of proposal can be found, for example, in Wood 1998; and Kagan 2019, 130–145.
11. Human centrists of this kind will want to characterize their position more carefully by saying that moral standing pertains to all and only humans who were born or who are older than x weeks or however else they want to characterize the distinction between abortable fetuses and tiny humans who have moral standing.

defense strategy against the speciesism objection. Taken on its own, the claim that a certain kind of standing that comes with various benefits and is understood to be grounded primarily in the possession of certain capacities also pertains to beings who merely have the potential for these capacities is simply implausible. If you do not know how to swim, you cannot argue your way onto the medley relay of the local swim team by insisting that you have the potential for being a kickass butterflyer.

In the face of these problems with the move to potential capacities, some human centrists try a different tack, move #2, by suggesting that moral standing does not only extend to beings who have the relevant capacities but also to all beings who belong to a species whose members typically or normally have them.[12] All and only humans, including children and cognitively impaired humans, have moral standing because moral standing is primarily grounded in, say, autonomy, to stick with our paradigm example, and the human species is the only species whose members typically or normally have autonomy.

This move is conceptually cleaner and comes with fewer promissory notes than the move to potential capacities—although one would like to hear a bit more about what "typically" or "normally" having certain capacities means. But it does not escape the charge of being both *ad hoc* and plainly implausible from an independent point of view. If your friend Ed is a lovely but extremely scrawny adult Clydesdale horse who can barely pull a wheelbarrow with a cat in it, you are not going to get him on a Budweiser commercial by insisting that he is a member of a breed whose adult members typically have an impressive peak burst power of well over 10 hp.

2.1.2.1.6   THE PROBLEM OF POSSIBLE ALIENS

Another general problem for any of the indicated attempts of human centrists to reply to the speciesism objection by appeal to the claim that moral standing is grounded in certain psychological capacities is the possibility of alien species whose members also have these psychological capacities. These aliens serve as a counterexample to the thesis that being a member of the human species is necessary for moral standing, which is integral to human centrism.

---

12. See, for example, Scanlon 1998, 185–186.

Given all of these problems, I conclude that the strategy of the human centrists to defend themselves against the speciesism objection by arguing that moral standing is grounded in certain sophisticated psychological capacities is doomed to failure.

2.1.2.2 Reply II: Moral Standing as Grounded in Human Social Relations

Another strategy for replying to the speciesism objection that can be found in the literature is built on the idea that human social relations are especially morally important.[13] This kind of reply also comes in two variants, like the reply just discussed. The first variant targets the claim that speciesism is morally wrong by calling into question the alleged similarity between speciesism, on the one hand, and racism and sexism, on the other hand. Unlike race or gender, species membership is morally relevant, and discriminating against non-human creatures on the basis of their species is neither an expression of a mere prejudice nor morally objectionable, so the reply goes, because all and only humans, including children and cognitively impaired people, are members of human society and culture and thus stand in various social relations to one another, which are especially morally important. The second variant targets the claim that ascribing privileged moral status to humans is a form of speciesism. Discriminating against non-human creatures by ascribing privileged moral status to humans is not a form of speciesism, so the reply goes, because the basis for this discrimination is, not the species of the non-humans, but their non-membership in human society and their non-participation in human social relations, which are especially morally important. For example, it has been suggested that, on account of not being part of human society, wild animals such as dolphins do not have a moral right to assistance from us, even in special situations where our help is their only chance for survival, whereas every member of human society has such a right since it is an essential commitment of any society to collectively assist its members.[14]

---

13. See, for example, Diamond 1978; Midgley 1984, chapter 9; Anderson 2004; Kittay 2005; and Williams 2006.
14. See Anderson 2004, 284.

Note that endorsing this reply strategy (on either variant) does not automatically commit one to human centrism. To be sure, the strategy is compatible with human centrism. One way for human social relations to be especially morally important is for them to delineate the group of beings who have moral standing at all. Similarly, one way for humans to have privileged moral status is for them to be the only creatures who have moral standing. But the strategy is also compatible with a weaker view that allows that animals have moral standing, while insisting that humans morally matter more than animals and thus have higher moral status on account of their membership in human society.[15] We will take a closer look at this weaker view under the title of "human exceptionalism" in section 3. Human exceptionalism is cut from the same cloth as human centrism in that it places humans on top of a hierarchy of moral considerability and grants them all sorts of rights, including basic rights, that are denied to other animals.

For present purposes, there is no need for us to try to determine which one of the indicated reply variants is preferable. The following critical remarks equally apply to both. I agree that social relations generate special reasons for action and that some of these reasons are moral reasons. For example, in virtue of the social relations that obtain between a teacher and her students, the teacher has reasons to be responsive to their learning needs and not to abuse her position of authority, reasons that can plausibly be regarded as moral. But I am highly skeptical about the claim that moral status, let alone moral standing, and the possession of basic rights such as the right to assistance in need can legitimately be seen as grounded in social relations.

First, there is the question of how exactly "human society" and "human social relations" are supposed to be understood in this context. Imagine a man who lives by himself on an unknown desert island where he was raised by wolves after having been swept ashore as a tiny baby. It seems very plausible to think that this man has moral standing and the same moral status and the same basic moral rights as all other human beings. But it is difficult to see in what sense this man is part of human society or stands in social relations to other humans. Relatedly, one might argue that there

---

15. Anderson (referenced in the previous note) explicitly endorses only the weaker view.

are several distinct human societies on this planet whose cultural norms and social customs differ considerably. Which one of these is the society whose members have special moral status and the moral rights associated with this status? Or is moral status supposed to be relative to a given society? In either case, it seems to follow that not all humans have the same moral status and the same rights, a consequence that many will consider unpalatable.

Second, even if these problems could be resolved, for example by understanding "human society" very broadly along the lines of "human fellowship," worries also arise about what the proposed view implies for our moral relations vis-à-vis members of possible alien species to whose society or fellowship we do not belong. There are two main worries. The first worry is that if the aliens endorse the proposed account, *mutatis mutandis*, we will have no grounds for complaint when they deny us basic moral rights that they accord to members of their own society and treat us in correspondingly shabby fashion. The second worry is that the proposed account also implies, implausibly, that there would not be anything wrong about denying assistance or other basic rights that allegedly depend on human social relations to aliens even if their psychological makeup and their basic interests were an exact match to ours.

Third, what reason is there to think that a being's membership or non-membership in human society determines its moral status and which basic rights it enjoys or even whether it has any moral standing at all? Merely pointing to the consensus that some human social relations are morally relevant falls far short of establishing this stronger claim. Proponents of the stronger claim may want to justify it by submitting that morality's main or even sole point and purpose is to regulate how humans live together in a community. But this alleged justification is really just a slight re-statement of the claim at issue. We still have not gained any insight into why we should believe that morality is so preoccupied with the human species.

This leads me to the most important shortcoming of the kind of strategy for replying to the speciesism objection presently under discussion. The strategy fails because it is itself speciesist and morally objectionably so. A racist or sexist could avail himself of the very same kind of strategy to defend himself against the charge that his position is morally wrong by replacing "human society/fellowship" with "white society/fellowship" or "male society/fellowship," respectively.

Race is morally relevant, and discriminating against non-white people on the basis of their race is neither an expression of a mere prejudice nor morally objectionable, so the first variant of the reply would go, because all and only white people are members of white society and culture and thus stand in various white social relations to one another, which are especially morally important. Similarly, discriminating against non-white people is not a form of racism, so the second variant of the reply would go, because the basis for this discrimination is, not their race, but their non-membership in white society and their non-participation in white social relations, which are especially morally important. Indeed, real-life racists from not long ago appear to have been expert at using this kind of strategy to legitimize their position by simply denying that non-white people are human in the relevant socio-cultural sense of the term, which, for them, included a restriction to white people. Dehumanization works best as an effective tool of exclusion and oppression in the context of the kind of account of moral status and basic moral rights presently under discussion, where "human" is understood, not in biological terms as a descriptive concept, but in socio-cultural terms as a normative concept. The attempt to ground moral standing or the possession of basic moral rights in special social relations or membership in a special social group is fundamentally misguided. It invites co-option by promoters of exclusion, and provides a hospitable breeding ground for the kind of biases and prejudices that we fought and are still fighting so hard to leave behind in our collective struggles against racism, sexism, and other forms of oppression.

In the foregoing discussion, I have not shown that it is impossible to defend human centrism against the speciesism objection. But our examination of the two most popular strategies for doing so—by way of proposing that moral standing is grounded in (a) certain sophisticated psychological capacities or (b) human social relations—has exposed both of them as resounding failures. So, I think it is fair to say that the prospects for salvaging human centrism look rather dim. In my assessment, human centrism is an ugly, invidious prejudice, which must be eradicated, just like racism, sexism, and other objectionable forms of discrimination on the basis of morally irrelevant features.

Another lesson from the previous considerations that will be useful to bear in mind as we continue our quest of figuring out who has moral standing is that inclusivity is a good-making feature of accounts of moral standing. More generally, when it comes to the question of who matters morally, it is a strongly advisable policy to adopt a course of caution and err on the side of overinclusiveness. All else being equal, there is nothing wrong with treating a being that does not have moral standing as if it did matter morally. But treating a being who has moral standing as if it was a mere thing is a grave moral crime.

2.2 All Sentient Beings Have Moral Standing

A more inclusive criterion for moral standing, which is not encumbered by speciesist prejudices and is quite popular in the animal ethics literature, is the sentience criterion.

> **Sentience criterion for moral standing:** X has moral standing if, and only if, X is sentient.

> X is **sentient** if, and only if, X is capable of experiencing pleasure and pain, understood broadly as positively or negatively valenced states of consciousness.

Like all other criteria, the sentience criterion must be justified; in particular, it must be explained what exactly sentience has to do with morality such that it can legitimately be regarded as demarcating who is and who is not morally considerable.

2.2.1 Welfare Utilitarianism

Endorsement of the sentience criterion is widespread among a certain type of utilitarians, and they are in a strong position to provide the desired justification. I will call these utilitarians "welfare utilitarians." Welfare utilitarianism can be characterized by its central tenet about what kind of actions are morally right.

> **Central tenet of welfare utilitarianism:** An action is morally right if, and only if, it maximizes the total amount of **flourishing** in the world.

In place of "flourishing" I could also have used "welfare," "happiness," or "wellbeing." I will mainly stick with "flourishing" in what follows.

There are several different proposals on the table about what exactly flourishing consists in. Proponents of classical hedonist utilitarianism in the nineteenth century, such as Jeremy Bentham and John Stuart Mill, identify flourishing with pleasure and absence of pain.[16] But people soon started to object that having pleasurable or painful experiences are not the only ways in which the lives of creatures can go better or worse for them.

Jeremy Bentham (1748–1832) was an English philosopher who is widely regarded as the father of utilitarianism.

John Stuart Mill (1806–1873) was one of the most important English philosophers in the nineteenth century. He was especially influential with respect to the development of liberalism in political philosophy. In ethics, he further refined Bentham's utilitarianism by offering a more sophisticated theory of pleasure.

Utilitarianism is one of the dominant positions in contemporary ethics.

This objection to classical hedonist utilitarianism is often made with the help of a thought experiment involving what has come to be known as an **experience machine**.[17] The experiment invites us to imagine having the option of being "plugged into" a machine for life that stimulates our brain to generate experiences, previously chosen by us, that are phenomenally indistinguishable from experiences that are generated in the usual way—where the usual way, roughly speaking, is through interactions of our brain and the environment, mediated by our sense organs. The machine is set up such that, if we were to plug in, we would spend our life enjoying exquisitely pleasurable experiences all day long. Would you plug in? Most people tend to say "no." This result is taken to show that there is more that

---

16. See Bentham 1780/1789; and Mill 1863.
17. See Nozick 1974, 42–45.

we care about than pleasurable experiences, as for example, being able to interact with our friends and family or to exercise our various bodily and mental capacities, and that our flourishing depends on more than how much pleasure and pain there is in our lives. Prompted by these and related considerations, many latter-day welfare utilitarians understand the flourishing of a being to be determined, not by how pleasurable its life is overall, but by how many of its preferences or desires are fulfilled or disappointed, or how many of its interests are realized or frustrated. According to these welfare utilitarians, it is thus not net pleasure but net preference fulfillment or net realization of interests that ought to be maximized according to morality.

2.2.2 Justifying the Sentience Criterion

Regardless of how exactly flourishing is understood, all welfare utilitarians can mount the following straightforward justification of the sentience criterion, which shows that, and how, sentience is morally relevant. From the point of view of welfare utilitarianism, a general characterization of the moral project would be to say that morality's fundamental aim is to make the world a better place by directing us to maximize flourishing in the world. But all and only sentient beings are capable of flourishing, so the argument goes. Therefore, all and only sentient beings have moral standing.

Why are all and only sentient beings capable of flourishing? This is immediately obvious if flourishing is identified with pleasure and absence of pain. But welfare utilitarians who understand flourishing in terms of preference fulfillment or interest realization can also insist that beings are capable of flourishing if, and only if, they are sentient by arguing that beings have preferences and interests if, and only if, they are sentient. The if-direction is uncontroversial. If a being is sentient, it obviously has preferences and interests, namely, minimally the preference for and interest in experiencing pleasure and not experiencing pain. To establish the only-if-direction, the most popular strategy of the utilitarians is to argue that (a) X has preferences and interests only if it matters to X what happens to it and (b) things matter to X only if X is sentient.

Endorsing the central tenet of welfare utilitarianism is compatible with subscribing to a criterion for moral standing other than the sentience criterion. But since all real-life welfare utilitarians of whom I am aware are committed to the sentience criterion, when I talk about welfare utilitarianism in the following, I should be understood as having a welfare utilitarian view in mind that includes the sentience criterion.

2.2.3 The Inclusivity of the Sentience Criterion

In contrast to the autonomy criterion, the sentience criterion does not have the objectionable implication of excluding young children and severely cognitively impaired humans from the realm of moral considerability. And it also includes animals.

There was a time when philosophers believed that animals are not sentient. For example, René Descartes held that animals are just like machines, such as clocks, and thus are incapable of feeling pain or pleasure. Today, there is broad consensus in the scientific community of people who investigate animal minds that at least mammals, birds, reptiles, amphibians, and fish are sentient, a group that includes all farm animals and the vast majority of animals in research labs and animal entertainment establishments. There is less consensus about invertebrates, but for some of them there is some positive evidence that they can feel pain, and for none of them is there conclusive evidence that they cannot feel it. It is impossible to know with certainty what, if anything, goes on in another being's mind, whether this is the mind of a shrimp or the mind of uncle Herbert. So, if in doubt, we should be charitable in all cases.

René Descartes (1596–1650) was a French philosopher, mathematician, and natural scientist. He is generally regarded as one of the fathers of modern philosophy. His work was of seminal importance, in particular, in the fields of epistemology, metaphysics, and the philosophy of science.

2.3 All Beings with a Good Have Moral Standing

I agree that the capacity for flourishing is both sufficient and necessary for moral standing. That is, I concur that X has moral standing if, and only if, X is capable of flourishing. At least, I agree with this claim if (a) flourishing is understood in terms of the realization of interests, and (b) for X **to have an interest** in α is understood to mean the same as for α to be in the interest of X, namely, that X has a stake in α such that X stands to gain or lose depending on what happens with respect to α.[18] Note that having an interest in this sense and taking an interest are not the same thing. For example, little Tommy may not take an interest in the proper working of his kidneys—he may not even know that he has kidneys—but it certainly is in his interest that his kidneys work as they are supposed to. Tommy has a stake in the proper functioning of his vital organs; if they fail at their job, he stands to lose a great deal, eventually maybe even his life. Since the realization or frustration of the interests of a being depend on what happens to it, its flourishing can also be positively or negatively impacted by what happens to it. This is the understanding of interests and flourishing that should be assumed from now on.

I also agree that sentience is sufficient for moral standing. Pain *is* bad for anybody who experiences it, and any sentient creature has a legitimate moral claim not to be caused undeserved pain all else being equal. However, I doubt that sentience is necessary for moral standing, at least if it is taken to entail the sort of consciousness that is familiar to us from our own experience. For I disagree with the claim that only creatures who are sentient in this strong sense have interests and can flourish. Relatedly, although I am happy to allow that a being has interests only if it matters to the being what happens to it, I do not believe that the latter requires the being to consciously process and evaluate what befalls it. There is not the least strain in saying that a butterfly has an interest in not having one of its wings pulled out and that a flower has an interest in being watered, for example, even if we assume that none of them are sentient. The butterfly has a stake in being able to use both its wings, and the flower has a stake in being watered; they stand to gain or lose depending on what happens with respect to the wings and the watering, respectively. Being able to use both its wings positively contributes to the butterfly's flourishing and matters to it, just as being watered positively contributes to the flourishing of the flower and matters to it.

More generally, on my view, all beings who are *striving* in the special way characteristic of all living things have interests and are

---

18. For a similar characterization of interests and further discussion, see Feinberg 1984, chapter 1, sections 2 and 3, esp. 38f.

capable of flourishing, regardless of whether they are sentient or not. What these beings are striving for and what ultimately determines their interests is their good, to put it in Aristotelian terms. In this context, the **good of a being** is to be understood teleologically as determined by what Aristotle calls the being's **characteristic function** or essential activity, which, on my view, centrally includes the maintenance of the being's own existence. More specifically, the good of a being consists in performing its characteristic function, its essential activity, well or excellently. When that happens, the being flourishes. For example, the characteristic function of an (able) elephant, roughly speaking, is to engage in all of the activities that elephants naturally engage in and exercise all the capacities that elephants naturally exercise, such as roaming around in the savanna, foraging for food, eating about 300 pounds of plant matter per day, making and caring for little elephants, maintaining close social relations to other elephants, and so on, activities many of which contribute to keeping the elephant alive. It is in the interest of an (able) elephant to engage in these activities and exercise these capacities, and if she is prevented from doing that, the realization of her good is put in jeopardy and her flourishing is negatively impacted.

Aristotle (384 BCE–322 BCE) was a Greek philosopher who, together with his teacher Plato, is one of the most well-regarded philosophers of all time. He made contributions to and invented many different areas of philosophy. In ethics, he defends a version of virtue theory. He develops his account of the good of a thing in his famous "function argument" in chapter 7 of Book I of the *Nicomachean Ethics*.

This account of flourishing is what is sometimes called an objective list view in that it characterizes what it means for a being to flourish by listing all the things that are objectively good for it. On the present account, the **goods for a being** are whatever things realize its various interests, interests that are objective in the sense of not depending on subjective preferences but being determined by the being's good, which, in turn, is determined by its characteristic function. Similarly, the bads for a being are whatever things frustrate its various interests. (In the following, this is how "being good/

bad for X" is supposed to be understood.) Note that, even though the proposed account does not explicitly mention pleasure and pain in its characterization of flourishing, it can accommodate the commonsense judgment that pain is bad and pleasure is good for sentient beings. Since pain and suffering are natural concomitants of compromised functioning, and pleasure is a natural concomitant of well-functioning, it typically goes against the interests of and thus is bad for sentient beings to suffer or experience pain, and it typically is in the interest of and thus is good for sentient beings to experience pleasure.

It is important to emphasize that not all things that have a telos or function count as having a good for which they strive. For example, a thermometer is designed to perform the function of measuring temperature. But it does not strive for excellent temperature measurements, nor does measuring temperature well qualify as its good. For its function does not include maintaining its own existence; that job falls to a mechanic who is versed in thermometer maintenance. But why is that relevant? Why must the function of a being include the maintenance of its own existence in order for it to count as having a good in the relevant sense? For reasons of space, I cannot provide an exhaustive defense of this claim here but the key thought is that all beings whose characteristic function includes maintaining their own existence have in common that they are engaged in a special overarching project, namely, the project of striving to make as good a living as they can, as one might put it. They are striving to stay in existence and make the best of the time they have got, where what is best in this context is also determined by their respective characteristic function. That these beings are engaged in the special project of striving to make as good a living as they can makes it plausible to say that it matters to them what happens to them and to ascribe the capacity of flourishing to them—regardless of whether they are sentient or not.

So, my favorite criterion for moral standing can be formulated as follows.

> **Good criterion for moral standing:** X has moral standing if, and only if, X is capable of flourishing, which, in turn, is the case if, and only if, X has a good for which it strives.

This criterion classifies all sentient beings as belonging under the scope of moral considerability, but it also includes quite a few more beings. For the present, the boundary of moral considerability delineated by the criterion largely coincides with the boundary between living and non-living things (barring alien-designed non-living beings with a good for which they strive). All living organisms matter morally. This includes all animals, but also plants and members of extra-terrestrial living species, be they smart or dumb, sentient or non-sentient. If in the future we were to design teleologically structured cybernetic organisms that are capable of self-maintenance so that they qualify as having a good for which they strive, these artificial organisms would count as having moral standing as well. The considerable length of this list of beings with moral standing is a good thing. It may be overinclusive but erring on the side of caution is the right policy, given the high cost of mistakenly leaving a being off the list that should be on it.

The good criterion could be justified along utilitarian lines in the same way as the sentience criterion, as sketched above, with the only adjustment concerning the final step about what is required for a being to be capable of flourishing—namely, not sentience but having a good for which it strives. I want to end this section by distancing myself from this utilitarian justification, not only because I am not a utilitarian but also because I am uncomfortable with what moral considerability ultimately comes down to on the utilitarian account.

2.3.1   Moral Considerability Reconsidered

In a standard utilitarian framework, it does not make sense, strictly speaking, to say that we owe anything to anybody. To be sure, all sentient beings have to be taken into account in our utilitarian calculation of which action maximizes flourishing because all of them are capable of flourishing. This is the sense in which all sentient creatures are morally considerable or have moral standing according to welfare utilitarianism. But we do not really owe it *to these beings* to take them into consideration in this way. We must consider them, not on account of themselves, but on account of the flourishing that is contingently contained in them.[19] This is why I said in the

---

19. It is essential to all sentient beings to have some pleasures and pains, but no particular pain or pleasure and no particular amount of pain or pleasure is essential to any sentient being; *ditto* for preference fulfillments and non-fulfillments and interest satisfactions and frustrations.

introduction that the question to whom we owe something and the question of who has moral standing are closely connected, rather than saying that they are equivalent, and why I provided a disjunctive definition of what it means to have moral standing (according to which X has moral standing if, and only if, all moral agents (a) have moral obligations to X or (b) are morally obligated to take X's interests into consideration in their moral deliberations). On the utilitarian view, we have an obligation to take the interests of all sentient beings into consideration in our moral deliberations, but we have no obligations to sentient beings, strictly speaking. Sentient beings are mere "receptacles" for something of intrinsic value, as the point is often presented. What ultimately morally matters is the relevant intrinsic value, that is, the flourishing, not the receptacle.[20]

It is instructive to contrast this utilitarian conception of moral considerability with the Kantian conception. On Kant's view, it does make sense, strictly speaking, to say that we owe certain things to autonomous beings and that we have obligations to them. Autonomy, which is the special intrinsic value at the center of morality on the Kantian account, is not merely contingently contained in these beings; autonomy is one of their essential features. Autonomous beings themselves are intrinsically valuable on account of essentially having a capacity that is intrinsically valuable.

While I am much more sympathetic to the welfare utilitarian criterion for moral standing in terms of sentience than I am to the Kantian criterion in terms of autonomy, my sympathies on the question of how to think about moral considerability lie with the Kantians.[21] To my mind, talk of obligations is ultimately meaningful only if there is somebody to whom one is obligated, and the special status of morally considerable beings is grounded in that

---

20. X is **intrinsically valuable** if, and only if, it is valuable on its own, or in its own right. X is extrinsically valuable if, and only if, X is valuable in virtue of its relation to other things.

21. An account of moral standing that includes both Aristotelian and Kantian elements is also defended by Christine Korsgaard (e.g., in Korsgaard 2018) and Martha Nussbaum (e.g., in Nussbaum 2006). But in contrast to me, they both take sentient beings to have special moral status, despite their Aristotelianism (although Korsgaard hedges her view in this respect). Their accounts also differ from mine (and from each other's) with respect to the question of what sort of claims or entitlements are associated with moral standing, on which more in the following sub-section and section 4.

they themselves are intrinsically valuable in a morally relevant way and not in that they are contingently connected to some intrinsic value that is morally relevant. On my view, all beings who possess a capacity to flourish are intrinsically valuable because this capacity is intrinsically valuable and essential to them. Why is the capacity to flourish intrinsically valuable? In a nutshell, it is intrinsically valuable because it is a necessary condition for the existence of any goods in the world. The basic idea is that, apart from the capacity to flourish itself (which also may be called a good by extension), any good is a good *for* somebody, and there would not be any goods for anybody if it were not for beings with the capacity to flourish.[22]

2.3.2 Justifying the Good Criterion

The claim that beings with the capacity to flourish, understood as beings with a good for which they strive, are intrinsically valuable also provides the basis for a justification of the good criterion, according to which all and only beings of this kind have moral standing. As before, the crucial bit in this justification is to explain what having a good in this sense has to do with morality so that it can legitimately be regarded as the ground of moral standing.

Above I noted that, from a welfare utilitarian point of view, a general characterization of the moral project would be to say that morality's fundamental aim is to make the world a better place by directing us to maximize flourishing in the world. An even more general characterization would be to say that morality's fundamental aim is to make the world a better place by directing us to promote and protect some special intrinsic value. Proponents of various different moral theories can accept this general characterization, not only welfare utilitarians; I am partial to it as well. But there is disagreement between these different groups about what the special intrinsic value is and what promoting and protecting it is supposed to look like. Welfare utilitarians hold that the special intrinsic value is flourishing, which ought to be maximized, while Kantians hold that the special intrinsic value is autonomy, which ought to be respected (in a sense to be explicated in a minute).

---

22. More would have to be said to spell out and defend the argument hinted at in this sentence but, for reasons of space, the hint will have to do in the present context.

It is straightforward to see how one can utilize this conception of morality to justify a specific criterion for moral standing. The conception entails that morally considerable beings are beings who embody or are otherwise closely associated with the special intrinsic value that morality directs us to promote and protect, such as autonomous beings on the Kantian view or beings who are capable of flourishing on the utilitarian view. My justification of the good criterion also proceeds along these lines. But before I can spell out this justification, I must say a bit more about how I understand morality's directive for us to promote and protect some special intrinsic value.

As already noted, I agree with the Kantians that the privileged status of morally considerable beings is grounded in their own intrinsic value, rather than in their contingent association with something that has intrinsic value as on the utilitarian view. So, I agree that the special intrinsic value at the heart of morality is the intrinsic value of morally considerable beings. But I also disagree with the Kantians in various respects. In addition to favoring a different ground of the intrinsic value of morally considerable beings—which the Kantians identify with autonomy and I identify with the capacity to flourish and, more fundamentally, with having a good for which to strive—I also deviate from the Kantian position with respect to the question of how best to understand the promotion and protection of the special intrinsic value to which morality admonishes us. As just mentioned, the Kantians hold that we are obligated to **respect** autonomous beings. They mean by this that we are obligated to recognize these beings as ends in themselves and thus never treat them as mere means but always at the same time as ends. The latter principle, which is Kant's famous **categorical imperative** stated in its third formulation, the so-called formula of humanity, can be rendered more explicitly (if a bit roughly) as saying that we are obligated to never treat autonomous beings in ways to which they would not consent if they expressed a view. I have no qualms about this characterization of respect and agree that it is something that we owe beings with moral standing or, at least, those beings with moral standing who are capable of consent. But I have reservations about an aspect of Kantian respect that emerges only against the wider background of Kant's understanding of moral worth.

On the Kantian view, the moral law is a law based on pure reason that autonomous beings necessarily give to themselves, which finds expression in the categorical imperative. For Kant, an action has positive moral worth if, and only if, it has no other motive than respect for the moral law—where "respect" in this instance is to be understood, roughly, as a feeling of being impressed by the law's normative force. On the Kantian picture, when all is said and done, that autonomous beings ought to be respected is ultimately grounded, not in their intrinsic value, but in the moral law. We ought to respect autonomous beings because we ought to respect the moral law. Concern for other beings on account of their intrinsic value turns out not to be fundamental on the Kantian account of morality. Once we get down to brass tacks, all that matters is the moral law and the duties arising from it.[23]

To my mind, this view gets the order of priority wrong. Concern for intrinsically valuable beings is morally fundamental, and all moral obligations are ultimately grounded in that. More generally, on my view, living a morally decent life is not or at least not primarily a matter of acting based on abstract universal principles, such as the Kantian moral law. Rather, it is a matter of morally appropriately relating to particular beings in concrete situations, beings who are intrinsically valuable on account of being capable of flourishing. It is a complex business to figure out what is required for morally appropriately relating to other possible flourishers in a given situation. To my mind, a crucial necessary element in all situations, in addition to the exercise of practical judgment, is that we show them **compassion**. In this context, compassion for others is to be understood as empathic concern for their flourishing, that is, concern for their flourishing that is based on **empathy**. Empathy here means a capacity for recognizing others as beings with a good for which they strive and for emotionally identifying with them in such a way that what is good and bad for them affects us in the same kind of way as what is good and bad for ourselves.[24] All beings capable of flourishing are essentially vulnerable and dependent on vagaries of

---

23. See, for example, Kant 1785, sections I and II, 4:393–445.
24. Note that the exercise of this basic kind of empathy does not require imagining what it is like to be the other, nor does it require the other to have conscious mental states of the kind familiar to us from our own experience. It is possible to empathize with, say, a plant in the indicated sense, even if we assume that it is impossible for us to imagine what it is like to be a plant and that plants do not have conscious mental states like we do.

fortune not under their control. Showing them compassion is essential to morally appropriately relating to them.

In line with these considerations, on my view, an action has positive moral worth if, and only if, (a) the action is altruistic in the sense that at least one of the motives on which it is based embodies reason-guided compassion for others, and (b) none of the action's motives embodies the desire to negatively impact the flourishing of others or expresses disregard for how it could negatively impact their flourishing. Treating others with compassion entails respecting them and thus not using them as mere means but also goes beyond it in various ways. For example, it places more challenging demands on us as far as helping them in need is concerned (on which more in section 4).

So, here then is my non-utilitarian justification for the claim that all and only beings who are capable of flourishing have moral standing. On my view, the fundamental aim of morality is to make the world a better place by directing us to show all beings who are capable of flourishing compassion. This conception of morality directly entails that all and only beings who are capable of flourishing have moral standing. And since all and only beings who have a good for which they strive are capable of flourishing, as argued earlier, the good criterion is thereby justified as well. Indeed, for the reasons explicated in the preceding sub-section, the stated conception of morality also has the great advantage of not only underwriting the good criterion but also the stronger claim that the group of beings with a good for which they strive is coextensive with the group of beings to whom we owe things, strictly speaking.

The indicated account of morally worthy actions as altruistic actions based on reason-guided compassion agrees well with many people's judgments about what kind of actions are morally praiseworthy. But, of course, much more would have to be said to mount a full-scale defense of the sketched conception of the moral project, for which this essay, however, is not the right place.[25] Apart from putting my cards on the table, the main purpose of outlining this conception in the present context was to indicate a different line of justification for the good criterion for moral standing that does not rely on the assumption of utilitarianism and, moreover, suffices to

---

25. My specific version of an ethics of compassion is inspired by Schopenhauer who may be consulted for further discussion; see Schopenhauer 1841.

establish the even stronger claim that we owe something to X if, and only if, X has a good for which it strives.

> In sum, all and only beings with a good for which they strive have moral standing and are included in the group of beings to whom we owe things and who can be wronged. This also means that we owe things to animals and can do them wrong.

3 Moral Status and How to Value Lives and Interests

3.1 Human Exceptionalism and Status Egalitarianism

All animals, human and non-human alike, have moral standing. But do they all have the same moral status? That is, do they all matter equally from the moral point of view? Many people, especially people who are attracted by human centrism and do not want to admit defeat after having lost the battle over moral standing, answer this question in the negative. Some beings who are morally considerable morally matter more than others, and human beings matter most. I will call this view "human exceptionalism" and the opposing view "status egalitarianism."

> **Human exceptionalism:** There is a hierarchy of moral considerability among beings with moral standing, and human beings are at the very top in that they have higher moral status, or morally matter more, than all other beings.

> **Status egalitarianism:** There is no hierarchy of moral considerability among beings with moral standing.

Endorsing the view that there is a hierarchy of moral considerability is compatible with holding that it is not human beings but some other kind of beings whose moral status is higher than anyone else's. But I am not aware of any scholars who advocate such a position. Also note that in order for there to be a hierarchy of moral considerability, there must be at least two degrees of moral status but there could be more. For example, it might be that humans rank higher than non-human mammals who rank higher than invertebrates who rank higher than plants.

3.1.1   Defining Higher Moral Status

In order for human exceptionalism to stake out a well-defined position, it must be spelled out more explicitly what it means for a being to have higher moral status compared to another. One attempt at doing this, which is unhelpful and misguided but can be encountered in the literature, is to conceive of the moral status of X as corresponding to X's profile of interests, as one might put it, and understand higher moral status as reflecting a richer interest profile. Call this "the interest-profile conception" of higher moral status. On a view of this kind, humans have higher moral status than, say, pigs because, while pigs and humans share some interests, such as the interests in meeting their basic bodily needs and not suffering, humans have many interests that pigs do not have, such as the interest in learning to read and write and being able to participate in political elections.

The interest-profile conception is unhelpful because (a) it renders moral status an idle cog in that it does not add anything to the description of the interests of a being, and (b) on its assumption, it turns out to be trivially true that not all beings with moral standing have the same moral status since, obviously, not all beings with moral standing have an equally rich interest profile. Similarly, since it is fairly uncontroversial that humans have a richer interest profile than animals and plants, on the proposed conception, human exceptionalism turns out to be a disappointingly weak and toothless view, with which pretty much everybody agrees as a matter of course and which is thus not worth making a big deal about.

Furthermore and most importantly, the interest-profile conception fails to capture the thought that beings with higher moral status morally matter more, which, however, is the main thing that a conception of higher moral status is supposed to accomplish. How much a being morally matters depends on whether and to what extent its interests are relevant for our moral deliberations, not on how rich its interest profile is. If all interests of pigs are appreciated and given appropriate consideration and all interests of humans are appreciated and given appropriate consideration, then pigs and humans are treated as mattering equally, despite the fact that humans have a richer interest profile than pigs. By way of an analogy, if everybody leaves the family dinner table satiated and satisfied, everybody was treated as mattering equally with respect to the meal even if mom and dad, due to their richer food interest profile, so to speak, were offered and ate many more dishes than the three-year-old twins. For all these reasons, I will set the interest-profile conception of higher moral status aside.

Another conception of higher moral status, which is widespread in the literature and avoids these worries, defines it in terms of greater weight of **similar interests**. One is hard pressed to find precise characterizations of what it takes for interests to be similar in the relevant sense. But the basic idea seems to be something like the following. All interests (a) belong to a certain type and (b) have a certain magnitude, which is determined by the magnitude of the associated goods/bads. Interest I_A and interest I_B are similar if, and only if, I_A and I_B are of the same type and equal in magnitude. For example, your interest in not suffering to degree x is similar to my interest in not suffering to degree x because these interests are of the same type, namely, the type "not suffering," and equal in magnitude in that the same amount of badness, namely, suffering to degree x, is at stake for both of us. The weights of interest can then be thought of as coefficients by which their magnitude is multiplied. If the coefficient with which the magnitude of my interest in not suffering to degree x is multiplied is 1, while the coefficient with which the magnitude of your interest in suffering to degree x is multiplied is 2, your interest has more weight, namely, twice the weight, compared to my similar interest.

Using this terminology, we can record the following definition of what it means to have higher moral status:

> A has **higher moral status₁** than B if, and only if, there is at least one interest of A that has more weight than a similar interest of B, and there is no interest of B that has more weight than a similar interest of A.

Yet another conception of higher moral status that is sometimes at play in the discussion in the literature ties moral status to the intrinsic value of a being.

> A has **higher moral status₂** than B if, and only if, A's intrinsic value is greater than B's intrinsic value.

In order for this conception to have any practical relevance and capture a sense in which beings with higher moral status matter more from a moral point of view, more details need to be filled in about how this greater intrinsic value manifests itself such that it affects how the being ought to be treated. One way of doing this would be to combine the present conception of higher moral status with the one just discussed and say that the greater intrinsic value of A compared to B manifests itself in that A has some interests that weigh more than similar interests of B, while B does not have any interests that weigh more than similar interests of A. This is a plausible way to proceed, but since it basically amounts to falling back on the conception of higher moral status$_1$, we will not pursue it.

Another option is to go minimal, so to speak, and say that the greater intrinsic value of A compared to B manifests itself in nothing more than that A's existence is intrinsically more valuable than B's existence. This option has the practically relevant implication that the outcome of an action that leaves A destroyed but B intact would be worse than the outcome of an action that leaves A intact and B destroyed, all else being equal. This conception of higher moral status is also not particularly helpful since we might as well directly talk about the different intrinsic values of the existence of different beings, but it at least captures a sense in which beings who have higher moral status morally matter more.

3.2 A Challenge to Status Egalitarianism: The Lifeboat Case

In the dispute with the status egalitarians, human exceptionalists like to appeal to a certain kind of thought experiment that generates intuitions that, they think, strongly tell against their opponents. The thought experiment is a version of the so-called **lifeboat case**. Imagine that the ocean liner on which you are traveling rammed an iceberg and is about to sink within the next two minutes. The water is freezing, so it is certain that whoever does not get on a lifeboat will surely die. You were smart enough to bring your own instantaneously self-inflating lifeboat but the boat is very small and there is only room for one more in addition to yourself. There is nobody on deck with you except a large (friendly) dog and another human. Whom will you save? And whom ought you to save?

According to the human exceptionalists, most people will say that they would and ought to save the human. And I agree that this assessment about what most people would say is probably correct. This kind of thought experiment is presented as a challenge to status egalitarians who hold that animals have moral standing because, so the argument goes, they are committed to the view that one ought to toss a coin to determine who gets saved, putting them at variance with most people's reactions to and intuitions about the case. By contrast, human exceptionalism is in harmony with these reactions and intuitions since it implies that one ought to save the human over the dog. One ought to save the human either because, due to his higher moral status$_1$, his interest in not dying has more weight than the similar interest of the dog in not dying, or because, due to his higher moral status$_2$, his existence is intrinsically more valuable than the existence of the dog.

3.2.1 Reply I: Greater Benefit of Human Lives to Humans

There are different ways in which status egalitarians can reply to this challenge. One frequent response in the literature is to deny the assumption, implicit in the challenge, that the interest in not dying of the dog is indeed similar to the interest in not dying of the human. The interests are not similar, so the reply goes, because their magnitudes are not equal. This point is often made by arguing that the human has more to lose by death than the dog because the lives of humans, thanks to their more sophisticated psychological capacities, are typically of greater benefit to them than the lives of animals are to animals.[26] There is more flourishing in an average human life than in an average animal life. Humans have many additional kinds of good things in their lives compared to animals: deeper and more meaningful social relationships, achievements of long-term projects and ambitions, knowledge, virtue, aesthetic appreciation, creative and artistic pursuits, and so on.

Status egalitarians who hold that all living beings are equal in that their similar interests weigh the same and their existence has the same intrinsic value can thus still agree with the commonsense intuition that one ought to save the human over the dog. On their analysis, one ought to save the human, not because the human's existence is intrinsically more valuable, nor because the human's interest in not dying weighs more than the similar interest of the dog in not dying, but rather because the human's interest in not dying has greater magnitude than the dog's interest in not dying since the human has more to lose by death.

---

26. For different versions of this view, see Mill 1863, 10–16; Singer 1975, 18–21; DeGrazia 1996, 251–254; McMahan 2002, 189–199; and Regan 2004, 324–325.

Given that I am a status egalitarian, I wish I could warm up to this kind of response, but I just find it unconvincing. First, there is the by now familiar kind of trouble that if we modify the example and add that the human on deck is cognitively impaired to such a degree that his psychological capacities are on a par with the psychological capacities of the dog, the indicated response is no longer available. But most people, I reckon, would persist in having the intuition that we ought to save the human over the dog.

Second, it is striking to me that, in this kind of discussion, people tend to focus almost exclusively on how much *better* the lives of humans typically are for them, thanks to their sophisticated psychological capacities. This is striking because, if the possession of sophisticated psychological capacities opens up the possibility of additional good things for a being, such as deep love and friendship, achievement of long-term goals, knowledge, and virtue, it also opens up the possibility of additional bad things for it, such as jealousy, betrayal, and bereavement, crushing failures, ignorance, and vice. So, it is not clear to me at all that the lives of humans typically benefit them more than the lives of animals typically benefit them—even if we grant that the flourishing of members of different species can be compared (on which more presently). On the contrary, as far as I can tell, typical people are not really great flourishers.

Third, I am skeptical about the claim that it is generally possible to compare the flourishing of members of different species. The flourishing of a being depends on all the things in its life that are good or bad for it, that is, all the things in its life that are in or contrary to its interests. Accordingly, whether the comparison of the flourishing of members of different species makes sense depends on whether the goods and bads for them can be compared. Some people think that such a comparison is impossible on account of the relational nature of these goods/bads.[27]

A good/bad is **relational** if, and only if, it is good/bad for a particular being or a particular group of beings. A good/bad is **absolute** if, and only if, it is good/bad *simpliciter*.

---

27. For discussion, see Korsgaard 2018, chapter 1.

It is plausible to hold that two goods/bads X and Y are comparable only if (a) X and Y are absolute goods/bads, or (b) X and Y are goods/bads for the same being. By way of an analogy, think of motions in the context of Newtonian mechanics. Suppose that we want to compare the motions of bodies B1 and B2. Unless B1 and B2 are both in absolute motion—which, in the Newtonian context, means non-inertial (that is, accelerated) motion—or there is a common frame of reference to which the motions of B1 and B2 can be related, we cannot compare them. Assuming the indicated plausible claim about comparability, if absolute goods/bads were impossible or no relational goods/bads could be absolute goods/bads at the same time, it would directly follow that goods/bads for different beings are incomparable.

While I feel the pull of this consideration, I am prepared to admit both that absolute goods/bads are possible and that it is possible for relational goods/bads to be absolute goods/bads at the same time. More specifically, I agree that if something is good/bad for an intrinsically valuable being, then it is good/bad absolutely for the being to have it. And since I believe that all beings with moral standing are intrinsically valuable, I agree that it is good/bad absolutely for these beings to have what is good/bad for them. But this is just another way of saying that goods/bads for beings with moral standing are absolute goods/bads at the same time. Going yet further, I am even prepared to admit that some particular goods/bads for members of different species appear to be comparable in that we have strong intuitions about how to rank them with respect to being better or worse. For example, it seems intuitively obvious not only that the suffering endured by a chicken on an average day in a factory farm is very bad as far as chicken suffering goes, and that my suffering from a mild headache for five minutes is not very bad as far as human suffering goes, but also that the suffering of the chicken in the factory farm is much worse than my suffering from the mild headache.

Nevertheless, despite all of these concessions, I contend that the flourishing of members of different species generally cannot be compared. I believe that cases of interspecies comparability of goods/bads are quite rare—if, indeed, they exist at all. (Our intuitions about these cases may well be misleading.) When asked whether it is better for a human to be able to think for as much as she wants (assuming that thinking is an integral part of the characteristic function of humans) than it is for a tiger to be able to run for as much as he wants (assuming that running is an integral part of the characteristic function of tigers), most of us will draw a blank. Trying to compare the good of thinking for humans and the good of running for tigers is like trying to compare apples and oranges. And the same goes for a great many other goods/bads for humans and other animals. Only very few, if any, of the goods/bads for members of different species can be compared with respect to being better, worse, or equal. And since the flourishing of a being is determined by all goods/bads for it in its life, this means that the flourishing of members of different species generally cannot be compared either.

3.2.2 Reply II: Rejecting the Challenge

The following three-pronged reply to the lifeboat challenge on behalf of status egalitarianism seems more promising to me. First, all that the thought experiment shows is that most people are inclined to and most people's intuitions are favorable to human exceptionalism. But nobody denies that. The mainstream culture of industrialized nations tends to be human exceptionalist if not human centrist, and most of us are brought up and educated by human exceptionalists if not human centrists. It is thus no surprise at all that most people believe that they would save the human over the dog, and have the intuition that they ought to do so. The prevalence of this reaction and intuition cannot be counted as evidence for the truth of the claim that one ought to save the human over the dog, let alone for the truth of human exceptionalism.

Second, the challenge includes the claim that status egalitarians who hold that animals have moral standing are committed to asserting that, in the described situation, one ought to flip a coin to determine who gets saved. This claim is false. Status egalitarians who deny that the claim to life of the human is greater than the claim to life of the dog—because their interests in not dying are similar and have the same weight or their existence has the same intrinsic value or their interests are incommensurable—can hold that it is morally permissible to save the human over the dog without a coin flip. They could argue, for example, that, in a moral dilemma situation, such as the one described in the thought experiment, where one cannot but fail to help one of two beings whom one ought to help, one does not make things worse by choosing who the violated party is going to be. Status egalitarianism is thus not necessarily at variance with most people's reaction to the thought experiment that they would save the human. It can accommodate this reaction by classifying the saving of the human as morally permissible.

Third, the indicated type of status egalitarians (who deny that the claim to life of the human is greater than the claim to life of the dog) can even hold that one ought to save the human over the dog. They could argue, for example, that social relations matter morally in the sense of creating special obligations to members of one's social group, obligations that, although incapable of trumping basic rights, come into effect once all basic obligations that are grounded in basic rights have been discharged to the extent possible in the situation in question. Status egalitarianism is thus also not necessarily at variance with the prevalent intuition that one ought to save the human over the dog.

The first prong of this response by itself is already enough to deflate the challenge by the human exceptionalists. Prong two and prong three are optional and will be welcomed by status egalitarians who are reluctant to dismiss most people's reactions and intuitions as misguided. Personally, I am less prone to be affected by these kinds of scruples but I am also sympathetic to the second prong and sometimes even to the third.

3.3 Two Objections to Human Exceptionalism

In the dispute with the human exceptionalists, status egalitarians are not reduced to parrying the attacks of their opponents. They can go on the attack themselves by launching objections, of which we will consider the two that I take to be most damaging.

3.3.1 The Formulation Objection

The first objection is that the prospects for providing a more explicit formulation of human exceptionalism by spelling out what exactly it means for a being to have higher moral status than another such that this formulation (i) captures the thought that humans morally matter more than all non-humans and (ii) is both meaningful and defensible, are rather bleak. Some formulation attempts fail right out of the gate on account of not satisfying condition (i). For example, this holds for the attempt that utilizes the interest-profile conception of higher moral status, as we saw in section 3.1.1. The other two formulation attempts introduced there also fail, but their downfall is that they do not satisfy condition (ii).

Upon closer inspection, the spelled-out formulation of human exceptionalism that utilizes the conception of higher moral status$_1$ turns out not to make any sense or to render human exceptionalism necessarily false at best. For humans to have higher moral status$_1$ than all other beings with moral standing it is a necessary condition that, for every non-human species of beings with moral standing, humans have at least one interest that has more weight than a similar interest of members of this species. And for the latter to be the case, it is a necessary condition that, for every non-human species of beings with moral standing, there is at least one interest of members of this species that is similar to a human interest. The problem is that the latter claim does not make any sense or is necessarily false at best. Interests are similar only if their magnitudes are equal. As explicated above, on my view, only very few, if any, of the goods/bads for members of different species are comparable with respect to being better, worse, or equal, which also means that only very few, if any, of their interests are comparable with respect to having greater, smaller, or equal magnitude. As I see it, either no interspecies comparisons of interests are possible at all or such comparisons are possible only for interests that are associated with goods/bads that are extremely good/bad for members of the one species and only slightly good/bad for members of the other species (or *vice versa*), such as the interest of a chicken in not undergoing suffering in a factory farm for a day compared to my interest in avoiding a mild headache that barely lasts five minutes. In the first scenario, talk about similar interests of members of different species makes no sense. If none of the magnitudes of interests of members of different species are comparable, it is clear *a fortiori* that trying to classify such interests as similar or dissimilar is a meaningless undertaking. In the second scenario, there are some interests of members of different species whose magnitudes are comparable. But these interests necessarily differ with respect to their magnitudes and thus necessarily are not similar. Since all other interests of these beings are incomparable with respect to their magnitudes, it follows that the claim that, for every non-human species of beings with moral standing, there is at least one interest of members of this species that is similar to a human interest is necessarily false. And this, in turn, means that human exceptionalism, as formulated in the approach currently under discussion, is necessarily false. In sum, if I am correct with respect to the question of the comparability of the magnitudes of the interests of members of different species, the spelled-out formulation of human exceptionalism in terms of the notion of higher moral status$_1$ turns out to be meaningless or indefensible.

The other spelled-out formulation of human exceptionalism that cleared the initial hurdle of capturing the thought that humans morally matter more than all non-humans utilizes the conception of higher moral status$_2$, which is defined in terms of the greater intrinsic value of a being. The problems with this formulation are that (a) it makes sense only on an implausible conception of the intrinsic value of beings with moral standing, and (b) it fails to capture the vision of much greater moral importance of human beings compared to all other beings with moral standing that typically animates people with human exceptionalist leanings. So, this spelled-out formulation of human exceptionalism is also indefensible, if not meaningless.

Starting with problem (a), to my mind, the intrinsic value that beings with moral standing have is not a kind of value that is comparable. This is another respect in which I am sympathetic to Kant's moral philosophy. Kant distinguishes between the kind of value that beings with moral standing have—who, for him, are beings with autonomy, as we saw before—and the kind of value that goods have that are pursued by beings like us. Goods have a *price*, but autonomous beings have *dignity*. A price is a relational value that can be measured, and things with a price are fungible in that they can be replaced by other things with the same price. By contrast, dignity is an absolute value that cannot be measured, and beings with dignity are not fungible, which, I take it, entails that their value is not of the comparable kind.[28] As already noted, I do not agree with Kant's contention that all and only beings with autonomy have moral standing—on my view, all and only beings with a good for which they strive have moral standing—but I do agree with his account of what kind of intrinsic value beings with moral standing possess, namely, dignity, which is an absolute value that cannot be

---

28. See Kant 1785, 4:435. If the value of beings with dignity were of the comparable kind, one would expect them to be replaceable by one another if their respective values are the same.

measured or compared. If the intrinsic value of beings with moral standing is incomparable, it does not make any sense to say that one of them has greater intrinsic value than another. Anybody who is partial to this Kantian account will thus reject the conception of higher moral status$_2$ and, with it, the spelled-out formulation of human exceptionalism currently under discussion on the grounds that either it is meaningless or ascribes the wrong type of value to beings with moral standing.

As for problem (b), the formulation in question can be expected not to be very attractive to typical human exceptionalists on account of the rather limited scope of the greater moral considerability of human beings compared to other beings with moral standing that it underwrites. On the proposed spelled-out formulation of human exceptionalism, humans morally matter more *only* in that their existence is intrinsically more valuable. But human exceptionalists typically think of the greater moral considerability of humans as much more extensive in scope. Humans are to be given preferential treatment not only when it comes to matters of life and death but across the board.

These considerations do not show that it is impossible to provide an acceptable, more explicit formulation of human exceptionalism that satisfies both conditions stated at the beginning of this subsection. But since our considerations establish that the most popular formulation attempts fail, we can conclude that the prospects for this formulation project do not look promising at all.

3.3.2 The Speciesism Objection

This result already puts considerable pressure on human exceptionalism, but some especially thick-skinned proponents of this view might still want to persist in their ways. This is where the second objection comes in, which is already familiar to us from our previous discussion. It is the speciesism objection. Human exceptionalism is a way of discriminating against non-human creatures on the basis of their species. It is thus a form of speciesism. Since speciesism is morally wrong, human exceptionalism is morally wrong as well. Giving more weight to the interests of members of the human species than to similar interests of members of other species (assuming that this makes sense) or treating the existence of humans as intrinsically more valuable than the existence of non-humans (assuming that this makes sense) is an expression of bias and a morally objectionable form of discrimination, just as it would be an expression of bias and a morally objectionable form of discrimination to give more weight to the interests of white men than to similar interests of non-white people or women or to treat the existence of white men as intrinsically more valuable than the existence of non-white people or women.

In the face of this criticism, human exceptionalists will scurry to dust off the replies to the speciesism objection offered by human centrists that we examined in the second main section and try to recycle them, suitably adjusted, for the purposes of their own defense. But some things just do not get better with age. The replies remain as unconvincing as they were at their first airing. The speciesism objection deals a fatal blow to human centrism and human exceptionalism alike.

> The bottom line is that human exceptionalism is untenable. It is very much questionable whether a notion of higher moral status can be identified that captures the thought that beings with higher moral status matter more from a moral point of view and is both meaningful and defensible. But even if this considerable hurdle could be overcome, human exceptionalism is felled by the speciesism objection. Human exceptionalism is an invidious prejudice and morally objectionable form of discrimination, just like human centrism. There is no hierarchy of moral considerability among beings with moral standing. All beings with moral standing, human and non-human alike, are equal in the sense of morally mattering equally.

4 What Do We Owe Other Animals?

4.1 Compassion

Since all humans and animals have moral standing and morally matter equally, there is a sense in which we owe animals exactly what we owe other humans. By saying this I do not mean to suggest that we owe humans and animals the same treatment. What treatment is owed to a being depends on what its interests are, which, in turn, depends on what kind of being it is. We owe it to human children to teach them to read and write but we do not owe it to the children of elephants to teach them to read and write.

So, what is it that we equally owe all beings with moral standing? One's answer to this question will vary depending on what moral theory one subscribes to. My answer is that we owe them reason-guided compassion, where compassion is understood as empathic concern for the flourishing of others. As explicated in section 2.3.2, I take compassion to be the only moral motive, that is, the only motive on which all actions that have positive moral worth must be based. What exactly showing compassion to others amounts to in a given concrete situation depends not only on what kind of being they are but also on their individual features and the particular circumstances in which we encounter them. Nevertheless, it is possible to describe a common core of showing compassion that is invariant across different particular beings and situations by way of identifying two basic reasons for action by which one is moved if one is empathically concerned for the flourishing of others. Showing compassion to others minimally entails appreciating and being moved by these basic reasons.

Before taking a look at what these basic reasons are, in order to forestall confusion, it is important to highlight that I conceive of them as strong but merely **pro tanto reasons**. Pro tanto reasons are reasons that speak for/against doing something and indicate the extent to which doing it would be a good/bad thing but can be outweighed by other relevant reasons. For example, the fact that you would get pleasure from eating a bucket of ice cream speaks for the feast, the fact that you would be sick afterwards speaks against it; but neither one of these reasons is decisive on its own. Whether you have overall reason to eat a bucket of ice cream will depend on how you assess the relative strength of these and other relevant pro tanto reasons, such as that you still have dinner plans that day or that you are in want of a credible excuse for not having to join your spouse on his evening run. Similar remarks apply with respect to a possible alternative characterization of the invariant common core of showing compassion to others in terms of the basic moral rights that these others have. It is acceptable to say that showing compassion to others minimally entails appreciating and respecting the others' basic moral rights, as long as "right" is understood in a lightweight sense as a strong, albeit defeasible, claim that corresponds to a pro tanto reason for doing whatever the right demands.

4.1.1   The Reason Not to Harm and the Reason to Help in Need

The two basic reasons that one appreciates and by which one is moved if one shows compassion to others are: (1) a reason **not to harm** them and (2) a reason **to help** them **in need**. The first reason corresponds to the right to freedom from harmful interference, the second corresponds to the right to assistance in need. What exactly does it mean to harm or help somebody in this context? The basic idea is that by harming somebody you make him worse off than he would have otherwise been, while by helping him you make him better off. More precisely, we can say that X harms/helps Y if, and only if, X acts in a way such that Y flourishes less/more than she would have flourished if X had not acted in this way.

There is no precise formula to determine whether, in a given situation, a creature is in need in the relevant sense. As much else in our moral lives, this determination ultimately is a judgment call that we all must make on our own as best we can. But by way of offering a general guideline, one can say that a creature in need is in a situation in which its capability to satisfy its **basic interests** is threatened or compromised. The basic interests of a being are those interests that must be satisfied for it to be able to live what amounts to a minimally decent life for a creature of its kind, interests such as access to adequate nutrition, living in a species-appropriate habitat, and being able to properly exercise its capacities.

It is also useful to make explicit that, typically, the reason for not harming others will also be a reason for not killing them because, typically, a being's flourishing is negatively impacted by its death.[29] Indeed, since being alive is a necessary condition for any kind of flourishing (at least for living organisms), in ordinary circumstances, killing a being constitutes one of the greatest harms that one can inflict on it. Note, though, that this is not necessarily the case. There could be and are tragic situations where a being's flourishing is compromised to such an extent that its life is a burden to it and not worth living anymore and where there are no other options for helping it apart from killing it. Killing a being in such a tragic situation does not negatively impact its flourishing (provided the being gave its consent if it is autonomous).[30] The compassionate thing to do and the proper means by which to respect its dignity would be to

---

29. It is a bit tricky to formulate this point precisely given that, once the being is dead, there is nobody around anymore for whom things can be good or bad. For our present limited concerns, the rough and ready characterization in the main text will do since it is sufficient to convey the relevant basic idea.

30. In the case of an autonomous being, without its consent, the killing would constitute a violation of its autonomy and thus negatively impact its flourishing since the exercise of this capacity is an integral part of its flourishing.

end the being's life (provided it gave its consent if it is autonomous) because this is the only way to positively impact its flourishing in the sense of making the situation better for it.[31]

In keeping with my view that living a morally decent life is not a matter of following general rules but of morally appropriately relating to particular intrinsically valuable beings in concrete situations, I regard it as futile to try to come up with an exhaustive characterization of all possible factors that could affect the degree of moral failing of harming or not helping others or with general universal rules for how to adjudicate between conflicting demands made on us by different beings with moral standing. How much weight we accord to the different morally relevant reasons in play in a given situation and how we combine these reasons to arrive at an overall assessment of what we have most reason to do from a moral point of view are also, to a significant extent, judgment calls that we all must make on our own and for which we must take responsibility. But I do agree that some rough generalizations concerning the weight of the reasons associated with moral standing and possible overriding factors seem defensible. These generalizations include, most saliently, that the reason for not harming a being with moral standing is extremely weighty and much weightier than the reason to help it when it is suffering a comparable need and can be overridden or outweighed only in special circumstances. These special circumstances comprise, for example, situations in which the inflicted harm is a side-effect of self-defense and (maybe?) situations where the only way to provide badly needed help to a very large group of beings with moral standing is to inflict a small amount of harm to a small number of others.[32] In ordinary circumstances, the reason not to harm trumps all other reasons.

The reason not to harm (or the right to freedom from harmful interference) and the reason to help in need (or the right to assistance in need) or at least closely related reasons (or rights) also

---

31. Of course, in practice it might be very difficult, if not impossible, to tell whether killing X indeed makes the situation better for X (even if we assume that death truly is the end). But this is an epistemological problem, not an ethical one.

32. The determination of the circumstances in which and the threshold at which the reason not to harm is overridden or outweighed is, again, a judgment call that we all must tackle on our own. The examples that philosophers like to think about in this context are contrived scenarios of the kind where we can save millions of people from dying of a painful disease by causing one person to suffer a slight cold or something along those lines.

reliably appear in the literature in non-utilitarian characterizations of moral standing in terms of the reasons (or rights) associated with it by people for whom an ethics of compassion is anathema. It is also quite common for people who recognize these reasons (or rights) as being entailed by moral standing to endorse the view that the reason not to harm (or the right to freedom from harm) is extremely weighty and that harming somebody to help others in need typically is morally impermissible.[33] So, despite my starting point from an ethics of compassion, which, it is fair to say, lies some way off from the beaten path, my account of the reasons and rights that come with moral standing and of their respective weight is not at all idiosyncratic. (From now on, for the sake of a less clumsy presentation, I will be talking only about reasons, not rights; but it should be sufficiently clear from the foregoing remarks how to translate reasons-talk into rights-talk.)

4.2 Worries About Overdemandingness

On my account, we owe all beings with moral standing compassion, which, in turn, entails minimally that we appreciate and are moved by the reasons not to harm them and to help them in need. Given the extensive size of the group of beings that are morally considerable on my view, one might worry that even these minimal requirements already go way too far to be acceptable as morally obligatory. More specifically, one might worry that the no-harm directive is over-demanding and thus cannot express a moral obligation since we cannot survive without harming at least some living beings. After all, we must eat something. Furthermore, one might worry that the help-in-need directive is overdemanding and thus cannot express a moral obligation since at any given moment vast numbers of living beings are in need, some of whom we thus cannot but fail to help. I will address these worries in turn, starting with the latter.

4.2.1 Help as Much as You Can

None of what I have said implies that we have an obligation to help all living beings in need, as the second worry alleges. According to

---

33. In the animal ethics literature, a strong version of a rights account that incorporates these claims is, for example, defended in Regan 2004, esp. chapter 8.

my view, for every living being, we have an obligation to appreciate and be moved by the reason to help it in need. But, as noted, by itself this reason is not decisive but merely pro tanto and thus does not directly translate into a general obligation to help. What we ought to do in a given situation depends on all moral reasons in play.

Moreover, I agree that there are limits on what can reasonably be regarded as morally required of us. These limits are largely circumscribed by a principle that is known as the ought-implies-can principle—although, on my view, there are certain conditions under which the principle does not apply (on which more shortly).

Ought-implies-can principle: X is morally obligated to do something only if it is possible for X to do it.

Requiring somebody to do something that she cannot possibly do clearly would be overdemanding. A requirement that is overdemanding in this sense is not morally obligatory. For example, the requirement for members of congress to fly on their own power for an hour every Tuesday violates the ought-implies-can principle and thus is not even a candidate for being morally obligatory since, hard as they may try, members of congress simply cannot fly on their own power.[34]

Without having to get embroiled in an analysis of specific competing reasons and their respective weight that could come into play in different situations when we are trying to determine what we ought to do, based on the ought-implies-can principle we can conclude straightaway that we do not have an obligation to help all living

---

34. There is a question about what kind of possibility is at play in the ought-implies-can principle. Obviously, it must be stronger than mere logical possibility. It is logically possible for humans to fly on their own power. But most people who endorse the ought-implies-can principle would agree that the obligation to fly on one's own power for an hour every Tuesday conflicts with the principle. The assumption that the relevant kind of possibility is physical possibility, understood as what is possible according to the laws of nature or something even slightly stronger, such as physical possibility given the current state of affairs in the actual world, coheres much better with most people's intuitions about which kind of obligations are ruled out on account of their violation of the ought-implies-can principle. This is also how I understand "possible" in the ought-implies-can principle here.

beings in need—although the relevant argument is a bit more complicated than it might initially appear. On first glance, one might think that the argument consists in the following straightforward line of reasoning. Given the overwhelmingly large number of living beings in the world who are having a tough time, it is impossible for us to help all of them. On the assumption of the ought-implies-can principle, it thus follows that we are not morally obligated to help all of them. On second glance, it transpires, however, that we must be a bit more careful about specifying precisely which living beings in need we are talking about because the ought-implies-can principle does not apply in all possible situations where we find ourselves confronted with more living beings in distress than we can help. The conclusion of the sketched argument is correct, but the reasoning needs to be spelled out more carefully. So, let us take a closer look.

Humans have brought and continue to bring enormous amounts of suffering and destruction upon other living beings, be it through direct interference or interference mediated by human-caused climate change. Whether we like it or not, all of us who live in civilized societies in industrialized countries are to some extent implicated in this sad business and thus bear part of the responsibility for it. The number of living beings who are in need because of this kind of harmful human interference is very large. So, unfortunately, we find ourselves in a situation where it is impossible for us to help all living beings in need who require assistance because of harmful interference for which we are partly responsible. But, as I see it, this impossibility does not get us off the hook, morally speaking, precisely because we are partly responsible for bringing it about. That X is partly responsible for his inability to do what is asked of him is a *defeating condition* for the ought-implies-can principle. If Billy, contrary to his promise, cannot pay back a loan to his best friend Bobby on the first of the month because he directly spent his entire paycheck on a new plasma TV, Billy cannot appeal to the ought-implies-can principle to argue that he has no obligation to pay back his friend. Similarly, the ought-implies-can principle does not apply in a situation in which there are more beings in need than we can help where these beings are in need because of harmful interference for which we are partly responsible. Moreover, that we are partly responsible for the other beings' plight also adds a lot of weight to our reason for helping them. Indeed, on my view, it adds enough weight so that it is fair to say that, except in special circumstances, we have a moral obligation to help all living beings in need who require assistance because of harmful interference for which we are partly responsible. That in the current circumstances we are unable to meet this obligation is tragic, but since the inability in question is at least partly our own fault, it is not a reason to conclude that we do not actually have the obligation.

We are now in a position to answer the question of whether we are morally obligated to help all living beings in need in an appropriately more careful way. Even if we set aside those living beings who are doing badly because of harmful human interference, it is still impossible for us, through no fault of our own, to help all remaining living beings in need. Some of them are beyond our reach, in oceanic depths, on mountain tops, in remote jungles, and other far-flung places. But the main problem, again, is that there are just too many of them. The world is full of suffering and destruction even if we disregard the huge amounts of suffering and destruction caused by humans. Nature indeed is red in tooth and claw, and natural disasters, on a small or grand scale, are par for the course. In this case, no defeating conditions obtain and the ought-implies-can principle does apply. The requirement to help all living beings who are in need independently of harmful human interference is overdemanding in the sense of asking us to do something that is simply impossible for us. Accordingly, the requirement to help all living beings in need in general is also overdemanding in the sense captured by the ought-implies-can principle, which is why I agree with the assessment that it is not morally obligatory.

Which living beings to help who are in trouble independently of harmful human interference and how much to help them are questions of practical judgment that we all have to figure out for ourselves. It is deplorable that we cannot provide assistance to all of them, and we do fail every single one whom we do not lend a helping hand. But as long as we do our best to help as many and as much as we can without disregarding or failing to be properly moved by any other relevant moral reasons, we are not violating any obligations and are beyond moral reproach.

4.2.2 Do No Harm

Just as none of what I have said implies that we have an obligation to help all living beings in need, none of what I have said implies that we have an obligation not to harm any living being, as the first of the two worries about overdemandingness alleges. But since I hold that the reason for not harming is extremely weighty and much weightier than the reason to help in need in a comparable situation and can be overridden or outweighed only in special circumstances, it is a fair question whether I am committed to the only slightly weaker claim that, except in special circumstances, we are obligated not to harm any living being. In the following, I will use the name "**no-harm obligation**" to refer to this qualified obligation.

To put my cards on the table, I do endorse the no-harm obligation. In contrast to the help-in-need case, the ought-implies-can principle does *not* apply in the do-no-harm case, not even in a restricted way. The principle does not apply here, not because of the presence of some defeating conditions, but simply because we are able to do what the requirement asks of us. While it is impossible for us to help all living beings who are in need independently of harmful human interference, it is possible for us not to harm any living being. Even if it were impossible for us to survive without harming any living being, we could still refrain from doing harm. We would die after a while, but we could do it.

Does that mean that we can fully live up to the demands of morality only by submitting to dying of starvation? On some gloomy days, I am prepared to admit that this is a real possibility, outrageous as this may sound. But let us first take a look at how one could argue for the more palatable answer that we can abide by the no-harm obligation while surviving at the same time.

The no-harm obligation says that we are obligated not to harm any living being, except in special circumstances. The obvious strategy to avoid having to say that we cannot survive unless we violate this obligation is to argue that (a) it is possible to feed ourselves without causing more than a minimal amount of harm to other living beings, and (b) a situation in which the only way to save our life is to cause a minimal amount of harm to other living beings constitutes one of the special circumstances in which harming is morally permissible.

So, is it possible for us to survive without causing more than a minimal amount of harm? On most days, I succeed in convincing myself that this is possible, at least in principle. We can survive on a diet that consists of synthetically produced foods and parts of plants whose removal from the plant does not constitute harm or can be performed in such a way as to constitute only a small amount of harm. To pick just two slightly simplified examples for purposes of illustration, an apple tree is not or almost not harmed if one carefully plucks an apple that is about to drop to the ground and eats it. Similarly, as long as one saves some grains from a barley plant, puts them back in the soil in the spring, and ensures, by carefully spacing them out and diligently watering them, that they produce about as many barley plants as would have been produced if one had not interfered, one is causing no or only a small amount of harm to the barley plant if one eats the rest of the grains. I will refer to the kind of diet that utilizes only synthetically produced foods and plant-parts that have been harvested in the indicated cautious fashion as "benign vegan diet." If desired, we could also supplement this diet with parts from animals who died of natural causes or through an accident. Whether or not we consume parts of these animals does not make a difference to them anymore.

But what about harmless bacteria and other non-pathogenic microorganisms? It seems inevitable that we kill a lot of them in the process of preparing and eating our food even if we restrict ourselves to a benign vegan diet.[35] And, as noted above, killing a living organism is one of the greatest harms that one can inflict on it. A comprehensive discussion of this question goes beyond the scope of this essay. But here is the short version of the gist of a possible answer. Different kinds of beings have different individuation conditions, i.e., conditions that specify what it means for beings of this kind to be the particular individual they are. This is not the place to get into an analysis of what these different individuation conditions are. For present purposes, we just need to appreciate that it can be argued that the individuation conditions of bacteria and other microorganisms allow that there can be more than one copy or instance of a particular microorganism at the same time. For example, if Helmut, the bacterium, reproduces through binary fission, the result of the process is two copies of Helmut. (Note, in passing, that similar remarks can be made about many plants and their offspring. The original plant and its offspring are all the same plant.) Moreover, microbes are prolific reproducers. For example, depending on the species, bacteria can double every 4 to 20 minutes.

---

35. I focus on non-pathogenic microbes here since the destruction of pathogenic microbes through our stomach acid and the cooking process could be regarded as a form of morally permissible self-defense.

This means that, even if Helmut is going at a comparatively slow pace, there will be well over 68 billion copies of Helmut after only 12 hours. Accordingly, it is quite unlikely that we will destroy all copies of a given microbe as a result of activities related to meeting our nutritional needs, which, however, would be required to kill it. So, despite the fact that the procurement of our nourishment inevitably brings with it the destruction of a lot of copies of non-pathogenic bacteria and other microbes, it is possible to get our fill without having to kill anything.

Even if we stick to a benign vegan diet, some infliction of harm seems unavoidable. Cultivation and harvesting require interference with the natural life of plants, and some of that interference might well constitute a form of harm. Similarly, since, arguably, the more copies a bacterium has, the more it flourishes, we do cause it some harm if we destroy some of its copies even if we do not kill it. At the same time, it is not entirely implausible to hold that, in all of these cases, the inflicted harm is minimal enough so that the reason not to inflict it is outweighed by the reason to help ourselves not to starve given that there is no other, less harmful way in which we could achieve that end. If that is correct, we can survive without violating the no-harm obligation.

As anticipated above, although I tend to buy this line of reasoning most of the time, there are some dark days on which I find it not entirely reassuring. This is mainly a result of my skepticism concerning our ability to gauge how bad the required harms for the affected beings are. Maybe the harm done to a plant during harvest and the harm done to a bacterium by destroying some of its copies are not as minimal as they appear to be after all? On these skeptical days, I am prepared to take seriously the possibility that we can fully live up to the demands of morality only by submitting to dying of starvation. I agree that this claim is outrageous, but it still might be true. According to an adage with a venerable history in philosophy, the actual world in which we live is *the best of all possible worlds*. But, to an unbiased observer, it looks more like an unmitigated disaster. It is a disaster because of how much misery and suffering it contains, but also because, given how it is set up, our survival can be bought only at the price of harming other living beings, which, however, we ought not to do. It is easy to imagine other possible worlds in which the same moral obligations obtain as in the actual world but whose inhabitants are not faced with this diabolical choice between starving themselves and harming others.

Gottfried Wilhelm Leibniz (1646–1716) was a German philosopher, logician, mathematician, scientist, engineer, and dip-
lomat. The thesis that the actual world is the best possible
world is one of his most well-known doctrines. This doctrine
is ridiculed in Voltaire's acerbic satirical novel *Candide, Or
Optimism* (1759), which recounts young Candide's progres-
sive disillusionment as he learns more about the horrors and
calamities that characterize our world.

Of course, I am not recommending that we starve ourselves—I
certainly have no plans to do so any time soon—but I think it is
important to be honest about what we are willing to do to survive, namely, (possibly) violate some of our moral obligations, and
to take responsibility for it. Note that this does not mean, however, that if we choose not to starve ourselves, we might as well
be hanged for a steak as for a copy of a bacterium, so to speak.
Not every moral failure is equally morally bad; there are degrees of
moral badness. If we want to minimize the moral badness of our
failures in connection with meeting our nutritional needs, adopting a benign vegan diet is our best bet since, as far as we can tell, it
causes the least harm of all possible diets that are open to us.

Relatedly, it is also useful to note that the fact that our life hangs
in the balance can reasonably be seen as a mitigating circumstance
when it comes to the evaluation of our blameworthiness for the
violation of the no-harm obligation in the course of procuring our
food. Our life is our most precious possession—once our life is lost,
everything else is lost for us as well—and so it is quite understandable that we want to hold on to it. That is to say, even if consuming
a benign vegan diet were to amount to a violation of the no-harm
obligation, people who take that path could plausibly be seen as
deserving only a limited amount of blame, given that they are doing
the best they can short of making the ultimate sacrifice.

It is worth acknowledging that most people in industrialized
countries do not currently have access to foods that are produced
in the indicated cautious, harm-minimizing way. This holds even for
people who have adequate access to vegan food options because of
the great amount of harm that is inflicted by industrial-scale crop
farming on all sorts of living beings, including small mammals, birds,
insects, and other plants. This means that a lot of people nowadays

cannot survive without being implicated in causing and thus being partly responsible for quite a lot of harm. But even though our lives are at stake, this situation quite clearly does not constitute a special circumstance in which the inflicted harm is morally permissible, not least because the harming in question comprises a lot of killings. The unavailability of a benign vegan diet in our society can plausibly be cited as a mitigating circumstance that reduces our blameworthiness for failing to adopt such a diet, but it does not make our current food choices morally innocuous. The lesson here is that the no-harm obligation brings with it the obligation for all of us to work toward freeing ourselves from our current predicament and creating living conditions that will allow us to do what compassion demands of us, including, in particular, not inflicting or at least minimizing impermissible harm. (A crucial step in that direction would be aggressive population control, for starters.)

4.2.3   The Demandingness of Morality

From experience I know that there are people who will not be swayed by the foregoing considerations. Citing their intuitions, they will insist that the requirements entailed by my view are still too demanding to be acceptable as morally obligatory. The requirement to help as many living beings in need as much as we can without failing to appreciate or be properly moved by any other relevant moral reasons may not conflict with the ought-implies-can principle and may be much less demanding than the requirement to help all living beings in need without qualification, but it is still far too much to ask, they will say. On their view, as long as one offers some help to the needy once in a while, one has discharged one's moral obligations as far as helping is concerned and cannot be expected to do any more. For example, making an annual charitable donation of a few percent of one's salary would suffice for the purpose.[36] Similarly, while the requirement not to harm any living being, except in special circumstances, may not conflict with the ought-implies-can principle either and may be satisfiable without

---

36. This is one of the respects, noted in section 2.3.2, in which my compassion-based account of our obligations goes beyond the Kantian account. According to the latter, we are obligated to engage in some helping, but it is left to our discretion how many others and how much we want to help.

submitting to starvation, it still goes far beyond what can reasonably be expected of us, they will claim. Indeed, for many people, the degree of demandingness of the requirement to adopt a vegan diet, let alone a benign vegan diet, is already far greater than the greatest degree of demandingness that they judge acceptable for a moral obligation.

My first question for people such as these would be whether they can produce some other plausible principle that underwrites their intuitions in the style of the ought-implies-can principle. If not, my second question would be why we should think that their intuitions about overdemandingness are a reliable guide to which candidate requirements are morally obligatory. That a certain requirement that does not violate the ought-implies-can principle seems overdemanding to us might simply be an expression of our own laziness, weakness, or self-indulgence, rather than a trustworthy indication that the requirement is not morally binding.

Other than that, I do not have much to say to the non-swayed who rest their case on their intuitions about overdemandingness, except that morality may well be a demanding business, like it or not. If we really want to continue our moral progress, we need to get over our so-called commonsense intuitions. We should not assume that living a morally decent life is easy. There are bound to be many failures—I am certainly accumulating a lot of them. But it is important to take responsibility for our shortcomings and try to do better, instead of letting our commonsense intuitions about what seems too much to ask lure us into complacency.

4.3 Concrete Practical Consequences

Given what I have said before about my conception of a morally decent life as being a matter of morally appropriately relating to particular intrinsically valuable beings in concrete situations, it should not come as a surprise that I do not believe that very much can be said *in abstracto* about what treatment we owe other animals. But the result just derived, that our obligation to show compassion to every being with moral standing implies that we are obligated not to harm any living being, except in special circumstances, allows us to draw one important general conclusion that speaks to this question. Unless we find ourselves in special circumstances, we owe every animal not to subject it to treatment that harms it in any way.

This general conclusion, in turn, puts us in the position to identify several important concrete practical consequences that are entailed by the proposed account of what we owe other animals. There are some kinds of harmful treatment of animals, such as experimentation for the purpose of medical research, where it will have to be worked out on a case-by-case basis through careful practical deliberation whether the relevant circumstances are such that the extremely weighty reason not to harm is outweighed by the combined force of all other morally relevant reasons. But there are also some kinds of harmful treatment of animals where this call can be made fairly easily from a general point of view and, more specifically, where it can be quickly decided that the circumstances do *not* qualify as special in the relevant sense. The atrocities against animals mentioned in the introduction fall in this category.

If there are any morally relevant reasons at all that speak for the development of yet another shampoo or deodorant that must be tested on animals, their weight is minuscule. They are easily trumped by the reason not to harm. The reasons that are usually cited in support of using animals for entertainment in circuses, rodeos, bull-fighting rings, and species-inappropriate exhibitions and the reasons that are usually cited in support of factory farming are largely the same. They include, above all, that experiencing these entertainments or consuming large quantities of meat, eggs, and dairy brings pleasure to people and allows them to engage in culturally valuable traditions.[37] In order for these reasons to carry weight in our deliberations about the moral permissibility of the harmful practices in question, they would have to be morally relevant, and it would have to be the case that there are no harm-free alternatives to said entertainments and food products that would provide comparable pleasures and comparable ways of engaging in culturally valuable traditions. It is far from clear that either one of these conditions is satisfied. But even if, for the sake of the argument, we

---

37. The alleged reason that factory farming is required to provide adequate nutrition for large numbers of people is spurious and can directly be set aside. Not only are vegan diets nutritionally adequate, the production of plant-based foods is also more efficient than the production of animal-based foods. It is much more efficient to directly feed people with plants than feeding people with animals that had to be fed with plants. Vegan diets cut out the middleman, so to speak, which makes them better suited for feeding large numbers of people than their non-vegan counterparts.

grant as much, it is still obvious that the cited reasons, even in combination, are swamped by the reason not to harm, given how very weighty it is. Whatever weight pertains to the reason that eating steak is pleasurable and part of one's culture, it is dwarfed by the weight of the reason that torturing a cow in a factory farm causes it great harm.

All of these atrocities against animals constitute flagrant failures to show them compassion, which is the main thing that we owe them. By perpetrating these atrocities, we are thus not only acting in ways that are morally wrong, we are wronging the animals. To reiterate what I said in the introduction, it is high time to rectify this dismal situation, for the sake of the animals and for the sake of our souls.

To sum up: All animals have moral standing in virtue of having a good for which they strive. There is no hierarchy of moral considerability among beings with moral standing. All beings with moral standing are equal in the sense of morally mattering equally. This means that we owe the same to all beings who have moral standing. What we owe them is reason-guided compassion, which entails, minimally, that we appreciate and are moved by the reasons not to harm them and to help them in need. This entails that we are obligated not to harm any animal, except in special circumstances, and to help as many of them as much as we can without failing to appreciate or be properly moved by any other relevant moral reasons. Apart from these general guidelines, we are mostly on our own when it comes to figuring out how to treat a particular animal in a given concrete situation and must rely on our capacity of empathy and our practical judgment. But even these very general guidelines are already enough to determine that and explain why various atrocities against animals, in particular factory framing, are deeply morally objectionable and constitute grave wrongs against animals. We owe it to the animals to end these practices.

Chapter 2

Opening Statement

Bob Fischer

Contents

DOI: 10.4324/9781003441823-4

I Introduction

Let's cut to the chase. You've seen the undercover videos. You know things aren't great for animals in factory farms. And you get that farms aren't the only problem. Animals suffer in all sorts of ways at human hands—in research labs, in animal shelters, in marine parks and roadside zoos, in the wild spaces we've polluted. It's a dark and sad story.

I'm not here to defend much of what we do to animals. If I could wave a magic wand and change it, I would. There are people out there who will tell you that animals don't feel pain; or that animals do feel pain, but it doesn't really matter; or that if we don't mistreat animals in a thousand different ways, the sky will fall—we'll starve or become sickly or we'll never cure cancer. None of that's true. Animals do feel pain, their pain matters, and change is possible without catastrophe. We could do better. It would be wonderful if we did.

But Anja and I aren't here to debate what's better. We're debating what we *ought* to do—in the weird way that philosophers use the word "ought"—in the face of the discouraging facts about what humans do to animals. That is, we're debating what we're morally *obligated* to do, what morality *demands* of us. We're asking about the moral *minimum*—the threshold for not acting wrongly—rather than what it would be good to do. (Much less what it takes to be a moral model!) We're trying to figure out how *little* you can do without being guilty of failing to meet your responsibilities.

This is *not* because we're determined to be morally lazy. Instead, it's because once we get *beyond* the moral minimum, there's usually some flexibility. It's morally permissible to make some choices about what to prioritize. Other considerations may win out when deciding what to do, including your personal preferences and interests. When it comes to the moral minimum, though—when it comes to what you *ought* to do—your preferences never win. For instance, you shouldn't steal someone's car even if it's your birthday and you really *want* to steal it. (I'm sorry to be the bearer of bad news.)

Another clarification. This is a debate about what "we" ought to do. But who are "we"? College students? Americans? Members of the (upper?) middle class? Humanity as a whole? Thinking in terms of groups is messy, so let's not. Instead, let's think of this as a debate about what *each* of us ought to do, rather than some big collective "we." After all, maybe there is some sense in which "we" should ensure that everyone has healthcare. Even if so, though, and if you're a member of that "we," *you personally* don't have to ensure that everyone has healthcare. It's important to know what groups ought to do, but that information rarely tells us what individual members of the group should do. Here, we're focusing on individuals. And since you know the facts of your own life, you can consider how well the arguments we're discussing apply to your own particular circumstances.

Here's the upshot. People treat many animals very badly, especially in factory farms. It would be better if things were different. This book, though, isn't about what would be better: it's about what's morally required of *you*, dear reader, in response to a bad situation. And what's that?

> In my contributions to this book, I will use the expressions "ought," "should," and "obligated" as synonyms to refer to what morality *requires* of someone—not what it would be good or nice for that person to do.

1.1   Should You Go Vegan?

According to many philosophers and animal advocates, part of the answer is simple: you should go vegan, stop using products that were tested on animals, and generally stop supporting industries that harm animals. Seems sensible enough. After all, that's what many people say *whenever* they're concerned about an industry. "Was the cocoa in that chocolate harvested by children or slaves? Don't buy it." "Does that business have ties to groups that try to undermine LGBTQ rights? Boycott it." "Did that comedian make a joke that glorified rape? Cancel him." "Are fossil fuel companies harming the environment? Divest."

It's plausible that you ought to distance yourself from wrongdoing. However, most of us don't think that we have to do *all* the notbuying, boycotting, canceling, and divesting—or at least not all the time. There are just too many causes to take up. Maybe we should all do *some* of those things *some* of the time, but no one has to take on everything.[1] Perhaps it would be great if you did, but you'd be going above and beyond. Morality might *commend* doing all those things, but it doesn't require them.[2]

So, the case for going vegan—or not using products tested on animals, or anything else—needs to be better than, "Distance yourself from wrongdoing." There needs to be something special that makes *that* distancing especially important. For instance, it's probably less than ideal to buy a chicken sandwich, given the way chickens are treated on factory farms. Still, I don't think it's like paying someone to torture puppies. But there are people who think that buying a chicken sandwich *is* like paying someone to torture puppies—that paying for puppies to be tortured and ordering a chicken sandwich are morally equivalent actions.[3] If that were true, then it would be especially important to distance yourself from chicken production. It would be wrong—and *seriously* wrong—to buy a chicken sandwich.

I'll argue, however, that buying a chicken sandwich is not like that. My main focus in this opening statement, then, is on whether we ought to do what so many animal advocates say we ought to do—namely, go vegan. I'll make the case that you aren't failing to satisfy any of your moral obligations if you keep eating chicken. You might not win moral *awards* for it, but **abstaining** isn't morally required.

1.2 The Burden of Proof

How am I going to show that? Here's the basic idea. When you're in a debate, the person with the **burden of proof** is the one who has to establish something. The idea is familiar from the courtroom. In a criminal trial, the prosecutor has the burden of proof; it's his job to show that the defendant is guilty of a crime. The defense attorney

---

1. Alternately: maybe some of us should do some of those things all the time. But absent an argument to the effect that it is especially important to abstain from animal products, that won't establish a general duty to be vegan.
2. You might disagree; you might think we ought to do it all. I have things to say about that view, but no room to say them here. (The short version: you're still going to get some weird anti-vegan results; for details, see Fischer (2020).) So, I'll just register my more modest view of morality's demands as an assumption.
3. See Norcross (2004), among many others.

doesn't have to prove that her client is innocent; that's the default position. We're supposed to assume her client is innocent unless the evidence shows otherwise. This means the defense attorney only needs to show that the prosecutor has failed, that he hasn't met his burden: she just has to show that the prosecutor hasn't established her client's guilt beyond a reasonable doubt.

I think the same is true in ethics. In a **moral debate**, the person insisting that you have a moral obligation has the burden of proof; it's his job to show that if you don't act in a certain way, you're failing to do your moral duty. In the context of this debate, I'm the defense attorney. I don't have to prove that you can keep living the way you'd like; that's the default position. I only need to show that your critic hasn't met his burden. If not, then he hasn't shown that you've got a certain responsibility.

Of course, in the context of a criminal trial, we have a standard we're supposed to use to decide whether the prosecutor has met the burden of proof. How good does the evidence for guilt have to be? Answer: beyond a reasonable doubt. We don't have anything quite like that in ethics, but maybe we can fashion something similar. How good does the evidence for a *purported* moral obligation have to be before you should think you've *really* got that obligation? Answer: *beyond your (reflectively held) reasonable belief*. Let me explain.

Billy comes to you and says:

> Hey, I really think you ought to give a bunch of money to Tall Clubs International Foundation (TCI), which funds scholarships for 'students under 21 years of age, about to attend their first year of higher education, and who meet the height requirements of TCI—5' 10" (178 cm) for women, and 6' 2" (188 cm) for men'.[4] They do a lot of good for tall people; no one else is helping the tall crowd.

You might reply:

> Hey Billy, super cool foundation and all, but I'm not so sure that'd be the best use of my money. I think that if I'm going to give, it should be to foundations that will do as much good as

---

4. http://www.tall.org/tci-foundation.html.

possible with those dollars. Given the choice between giving to TCI and, say, a foundation that tries to prevent kids from getting malaria, I should probably support the latter. Even if no one else is helping tall people, it isn't clear that tall people need my money more than kids who might get malaria.

It sure seems like you've got some reasonable beliefs that imply that you aren't morally obligated to give half your income to TCI. Moreover, and I'll just assume this going forward, they are *reflectively held* reasonable beliefs: they're beliefs to which you've given some serious thought and they still seem right to you; they aren't just ideas you happen to have, but which you'd give up at the first challenge. So, unless Billy can show that it would be *un*reasonable for you to believe those things, he hasn't met his burden.

Of course, as in the courtroom, the guilty sometimes go free. So, it's *possible* that you're still obligated to give half your income to TCI even though Billy hasn't met the burden of proof. His argument for giving isn't great, but maybe there's a better one out there, just waiting for someone to discover it. (I wouldn't hold my breath, but it's *possible*.) Strictly speaking, then, we should say that if Billy hasn't met the burden of proof, then *it's reasonable for you not to believe* that you're obligated to give half your income to TCI— not that you *aren't obligated*, full stop. Your obligations depend on what's actually true, not what Billy can show to be true. Your *beliefs* about your obligations, on the other hand, should be sensitive to the evidence, and if there isn't enough evidence, you don't need to change your mind.

However, just as we usually ignore this wrinkle in legal contexts, saying that a person is innocent if guilt wasn't established, we're going to ignore this complication here, and just say that you don't have the obligation if we can't find a good argument for your having it. So I wasn't being as precise as possible when I said, a few paragraphs back, that I'll argue you aren't failing to satisfy any of your moral obligations if you keep eating chicken. Again, strictly speaking, what I'm arguing in this opening statement is that *it can be reasonable for you to believe* that you aren't failing to satisfy any of your moral obligations in consuming animal products. Going forward, though, we won't worry about this level of precision.

Let's sum up. Humans treat many animals badly, especially in factory farms. What are you morally required to do in response to that fact? According to many philosophers and animal advocates, the answer is that you ought to go vegan. I'll argue that they haven't met their burden; so, you have no such obligation.

1.3   Veganism: What It Is and What's at Issue

To make this conversation a bit sharper, we need to say a bit about what veganism is and what arguments for veganism are supposed to establish.

As I understand it, veganism is a *diet*, a way of eating. In particular, it's a diet that's defined by what it doesn't include: namely, any animal products. This means avoiding meat (including fish), dairy products, eggs, and a wide range of products derived from animals, such as gelatin (which is made by boiling animals' bones, skin, and cartilage) and glycerin (which is usually made from animal fat). Typically, veganism is also understood as a diet that excludes things like honey and carmine (a red pigment that's produced by crushing cochineal insects), as insects, of course, are animals too. There's room for debate about the exact boundaries of the diet: what, for instance, should vegans say about oysters—animals indeed, but arguably ones that can't feel pain? For the most part, though, we won't worry about these kinds of wrinkles. If we're at the point where we're worried about whether to eat oysters, the defenders of veganism have won.

Not everyone understands veganism as a diet. The Vegan Society, for instance, has a much more expansive definition:

> Veganism is a *philosophy and way of living* which seeks to exclude—as far as is possible and practicable—all forms of exploitation of, and cruelty to, animals for food, clothing, or any other purpose; and by extension, promotes the development and use of animal-free alternatives for the benefit of animals, humans and the environment. In dietary terms it denotes the practice of dispensing with all products derived wholly or partly from animals.[5] (emphasis added)

According to The Vegan Society, then, adopting an animal-free diet is a *consequence* of veganism, rather than the core feature. That core feature is the rejection of animal exploitation and cruelty, and if you're committed to that, then (given that animal products stem

---

5. https://www.vegansociety.com/go-vegan/definition-veganism.

from animal exploitation and/or cruelty) you're probably going to think you ought to avoid consuming animal products.

Different definitions are useful for different purposes. But since we don't want to make any assumptions about the moral foundations of veganism, The Vegan Society's definition isn't ideal. For our purposes, it's better to start with a morally neutral characterization—just in terms of the behavior that's involved (or, rather, not involved)—and then ask why that might be required. Of course, as The Vegan Society's definition suggests, veganism is not necessarily just about what we eat and drink. If the arguments for veganism work, they also have implications for the ethics of using a wide range of other products, including leather and many cosmetics. For the sake of simplicity, though, I'll adopt a diet-based definition here. It should be easy enough to see how to apply the same points to any other animal product.

We need to get one more issue on the table. When people get into debates about veganism, they're often arguing about *strict* veganism: no animal products at *any* time, under *any* circumstances, for *any* reason. That framing makes the debate very boring. "What would you do if you were starving on a desert island and you came across a hidden stash of beef jerky? Would you eat meat *then?*" "What if you were living on the frontier during a terrible winter and you had to choose between feeding your family and killing a deer. Would you kill an animal *then?*" "What if it was Grandma's dying wish that you have some of her chicken soup with her? Would you eat it *then?*" Last time I checked, though, you don't spend much time alone on desert islands or on the early American frontier; and, thankfully, very few grandmothers make such deathbed requests. If we want to have a serious conversation about the ethics of eating, we should ignore these hypotheticals.

The interesting question is about what we might call *ordinary* veganism. Ordinary veganism means having a veggie burger rather than a beef patty at the cookout. It means that when you go to Chipotle, you get tofu or beans rather than chicken or barbacoa (and you skip the cheese and sour cream). It means having your cereal with soy milk rather than cow's milk. It means bringing your own vegan lunch when you know your boss is going to provide pizza for everyone at work that day. In other words, it's opting for the animal-product-free option in everyday life, whether at home, at work, or out and about. Forget about what you should do on desert islands or when Grandma is dying. Should you be an ordinary vegan? Are you morally obligated to abstain from consuming animal products *nearly* all the time? That's the question we'll try to tackle here. (For simplicity's sake, I'll just talk about veganism going forward, but the "ordinary" will be assumed.)

1.4 Coming Attractions

With all these preliminaries behind us, what's next?

In just a minute, we'll turn to the two most common—and, I think, most powerful—arguments for veganism. The first is that you should stop eating animals to help animals. More accurately, it says that if you stop eating animals, you'll prevent some harm to animals. The second argument is that whether or not your choices make any difference, you shouldn't be **complicit** in *especially heinous* wrongdoing. And since eating animals is a way of being complicit in especially heinous wrongdoing, you shouldn't do it. I'll make the case that *even if animals are extremely important*, these arguments don't work. That is, I am *not* going to say: "Animals don't matter nearly as much as human beings, so it's fine if we harm them when we could avoid it" or "Animals don't matter nearly as much as human beings, so factory farming isn't an especially heinous form of wrongdoing." Instead, I'll try to show that even if we think animals matter just as much as people (in a sense to be specified), the "stop eating animals to help animals" and "don't be complicit" arguments aren't successful.

Of course, there are more than two arguments for veganism. What about all the others? My view, for what it's worth, is that the problems facing the two arguments I discuss are pretty common problems; they take down lots of other arguments for veganism too. But since I don't have room to show that, I'll try a different tack. In the second part of this opening statement, we'll take a closer look at the assumption I'm going to grant when discussing the "stop eating animals to help animals" and "don't be complicit" arguments— namely, the **Equal Consideration Principle**. Essentially, it says that animals' interests matter as much as people's interests. This assumption makes it *much* easier to argue for veganism. In essence, it lets veganism's defenders say: "But just imagine if we were treating *people* the way we treat animals. Would it be okay for you to buy products from companies that were abusing *people* like that?"

However, if animals' interests matter a lot less than people's, this move goes away, and that makes it tougher to argue for veganism. I'll argue that it's indeed reasonable to reject the Equal Consideration Principle. So, it's a lot less likely that there are decisive arguments for veganism out there.

> Humans treat many animals badly, especially in factory farms. What are you morally required to do in response to that fact? According to many philosophers and animal advocates, the answer is that you ought to go vegan. I'll argue that even if we grant a big assumption—the Equal Consideration Principle—they haven't met their burden. So, you have no such obligation. Then, I'll argue against the Equal Consideration Principle. If it's false, then it's less likely that there are other good arguments for veganism out there.

2 Two Arguments for Veganism

With those preliminaries behind us, let's turn to the two main arguments for veganism. As we've said, the first is that you should stop eating animals to help animals—that not eating animals somehow makes a difference to how things go for animals. The second argument is that whether or not your choices make any difference, you shouldn't be complicit in especially heinous wrongdoing.

2.1 You Make a Difference

In what follows, let's run through a few different versions of the idea that you should stop eating animals to help animals.

2.2 The Simple Argument

Let's begin with the Simple "You Make a Difference" Argument for Veganism (or "the Simple Argument," for short):

1. If you stop eating animal products, fewer animals will suffer.
2. If you can prevent suffering, you should.
3. So, you should stop eating animal products.

Is this a good argument for veganism?

The second premise might seem plausible enough, though we could press on it. Is it really true that you should *always* prioritize preventing suffering, which is what the premise seems to say? We certainly don't live that way most of the time. We invest our energies in many projects and activities that have no obvious connection to preventing suffering, such as taking walks, trying to improve the spaces in which we live, spending time with friends, and so on. But let's grant this premise for now, focusing on the first one instead.

Is the first premise true? There are lots of situations that look like counterexamples. Here's one of them:

> You're at Mom's for lunch one Saturday. Mom makes her famous egg salad sandwiches for the family. She always makes the same amount of egg salad, since she just follows Aunt Edna's recipe. ("You don't tinker with a classic.") And without fail, she ends up throwing away the leftovers. (No one likes leftover egg salad.) So, whether or not you have an egg salad sandwich, there's no change in how many eggs are bought, which means that there's no change in how many chickens are laying eggs.

There is nothing weird about this situation. We're in spots like this all the time. Here's another:

> Your boss always orders ten pizzas to feed the office, because even though you only need eight, he says it's nice to have a little extra. The real story: the local pizza place has a punch card deal; after ten pizzas, the eleventh is free. Your boss likes collecting maxed-out punch cards for his own use—a perk of buying lunch with company money. And without fail, the leftovers get tossed, as while the pizza is good enough for a work lunch when fresh out of the oven, it isn't even good enough for tomorrow's work lunch when reheated. So, whether or not you have any pizza, there's no change in how many pizzas are ordered, which means that there's no change in how much cheese, sausage, and pepperoni are used, which means that there's no change in how many dairy cows are milked or how many cattle and pigs are raised for meat.

Once you start noticing how common it is for food to be wasted like this, you realize how often your food choices don't make a difference to how many animals suffer. And if there are lots of cases where your food choices don't make a difference to how many animals suffer, then the first premise of the Simple Argument is false.

2.3 Supply Chains and Difference-Making

"Hold on," someone might say. "Sure: there are cases to which the Simple Argument doesn't apply. But there are *so many others* to which it *does* apply! You don't eat most of your meals at Mom's or thanks to your boss's discretionary spending account. Instead, you buy food at grocery stores and restaurants. And when you avoid buying animal products *there*, you make a difference to how many animals suffer."

That's a sensible reply. However, it isn't clear that it works. Let's think through the details.

Here's the crucial claim:

> When you avoid buying animal products at the grocery store, you make a difference to how many animals suffer.

Is that true? Pretty clearly not. When you buy a steak, no one calls a farmer and says, "Please kill another bull; we have to refill the meat case." Likewise, when you *don't* buy a steak, no one calls a farmer and says, "Please don't inseminate Cow #4793; we aren't going to need her calf in roughly three years" (which is approximately how long it takes to bring a calf to slaughter weight). Indeed, grocery stores never communicate with farmers directly. Let's try to get a better sense of how the system works.

Most grocery stores aren't independent anymore; they belong to chains. (And the remaining independent ones belong to associations that, for present purposes, make them tantamount to chains.) So, they get pallets of stock from their company's distribution center. The distribution center gets truckloads of stock—not just individual pallets—either directly from "processors" (that is, slaughterhouses) or from other companies that themselves source their products from processors. (Those companies might buy pork and turn it into sausage or buy chicken and incorporate it into frozen meals.) The processors are the ones dealing with the animals, killing thousands upon thousands of them each day. They are supplied, of course, by farmers, though often the farmers have very little control over how many animals they raise. Instead, farmers usually just do what they're told by enormous agribusinesses, such as JBS, Tyson, and Cargill. These businesses generally don't own the farms them-selves, largely as a way to externalize certain financial risks. Instead, they own the animals, trucking companies, and processing facili-ties, exerting enormous influence on other parts of the supply chain through a complicated system of contracts. The system is vast, intri-cate, and incredibly good at turning animal feed into money.

Here's the upshot for our difference-making claim. When you don't buy a steak, no one tells the farmer to do anything differ-ently. Farmers are a long, long way from the point of sale. But it isn't just that no one tells the farmers to do anything differently. Most of the time, the grocery store itself doesn't change a thing. It can't. The grocery store doesn't have the ability to adjust its order-ing by a single steak; that isn't the way the supply chain works. The store can only adjust by the box or pallet. What's more, the store doesn't *want* to adjust its ordering for every tiny fluctuation in demand. The store is not a *waste-minimizing* operation; it's a *profit-maximizing* operation. If it can make more money by wasting some meat, it absolutely will. And the evidence is clear: stores *do* make more money by wasting some meat. The store wants to ensure that the meat cases are full, as consumers buy more when cases are full and the meat is fresh. So, if you want to sell as much as possible, you overstock the meat case relative to projected sales and you turn it over regularly.

Of course, stores don't want to waste anything unnecessarily. So, the ground beef that no one's buying might become meatballs in the prepared food section, a bit of processing that both raises the price and extends the life of that product. But there's only so much of this that stores can do, and though the amount varies by product, a lot of food goes into the trash. (According to the latest estimate from the USDA, 12.6% of chicken, 11.2% of beef, and 8.9% of pork are lost at the retail level, with even more being lost earlier in the supply chain.)[6] So yes, stores work hard to minimize waste; yes, they track purchases intensely. However, it's clear that stores would rather sacrifice some product than lose a profitable sale. And once we rec-ognize that, we should also recognize that they have a powerful incentive *not* to change their ordering in response to an individual transaction, as that level of precision doesn't make sense given the amount of waste they're prepared to tolerate to maximize profits.

---

6. https://www.ers.usda.gov/webdocs/publications/44100/eib-155.pdf?v=663.5.

Instead, they change their ordering in response to sufficiently large and stable trends. And *that* means that when you don't purchase, nothing happens.

Or, at least, that's the way things work the vast majority of the time. Pick an average day: the odds are very good that your choices don't make any difference to how many animals suffer. But in principle, there could be *threshold* days. A threshold day is a day when, unbeknownst to you, many, many other people have been changing their shopping behavior for a good while too. And also unbeknownst to you, the store happens to be at an **order threshold**—a spot where the difference of one sale is going to be the thing that leads them to reduce their order for some animal product by a case, or pallet, or whatever their ordering unit is. Then, your decision not to purchase makes a difference.

But what, exactly, does it make a difference to? Not necessarily to the number of animals who suffer. It only makes a difference to the number of cases (or pallets, or whatever the relevant ordering unit is) that the grocery store requests from the distribution center. And distribution centers, of course, tolerate some waste to ensure that they always have enough relative to whatever grocery stores need. So, if the aim is to affect production levels, more stars need to align, and we need to hit an order threshold at the level of the distribution center as well. Then, your decision not to purchase makes a difference.

But again, what does it make a difference to? Not necessarily to the number of animals who suffer. It only makes a difference to the number of truckloads of the relevant animal product that the distribution center orders from the processor. So, if the distribution center orders one fewer truckload of the relevant animal product from the processor, does *that* make a difference to the number of animals who suffer?

It may. Again, though, not necessarily. This is because contemporary farming is a business with extremely thin margins. Insofar as there's any money to be made, it's in volume. So, farmers—or, rather, the corporations that largely dictate to farmers what they're going to do—have a strong incentive to find an alternative market for their products rather than reduce production levels. If, for instance, they can shift toward frozen foods rather than fresh, which obviously keeps longer, they'll do that. Then, they can hold the product until demand increases or find another market where demand is higher.

I'm not saying that your choice not to purchase a steak could *never* make a difference. Plainly, it could. But the vast majority of the time, it doesn't. So, recall the Simple Argument:

1. If you stop eating animal products, fewer animals will suffer.
2. If you can prevent animals from suffering, you should.
3. So, you should stop eating animal products.

It looks like the first premise is false. And if the first premise is false, then the Simple Argument fails.

2.4   The Expected Utility Argument

Maybe the Simple Argument is too simple. Is there a more complex argument for veganism that's still based on the idea that you can make a difference? As it turns out, there is. Let's call it the Expected Utility Argument for Veganism (or the "Expected Utility Argument," for short):

1. The **expected utility** of purchasing animal products doesn't maximize **utility**.
2. You shouldn't perform actions that don't maximize utility.
3. So, you shouldn't purchase animal products.

There's a lot going on here, so let's slow down and try to unpack it all.

First, a few words about the idea of expected utility. "Utility," here, is just a measure of something valuable. That could be something like *lives saved*. The *expected* utility of an action is how much of the valuable thing you expect to get multiplied by the probability of getting it. We can compare expected utilities to decide how to act. Imagine that one action has a 50% chance of saving 90 lives and another action has a 40% chance of saving 120 lives. Which is better? Well, do the math: 50% of 90 = 45 lives; 40% of 120 = 48 lives. "In expectation," then, it's better to choose the action that has a 40% chance of saving 120 lives.

Some ethicists—*utilitarians*—think that this is the way we should assess whether actions are right or wrong. But they think that we should understand utility as a measure of *wellbeing*, which is how well or badly things are going for particular individuals. On their view, impacts on wellbeing are what ultimately matter morally. In other words, when considering what to do, they think we should calculate the odds of particular outcomes given different courses of action, do our best to assess the wellbeing impacts of each outcome, and multiply.

This brings us back to the Expected Utility Argument. The idea goes like this. The probability of getting some pleasure from buying chicken wings is high, but all things considered, the amount of pleasure you'd get is pretty minimal. By contrast, the odds of making a difference to the number of chickens who suffer is very low, but in principle, the number of chickens you'd spare from suffering *if* you made a difference is huge. You'd be hitting a threshold—a tipping point—causing a change in the supply chain. It could be that an entire barn, which often hold 10,000 birds or more, goes empty for a full production cycle. So, as long as there is enough chicken suffering at stake, it can work out that the expected utility of purchasing chicken wings is less than it would be if you didn't purchase them—which means that purchasing chicken wings fails to maximize expected utility. So, should you buy the chicken wings? According to the Expected Utility Argument, you shouldn't.

How plausible is this argument? So far, not very. This is because it's one thing to show that the expected utility *could* be lower than it would be if you abstained; it's quite another to show that the expected utility *would* be lower. Lots of people enjoy eating chicken wings; indeed, they enjoy them far more than they enjoy the alternatives. (I eat the vegan alternatives regularly. They are good. But— I'm sad to say—they aren't nearly as good as the ones that come at the price of chickens' lives. I myself don't eat conventional chicken wings anymore, but I grant that they are tastier.) So, those people would be missing out on some positive utility if they were to eat the alternatives. If someone wants to show that those people should sacrifice that utility, they need to show something that sounds complicated, but isn't really. They need to show that the *extra* utility that people get from eating meat, multiplied by the probability of getting that utility, doesn't outweigh the *negative* utility generated by chickens on factory farms, which, again, is multiplied by the extraordinarily tiny chance of making a difference to their plight.

So, suppose you get 10 extra "utility points"—an imaginary unit of wellbeing that helps us compare how good and bad different outcomes are, wellbeing-impact-wise—when you eat chicken wings and you're certain to get them. Then, we multiply 10 (the number of "utility points") by 1 (the probability that you'll get those extra "utility points"). Suppose that if you happen to be the shopper who hits the right threshold, 10,000 chickens would be spared from losing 100 utility points as a result of being raised in a factory farm. But suppose the probability that you're that shopper is very low—just one in a million. Then, the expected utility of *not* purchasing chicken wings is 1, vs. 10 for purchasing and eating them. In that case, you maximize expected utility by eating the wings.

To make the Expected Utility Argument work, then, we need a reason to think that things aren't going to work out this way. I don't know of such a reason. And without it, the Expected Utility Argument doesn't succeed.

It doesn't really matter, then, whether the first premise is true—which is far more controversial than the first premise of the Simple Argument for Veganism, as utilitarianism is so controversial. You don't have to be a utilitarian to accept the first premise of the Simple Argument for Veganism, but only utilitarians are going to accept the first premise of the Expected Utility Argument. In any case, if the probability of making a difference is low enough, then even if there is a lot of chicken suffering at stake, the math doesn't show that it's a mistake to purchase animal products. And thus far, no one has shown that the math comes out any particular way.

2.5   The Negative Expected Utility Argument

Still, let's be charitable. There is *something* compelling about the Expected Utility Argument. At the very least, it might seem wrong to perform actions with *negative* expected utility—where the world would be worse, on the whole, in virtue of your choice. This gives us the Negative Expected Utility Argument for Veganism (or the "Negative Expected Utility Argument," for short).

1. Sometimes, the expected utility of purchasing animal products is negative.
2. You shouldn't perform actions that have negative expected utility.
3. So, sometimes, you shouldn't purchase animal products.

The first thing to observe is that this isn't an argument for veganism at all. It's an argument for not buying animal products *when the expected utility would be negative*, granting that sometimes it's positive. Still, the expected utility might be negative so regularly that this argument is still worth considering. It might not get us all the way to veganism, but it might get something near enough.

However, I think there are at least two serious problems with this argument. The first is that it isn't obvious that it's always wrong to perform actions that have negative expected utility. If it were, then it would often be wrong to start new businesses. Suppose, for example, that you and your partner have a successful fro-yo shop. I notice this and think: maybe there's enough demand for another! So, I start a fro-yo shop myself. But because I advertise better, I attract enough of your customers to drive you out of business. My wellbeing goes up as a result, of course, but you and your partner are much worse off. In terms of utility, this is a net loss: one person gains and two people lose—and they lose quite a lot. (Assume that the customers aren't sufficiently better off to offset your loss.) Now, I might have been able to predict that this would happen; if so, I'd have realized that starting my own fro-yo shop would have negative expected utility. Still, it doesn't seem to be wrong. So, even if your actions affect others,[7] your actions can sometimes have negative expected utility without being wrong.

The second is that lots of animal products probably are going to be condemned by the Negative Expected Utility Argument. Earlier, I focused on chickens because they make the best case for veganism. After all, they are much smaller than pigs or cattle, so you have to kill more of them for equivalent amounts of meat. More importantly, the lives of chickens are arguably far worse than those of many other animals that people farm. But as I mentioned, if the lives of chickens are even just *barely* worth living—that is, if they have even *slightly* more positive than negative experiences on balance—then it automatically comes out that the expected utility of getting the chicken wings is positive, as all their negative utility is offset by their positive utility. I am very confident that the lives of chickens are not good enough; I am not sure what to say about whether the lives of chickens are worth living. But in the case of some other animals, such as beef cattle and dairy cows, I suspect most of them do have lives that are worth living—even if their lives are far from being good enough. So, it probably works out that the Negative Expected Utility Argument permits eating beef and

---

7. ... and, not incidentally, even if you act without their consent, since you didn't agree to my new business!

dairy products, which isn't just "not veganism." It isn't even in the ballpark.

As you might imagine, we could always add wrinkle after wrinkle, ultimately generating the Modified Version of the Thrice Revised Yet-More-Modest Expected Utility Argument for Veganism. But I'm not sure we'd learn much more, as the central issue is clear. It's obviously true that large numbers of consumers *can* make a difference. However, it doesn't follow from this that any individual consumer *does* make a difference, either on a particular shopping trip or in general, or that any individual makes a difference that matters in expectation. And when we come to understand the complex relationships between individual shoppers, grocery stores, distributors, processors, and farmers—just to name a few of the relevant actors—we see that the "Go vegan, save a life" slogan isn't so plausible.

Of course, for all that, it's possible that you should go vegan—that it's morally required. All I've tried to show here is that one particular argument for veganism (or, rather, one particular family of arguments, all based on the idea that you make a difference via the way you shop) has problems. There are, however, plenty of other arguments for veganism worth considering. And in particular, there's an important argument for veganism that isn't supposed to depend on any assumptions about difference-making. Let's turn to it now. Its core idea is that we shouldn't be complicit in wrongdoing.

In this section, I've argued that the Simple Argument for Veganism fails because, even if you stop eating animal products, it's unlikely that fewer animals will suffer. I've argued that the Expected Utility Argument fails because it isn't clear that purchasing animal products fails to maximize expected utility. I've argued that the Negative Expected Utility Argument fails because there are too many animal products such that purchasing them probably has negative expected utility. In any case, I raised doubts about the moral premises in these arguments: that we should always prioritize preventing animals from suffering, that we should act so as to maximize expected utility, and that we should always avoid acting in ways that have negative expected utility.

3 Complicity

Maybe you've heard it said that a true friend is someone who will help you bury a body. I don't know a lot about the philosophy of friendship, so I'll let you sort out whether that's true. But either way, it seems pretty clear that the friend who helps you bury a body is *complicit* in the murde ... I mean ... *accident* ...

Anyway, someone is complicit, legally speaking, if they help or encourage another person to commit a crime. Similarly, we might say that someone is complicit, morally speaking, if they help or encourage another person to act wrongly. Let's have a look at an argument for veganism that's based on this idea.

3.1 The Anti-Complicity Argument

Here's an argument that isn't supposed to depend on your ability to make a difference. Some have claimed that it's attractive *precisely because* you can run it without getting lost in any complicated empirical questions.[8] The argument goes like this:

1. It's wrong to be complicit in an unjust practice.
2. Purchasing and/or consuming animal products make you complicit in an unjust practice.
3. So, it's wrong to purchase and/or consume animal products.

Let's call this the "Anti-Complicity Argument for Veganism" (or the "Anti-Complicity Argument," for short). A few clarifications are in order. The crucial idea behind the second premise is that animals deserve *respect*. People sometimes express the idea by saying that *animals aren't ours to use*. Raising them for food, of course, involves treating them as beings who *are* ours to use. If people were being used in that way, we'd say that the situation is unjust. The proponents of the Anti-Complicity Argument think the same about farming animals.

I'm going to bracket the question of *why* we might think that animals deserve respect (in this very specific, somewhat technical sense of "respect"). That's an important question, but I can't tackle it here. And as we'll see, we can make a lot of headway even if we grant this big moral assumption to some of veganism's defenders.

---

8. Tom Regan (2004), for instance, prefers it for exactly this reason (among others).

The short of it: let's assume that animals deserve respect and that farming them involves treating them unjustly; in other words, let's grant a big part of the second premise. Is that the end of the story? Does the argument go through?

Not obviously. To see why not, we should pause to note that there are more and less objectionable ways of being morally complicit. (Some of the cases that we will discuss are cases of legal complicity as well, but we can ignore that dimension here. There would be moral complicity in every case even if there weren't laws forbidding the relevant actions.) For instance, I can help you rob a bank by driving the getaway car. That's a very high level of complicity. On the other end of the spectrum, I can simply fail to say anything that discourages you from acting wrongly. For example, let's suppose that while you and I never go out to eat together, some very reliable mutual friends have informed me that you are a bad tipper, and I never call you out on it. I'm *not* saying that we finally go to a restaurant together, you decide not to leave a tip, and I just let it slide. I'm saying that while you and I are *never* in a situation where a tip has to be left, I just know this thing about you, and though I could discourage you from acting that way, I don't. There is still *some* sense in which I'm complicit in your bad tipping practices—it's the limit case where I "helped" you by enabling your behavior; I opted not to protest the way you operate—but it's obviously a very weak sense. And my guess is that very few of us think it's wrong to be complicit in that very weak sense.

The point: there are degrees of complicity, and depending on the action, the same degree of complicity might be more or less morally bad. As you might guess, there are lots of factors that seem relevant to where you fall on both spectrums. Here are some of them:

> *Knowledge.* Do you know that what the other person is doing is wrong? Or, perhaps more importantly, how good is your evidence that what the other person is doing is wrong?
>
> *Influence.* How much of a difference does your input make? Could the person pull off the wrongdoing without you? *Would* the person pull off the wrongdoing without you?
>
> *Intentionality.* Are you trying to help or encourage the other person to act wrongly? Alternately, are they simply being helped or encouraged by something you're doing, even

though you don't mean to help or encourage them? Suppose that you have very little influence, if any. Would you stop if you had more?

These three factors—knowledge, influence, and intentionality—are relevant to your degree of complicity. There are two others that are relevant to the overall moral badness of being complicit, independently of just how complicit you are.

> *Badness.* How bad is the action in which you're complicit? Really bad? Then all else equal, it's worse to be complicit in it. Not so bad? Then all else equal, it's less bad to be complicit in it.
>
> *Offsetting.* Are you doing anything to offset or somehow counterbalance your complicity? This question may not be relevant in all cases, of course: there might not be anything you can do to offset being complicit in a bank robbery. But lots of people think that, if you act in ways that have a significant environmental footprint—say, taking an international flight—you can "make up" for your complicity in climate change by purchasing carbon offsets. That is, you can fund projects that reduce carbon emissions elsewhere, and so make it less morally objectionable to fly.

When we lay out all these factors, it becomes apparent that "complicit or not" is the wrong way to think about complicity. We need a more nuanced approach. What does all this mean for the Anti-Complicity Argument?

In short, it means that we can reject the first premise of the argument: on the face of it, it isn't *always* wrong to be complicit in an unjust practice. It depends on what you know, on whether your action makes a difference, on your intentions, on the severity of the injustice, and on whether you make any effort to offset whatever you did. After all, as we said at the very beginning, we're *surrounded* by injustice: think about all the ways that businesses exploit their workers; institute policies that create or sustain gender, LGBTQ, and racial injustice; harm future generations via their environmental practices; assist other businesses in wrongdoing; and so much else. While it might be good to avoid complicity in every last injustice in every possible way, most of us don't think that we have to do *all* the not-buying, boycotting, canceling, and divesting, or at least not all the time. The alternative asks too much. So, the Anti-Complicity Argument fails.

3.2 The Revised Anti-Complicity Argument

Again, let's be charitable. The problem with the Anti-Complicity Argument is that it doesn't mention the various factors that affect both the degree of complicity and the badness of being complicit. This suggests the way forward for the Anti-Complicity Argument: namely, adding the relevant factors to the first premise.

This seems to be the view we get from Michael Huemer (2019), who offers an analogy designed to motivate the relevant tweaks. The analogy goes like this:

> You have a friend named "Killian," who happens to be a murderer. One day, you offer Killian $20,000 to get you a new car. Killian could carry out this task in a perfectly moral manner. But you know that the way he will in fact do it is by murdering some innocent person and stealing their car. You know this because Killian has performed tasks like this for you in the past, he always murders people along the way, and you always pay him for it afterward. You don't specifically tell him to murder anyone; you just know that that's the way he does things. So you tell Killian to get a car, he goes off, kills someone, steals their car, gives it to you, and you pay him $20,000 … [That's] like buying factory farmed meat. You didn't tell them to commit acts of extreme cruelty, but you know that that is how they do things, and you keep paying them for the product.[9]

According to Huemer, buying meat is like paying someone for a product that's acquired by murder. Being murdered seems to be a particularly awful injustice to the person who's killed. Paying someone with full knowledge of their role in murder seems like a particularly objectionable way of being complicit. Likewise, he thinks, the "extreme acts of cruelty" involved in factory farming are particularly awful injustices to animals. Moreover, paying grocery stores for products derived from this process seems like a particularly

---

9. Huemer 2019, 26.

objectionable way of being complicit. (It isn't just failing to criticize someone for acting less-than-optimally; instead, it's turning a blind eye to those "extreme acts of cruelty" and paying for their results anyway.) If Huemer is right, then both the badness of the action with which you're complicit (factory farming) and the type of complicity (with full knowledge, which is fairly objectionable) are of the type that don't just make complicity bad. Together, they make it wrong.

This gives us the Revised Anti-Complicity Argument for Veganism (or "the Revised Anti-Complicity Argument," for short):

1. If a practice is *extremely* unjust, then it's wrong to be *knowingly* complicit in it.
2. Purchasing and/or consuming animal products makes you knowingly complicit in an extremely unjust practice.
3. So, it's wrong to purchase and/or consume animal products.

This argument seems better than the last. But it isn't bulletproof, even if we ignore Premise #2, which is the one that makes the big moral claim about factory farming being an extremely unjust practice. Again, we're setting claims like that aside for now; we'll return to them in the second half of this opening statement. Here, we'll see how far we go with the premise that doesn't say anything about animals: namely, Premise #1. There are three issues with it that, jointly, seem to make it implausible.

Issue #1: *Influence.* Recall: your degree of complicity depends, at least in part, on how much influence you've got. But as we discussed when looking at difference-making arguments, you don't have much influence at all. So, you're less complicit than you would be otherwise. And if your purchases don't make any difference at all, then insofar as you've got *any* responsibility to avoid complicity, it seems pretty weak. In general, while it might be *good* to take symbolic stands, if it's really true that they're *just* symbolic stands, they're rarely obligatory.

Granted, it's often a good thing to take a symbolic stand. It's often bad not to. But it's also true that, at least when compared to actions that actually make a difference, it's pretty easy for other considerations to outweigh the reasons favoring the symbolic act. Imagine someone saying:

> Meat is tasty. I can get my kids to eat meaty meals without any fussing. So, although I *could* make some beans—which can be

delicious and I could get my kids to eat *with* some fussing—it's been a long day. So, I'm going to go into my backyard, shoot a few squirrels with the BB gun that I keep by the backdoor, butcher them, and cook them up.

Now imagine someone else saying:

Meat is tasty. I can get my kids to eat meaty meals without any fussing. So, although I *could* buy some beans—which are cheap, can be delicious, and I could get my kids to eat *with* some fussing—it's been a long day, my purchase doesn't make a difference, and I'd suck it up and deal if I really thought it *would* make a difference. So, I'm going to buy some chicken from the grocery store.

In the first case, not killing the squirrels is not just a symbolic stand. It makes a huge difference to the squirrels! In the second case, not buying the meat *is* just a symbolic stand. It makes no difference to any chicken. Whether or not we're satisfied by the reasoning in the second case, we should still acknowledge that the second justification is stronger than the first—not because the reason is much different, but because what's being justified is different. It's easier for practical considerations to trump symbolic considerations than non-symbolic ones.

Issue #2: *Intentionality*. Consider Meathead Mike. Meathead Mike knows what's happening on factory farms. He isn't upset about it. In fact, he's impressed by the efficiency of the system. He understands enough about the supply chain to recognize that his actions at the grocery store don't make a difference, but if they *did* make a difference, it wouldn't change how he shops. He likes meat, he likes it cheap, and he's happy to support the various actors that provide it. Meathead Mike doesn't make a difference, but he'd be happy to, as he's in favor of contemporary farming methods. It seems like Meathead Mike *intends to support* meat producers.

Let's contrast Meathead Mike with Sad Sally. Sad Sally also knows what's happening on factory farms. Unlike Meathead Mike, though, she hates it. Indeed, sometimes, the thought of what animals experience brings her to tears. She wishes she could prevent animals from suffering. However, she believes—rightly—that her choices as a consumer don't make any difference, and since some animal products are important to her because of the way she was raised, she buys them. That said, if Sad Sally thought her choices as a consumer *did* make a difference, she'd stop buying animal products immediately. Like Meathead Mike, Sad Sally doesn't make a difference. But unlike Meathead Mike, she *doesn't* want to cause more animal suffering, and she's *not* in favor of what factory farms do. It seems like Sad Sally *doesn't* intend to support meat producers.

Who's more complicit: Meathead Mike or Sad Sally? It seems to me that Meathead Mike deserves that title. And if so, then purchasing animal products itself doesn't guarantee equal levels of complicity. Your attitudes have some influence on just how complicit you are.

Issue #3: *Offsetting*. Sometimes, you can do something good to make up for something bad. And sometimes, that cancels out the bad entirely. Perhaps there's something analogous to carbon offsets for buying meat. Is there?

Arguably so. For instance, you could donate to an effective animal charity, of which there are many. Or you could encourage your friends and family members to reduce their animal product consumption, regardless of whether anyone stops entirely. Or you could volunteer at an animal sanctuary, freeing up their resources to help farmed animals. And so on.

However, someone might object that factory farming isn't like climate change. The point of buying carbon offsets, they might say, is to ensure that there is no net increase in carbon emissions as a result of your taking a flight (or what have you). The idea here is that it doesn't matter whether emissions are a bit higher in one location and lower in another; it's the net impact of total emissions that matters. When it comes to harming animals, though, net impacts *aren't* all that matter. It matters to *that chicken* that she not suffer, and you can't make that better *for her* by volunteering at an animal sanctuary. So, we might think that offsetting doesn't apply.

But suppose your purchases don't make a difference, as discussed earlier. It seems plausible that insofar as an action is a symbolic act, rather than a difference-making act, it's the kind of thing that can be offset. So, if not purchasing animal products is a good symbolic act, and you do the symbolically not-so-good thing of purchasing them anyway, you can probably make up for it by, say, donating to an effective charity—one that makes an actual difference to animals' wellbeing. After all, you haven't harmed *that chicken*, as you haven't harmed anyone. Moreover, if you do something good for animals that actually *does* make a difference, you've done something better than offsetting: you've actually improved the world relative to the way it would have been otherwise.

Where does all this leave us? The Revised Anti-Complicity Argument depends on this premise:

> If a practice is extremely unjust, then it's wrong to be knowingly complicit in it.

I'm granting that factory farming is extremely unjust. I'm suggesting, though, that not all kinds of complicity are morally equal. Sometimes, it's wrong to be complicit in wrongdoing; in other cases, it's bad or tragic or what have you—but not wrong. It seems to me that if you don't make a difference to the wrongdoing, don't want to cause it, and actively try to help in other ways, then your complicity isn't obviously wrong. Being complicit still might not be morally optimal, but as we said at the outset, that isn't the relevant standard here.

> In this section, I've argued that the Anti-Complicity Argument fails because it demands too much; it would require us to opt out of society entirely. I've argued that the Revised Anti-Complicity Argument fails because it ignores factors that are relevant to complicity, such as degree of influence, degree of intentionality, and the possibility of offsetting. In short, not all complicity is equal. Even if we grant that products are made in ways that involve serious injustices, there are ways of being complicit that aren't as bad and, as we've seen, may not even be wrong.

4   How Far Have We Come? Where Do We Need to Go?

Let's take stock. Humans treat many animals badly, especially in factory farms. What are you morally required to do as a result? According to many philosophers and animal advocates, you ought to go vegan. We've considered two basic kinds of argument for that claim. First, we looked at arguments that are based on difference-making: we should stop eating animals to help animals. Second, we examined anti-complicity-based arguments: factory farming is wrong and we ought to distance ourselves from wrongdoing.

The central problem with difference-making arguments is that individual consumers don't seem to make a difference. There are also problems with anti-complicity arguments, the main ones being that they're either too strong or too weak: on the one hand, they can fail by implying that we're just about always acting wrongly; on the other, they can fail by being insensitive to all factors that can mitigate both the degree and badness of complicity.

So that's it? You aren't obligated to go vegan?

Not quite. The first problem with drawing this conclusion is that we haven't considered every argument for veganism. Instead, we've just looked at some particularly significant examples. We can't infer that every argument for veganism doesn't work from the fact that a handful of arguments for veganism don't work.

For what it's worth, I do think that the problems we've discussed affect many other arguments for veganism. Notice, for instance, that the problem of not making a difference didn't just come out when we were talking about arguments based on difference-making: we also discussed it when considering anti-complicity arguments. As we saw, the moral significance of complicity is partially tied to your degree of influence and your ability to offset. If you don't make a difference, then either you are less complicit or it's less bad to be complicit. I think we're going to find the same thing when we examine other arguments: we'll find that your inability to make a difference weakens whatever reason people offer for not buying or eating animal products. Of course, it would take much more work to show that.[10] So, I can't conclude that defenders of veganism haven't met their burden.

The second problem with drawing this conclusion is that there seems to be a compelling challenge to my general approach. If those who defend veganism were being very charitable, they might say this about everything you've read so far:

Here's the thing, Bob. Sure, there are some puzzles when it comes to arguments for veganism. It's hard to figure out the odds that a particular purchase makes a difference. Yes, it's tricky to come up with a general moral principle that tells when

---

10. I've tried to do that work elsewhere: see Fischer (2020).

it is and isn't wrong to be complicit. But you're missing the forest for the trees. Factory farming is a moral tragedy of epic proportions; it might be humanity's greatest moral failing. *How could it be morally okay to support that?* Put differently, if there are problems with the arguments for veganism that we've offered, the reasonable thing is to accept that we need to spend more time tweaking the premises—not to abandon the conclusion. If animals matter as much as people, it just makes sense that we ought to be vegan. The challenge is to explain *why* it's wrong to consume animal products, not *that* it's wrong.

The upshot: I can't canvas all the possible arguments for veganism, and if factory farming is indeed humanity's greatest moral failing, it seems crazy to think that *every* argument for veganism fails. Put these two observations together, and you have a serious objection. If it seems plausible that there is at least *one* good argument for the view that we ought to be vegan, then who cares if a handful of them don't work?

My reply to this objection has two parts. The first is simple; the second will take the rest of my opening statement to develop.

The first and simple part of the reply is just a reminder of the methodological point I made in the beginning. I think you're entitled to assume that you are acting permissibly unless someone can show otherwise. The burden of proof is on those who want to establish moral wrongness, not on those who want to assume moral permissibility. So, until we have a good argument for veganism, it's reasonable to assume that we aren't obligated to be vegans, however awful the situation for non-human animals. (And I agree: it's really awful.) The objection is based on the opposite view: namely, that given how bad things are for animals on factory farms, we should assume that it's wrong to purchase and consume animal products until someone shows that it's okay. The objection says that the burden of proof is on the person who assumes that it is permissible to consume animal products.

I think we should reject this view. The world is full of terrible things to which we bear various direct and indirect connections. If we start assuming that it's wrong to have those connections even when we can't explain why it's wrong to have them, we will just end up condemning everything we do. Of course, a blanket condemnation of our actions is always an option; we can say that we're constantly engaging in wrongdoing in a world that's as dark as ours.

But I don't see the point of saying that. I think of ethics as helping us distinguish between what we should and shouldn't do in an imperfect world; it's supposed to help us live more decently in indecent circumstances. If our ethic just condemns all our actions, it isn't helping. It's blaming us for too much. So, I think we should set that approach aside.

The second part of my reply involves trying to address the core of the objection directly. The objection is based on the claim that animals matter as much as people. That's why the objection insists that animal agriculture is a moral tragedy. I sympathize with that conclusion. Around the globe, human beings raise and kill *trillions* of animals every single year. Moreover, those animals are raised in conditions, and killed in ways, that we would regard as horrifying if our pets had to endure them. If people had to endure them, words would fail entirely. If animals matter as much as people, then factory farms are a moral nightmare. There is nothing we do that's worse.

As I've indicated many times now, I agree that factory farming is terrible. But I don't think that animals matter as much as people. So far, we've been granting that something like that claim is true. Again, I haven't challenged the difference-making and complicity arguments by saying things like this:

> Sure, you make a difference when you shop, but animals don't matter as much as people, so it's fine to cause animals some harm.

Or:

> Sure, you're complicit in wrongdoing, but animals don't matter as much as people, so it's not a big deal to be complicit in wrongdoing toward animals.

Instead, I've *assumed* that animals matter as much as people, and I've argued that *even given that assumption*, there are problems with the arguments for veganism.

Now, though, we need to question the assumption. If we can show that it's reasonable to reject it, then we can go a long way toward addressing the objection that we've been considering. Here's the idea. Suppose, as I've argued, that there are problems with the standard arguments for veganism *even if we assume* that animals matter as much as people. Then, if animals *don't* matter as much as people—it becomes fairly plausible that the defenders of veganism won't be able to meet their burden. That is, if there are problems with the main arguments for veganism even when we grant a big assumption about the moral importance of animals, and that assumption turns out not to be true, it seems a lot less likely that we're going to find a good argument for veganism somewhere else. Not impossible, of course, but much less probable. Given the space available, that will have to do.

> In this section, we identified a serious objection to the argument thus far. I haven't explored every argument for veganism and, if animals matter as much as people, we might think that at least one argument for veganism has to work. My reply has two parts. The first is methodological: I think we need to see the positive case for the claim that it's wrong to consume animal products; the burden of proof is on the person who says you have an obligation. The second is to challenge the claim that animals matter as much as people.

5   The Equal Consideration Principle

Thus far, I've been using phrases like, "animals matter as much as people." Phrases like this give you a feeling for the idea I want to challenge, but they don't actually express it precisely. Now, however, we need to be precise. The relevant claim is:

> *The Principle of Equal Consideration of Interests* (or the "Equal Consideration Principle," for short). To the degree that interests are similar, they deserve equal consideration in our moral deliberations regardless of whose interests they are.

In other words, if a pig and a child are experiencing roughly the same level of hunger, then at least as far as their hunger goes, we have no reason to prioritize the child over the pig. Humans don't get special consideration simply because they're humans.

To be clear, the Equal Consideration Principle doesn't imply that humans and animals should be treated the same way. Depriving you of food for a week would be a big deal; depriving a python of food for a week wouldn't be a big deal at all, as they can go six months between meals. So, giving equal consideration to your interests and the python's would *look* like you were getting special treatment—you would get food every day and the python wouldn't—but that wouldn't be what's going on at all. Instead, that's what would be morally appropriate given the differences between your interests.

What's more, the Equal Consideration Principle doesn't imply that all interests matter the same. The claim is only that if some interests matter more than others, the difference in moral importance has nothing to do with whose interests they are. It's plausible, for instance, that *basic* interests—in food, in not experiencing pain, in staying alive, etc.—are especially important. By contrast, *non-basic* interests—in having a job we love as opposed to one that's just okay, in wearing certain styles of clothing over others—range from the moderately important to the trivial. When basic interests go up against non-basic interests, basic interests win. The cases we're interested in—namely, people buying and consuming animal products they don't need—involve basic animal interests competing with non-basic human interests. So, if basic interests matter more than non-basic ones, the Equal Consideration Principle implies that in these cases, animals' interests are more important.

But the Equal Consideration Principle goes much further. To get a feel for its implications, you can run through a little imaginative exercise. Begin by calling to mind a situation involving animals being harmed in some way—perhaps a lab where experiments are performed on mice. Then, swap out the animals for human beings. In the new scenario, people are experimenting *on other people*, perhaps giving these people some form of cancer to see how the disease progresses (without their consent, of course, since no one asks the animals). Would that be morally okay to sacrifice the relevant individuals' interests in this way? If you think it wouldn't be—and if the explanation for *why* it wouldn't be involves interests that humans and animals share—then the Equal Consideration Principle may well imply that it's wrong when such things are done to animals.

Granted, there are going to be many situations in which humans have interests that animals don't. For instance, people have an interest in religious freedom that, presumably, most animals don't have (on the plausible assumption that animals aren't religious). So, sometimes you'll need to control for that in your imagination. Don't just swap out the animals for random human beings; instead, swap them out for human beings who don't seem to have the interest that's complicating things. This might mean imagining that the humans are members of one of the groups we discussed earlier: third-trimester fetuses, month-old infants, people with severe cognitive disabilities, late-stage Alzheimer's patients, or those in permanent vegetative states. Would doing cancer research on late-stage Alzheimer's patients seem any less wrong? Suppose not, and suppose further that there are no other differences in the interests of late-stage Alzheimer's patients and non-human animals that could explain why it's wrong to experiment on these humans but not wrong to experiment on the animals. Then, the Equal Consideration Principle probably implies that it's wrong to experiment on the animals.

5.1 The Argument Against the Equal Consideration Principle

In philosophical circles, the Equal Consideration Principle is pretty common. Nevertheless, I don't think anyone can be faulted for rejecting it. The conclusions that follow are so extreme—so wildly contrary to our ordinary moral outlook—that it makes sense to insist on humans being morally special just to avoid them. That is, it makes sense to reject the Equal Consideration Principle in favor of a view we'll call *Human Exceptionalism*:

> *Human Exceptionalism.* Human interests matter more than the interests of non-human animals.

Human Exceptionalism is intentionally vague. It doesn't say how much more human interests matter than non-human animal interests. It doesn't say whether human interests always outweigh the interests of non-human animals. It doesn't say why human interests would matter more than the interests of non-human animals. It only says that human interests matter more; it's otherwise silent. As we'll see, there are good reasons for this.

Before we get there, though, we need to introduce the Argument Against the Equal Consideration Principle (or "the Anti-Equal Consideration Argument," for short). It's this:

1. If the Equal Consideration Principle were true, then various radical conclusions would follow.
2. Those radical conclusions are false.
3. So, the Equal Consideration Principle is false.

I won't have much to say about the second premise of the Anti-Equal Consideration Argument. It's basically a version of an argument that is sometimes given against *skepticism*, which is the view that we don't have all the ordinary knowledge we seem to have, such as that I'm currently in front of a computer, or that you are currently reading a book. That argument goes:

1. If skepticism is true, then I don't know that I'm in front of a computer.
2. But I do know that I'm in front of a computer.
3. So, skepticism is false.

In other words, I'm sure that I'm looking at my computer right now. If skepticism implies that I don't know that, then skepticism has to go. Similarly, I'm saying that if the Equal Consideration Principle implies all the radical things I think it implies, then I don't have to shrug my shoulders and accept all those radical conclusions. Instead, it makes sense to reject the Equal Consideration Principle.

The skeptic reasons like this:

> For all you know, you could be in the Matrix! You could be a brain in a vat that's controlled by a mad scientist! You could be a disembodied spirit who's being deceived by an evil demon! You could be living in one of those holodecks on Star Trek! You can't rule out those possibilities!

One common reply to the skeptic is to insist that being able to rule out those possibilities is the wrong standard for knowing that you *aren't* in the Matrix, etc., or at least the wrong standard for knowing various boring facts about, e.g., your own body or the weather.

In a sense, we've already seen one radical implication of the Equal Consideration Principle. You might have felt uncomfortable with the "swap out animals for humans with severe cognitive disabilities" imaginative exercise. If so, congratulations! The Equal Consideration Principle makes it hard to avoid the conclusion that if a human and a dog have roughly the same cognitive capacities— as can happen—then they have roughly the same interests. And if they have roughly the same interests, then if it's okay to do something to a dog based on the dog's interests, it's okay to do it to a human with severe cognitive disabilities based on the human's interests. That's an extreme result indeed.

However, we're only just getting started. Let's consider five other conclusions we can reach using the Equal Consideration Principle. Jointly, they make up my case for the first premise of the Anti-Equal Consideration Argument.

5.2   General Considerations about Alleviating Suffering

We begin with a more abstract, general point—one that sets the stage for many of the other implications we'll discuss. The short of it: if the Equal Consideration Principle is true, animals' suffering should receive far more attention than it does—which, of course, means that humans' suffering should get far *less* attention than it does. Why is this?

We have some moral reason to alleviate suffering. All else equal, the more intense the suffering, the stronger the reason to alleviate it. And all else equal, we have more reason to alleviate the suffering of a larger group of individuals than a smaller one. If the Equal Consideration Principle is true, then animals' suffering is no more or less morally important than humans' suffering. But there are, at any given time, many more animals suffering far more intensely than human beings are suffering: just think of all the pigs and cattle being castrated on factory farms, the hens having their beaks trimmed, and the countless fish infected with parasites in aquaculture operations. So, we have far stronger reasons to alleviate animals' suffering relative to humans' suffering. Insofar as we prioritize humans' suffering when we could be attending to animals' suffering, we are ignoring what we have most moral reason to do.

Just think about everything we do to alleviate humans' suffering. The networks of hospitals, clinics, doctor's offices, and primary care facilities. Unending medical research. The many kinds of first responders. Countless social programs. Charitable giving at the individual, corporate, state, and federal levels. Military-backed peacekeeping missions. The list goes on. I don't have the numbers, but I'd guess that if we were to make a pie chart representing all the dollars spent on humans' suffering vs. animals' suffering, animals would only get a sliver. If the Equal Consideration Principle is true, this arrangement is almost certainly wrong.

5.2.1   Wild Animals

It's one thing to say that we should allocate more resources toward alleviating animals' suffering. It's another to consider where, exactly, those resources should go. Here's another radical conclusion: a lot of those resources should go toward wild animals—and not to conserve them, but either to kill them or to genetically modify them.

We often think of the wild as an idyllic place, where animals roam free living the kinds of lives that are best for them. However, even when ecosystems are healthy, animals are living the kinds of lives that are best for propagating their *species*, not for maximizing their welfare as individuals. Wild animals regularly suffer from hunger, thirst, extremes of heat and cold, parasites, predators, stress from the threat of predation, inability to find mates, the loss of young, disease, injury, and any number of other factors. Humans don't cause this suffering; animals don't experience all these things because of climate change, pollution, or habitat destruction. Instead, this is simply the way the natural world works. Indeed, as Richard Dawkins says of all this suffering: "It must be so. If there ever is a time of plenty, this very fact will automatically lead to an increase in the population until the natural state of starvation and misery is restored."[11]

Given the Equal Consideration Principle, we have reason to alleviate animal suffering whenever we would have reason to alleviate comparable human suffering. Again, the greater the suffering and the greater the number of individuals suffering, the stronger the reason. In the case of wild animals, the suffering is intense and extensive indeed, giving us a very strong reason to act.[12] Unfortunately, though, we don't have many systematic remedies available. Quite often, it may be the case that the only thing we can do for animals is kill them. And in fact, some philosophers have suggested that this is exactly what we ought to do.[13] Others don't necessarily favor killing; they just think we should do what we can to prevent animals from coming into existence. If, for instance, we can reduce the total number of animals who come into existence by turning forests into parking lots, then that is, they say, a strong consideration in favor of creating more parking. The more optimistic philosophers don't favor either strategy: they think we should genetically modify

---

11. Dawkins 1995, 132.
12. Horta 2017.
13. Bramble 2021.

animals, perhaps turning predators into herbivores, and radically reducing birth rates so that animals don't reproduce beyond the carrying capacities of their local environments.[14] Obviously, this would require massive investments in research and wildlife management—resources that, of course, would have to be redirected from helping humans to helping animals. So not only is the idea of what we ought to do radical, but the resource reallocation that would be necessary is radical too.

5.2.2 Insects

We love lions, tigers, and bears. Perhaps we can accept that we should do far more for them than we currently do. But let's recognize that the Equal Consideration Principle doesn't just tell us to spend more money on large and lovely animals. We should also be worried about bugs.

It isn't clear whether insects have morally relevant interests. They might be little robots, ambling about their environments without actually experiencing anything. But if they *do* have experiences, then they have morally relevant interests, and the Equal Consideration Principle applies to them too. So now we face a hard question: how should we handle our uncertainty about whether insects have morally relevant interests?

There are two basic approaches: the expected utility approach and the precautionary approach.[15] You'll recall the core idea behind the expected utility approach from our discussion of various difference-making arguments for veganism. An expected utility calculation requires some values and probabilities to multiply together. We're assuming the Equal Consideration Principle, so if insects *do* suffer, their suffering gets the same weight we'd give to comparable human suffering. That, essentially, is the value portion. What about the probability portion? What we need is an estimate of the odds that insects can suffer. As you might guess, that's very difficult to provide—at least if we want to be at all precise. Thankfully, though, we don't need to be precise in this context. Instead, we can simply pick the lowest probability that doesn't seem totally crazy, which will give us a lower bound: it's *at least* that likely that insects have morally relevant experiences.

14. McMahan 2010.
15. Sebo 2018.

What probability should we use? Let's suppose that the probability of insects being able to suffer is just 1%—low odds indeed. According to one estimate, there are ten *quintillion* insects alive at any given time. That means that even if the odds of insects being able to suffer are just 1%, their suffering is morally equivalent to the suffering of *100 quadrillion* people, which is over 12 million times the global human population (which, as I write this, is around 8 billion). Once we realize this, we may find ourselves tempted to revise our probability estimate downward—say, to 0.1%, or even 0.01%. But first, let's note that at some point, the probability estimate becomes ridiculous. Do we *really* think the odds could be that low? Second, let's note that shifting the decimal over a few places doesn't change how uncomfortable the result is. Suppose we revise that probability estimate downward even further still: we'll say the probability that insects can suffer is just 0.001%. Now, the expected utility calculation says that the suffering of insects is morally equivalent to the suffering of *100 trillion* people.

Are things any less radical with the precautionary approach? Absolutely not. The precautionary approach says: if you don't know that a being *can't* suffer, treat it as though it can. So, since we don't know that insects can't suffer, we should treat each insect as though it can. When we combine that conclusion with the Equal Consideration Principle, we get the result that each insect's suffering should be given as much weight as we'd give to similar human suffering. If anything, then, this result is even more extreme than the one we get from the expected utility approach. (Just consider what this would mean for the ethics of crop production, which involves spraying pesticides that kill extraordinary numbers of insects every time they're used.)

5.2.3   Poverty

We spend huge amounts to alleviate humans' suffering. We spend comparatively little on animals' suffering, even though there are far more animals suffering far more intensely. If the Equal Consideration Principle is true, this is hard to justify. And it isn't just that we should reallocate resources: the Equal Consideration Principle suggests that we should actively try to *prevent* the alleviation of some human suffering, since it would be dramatically worse for animals if we did.

Here's one example of this problem. Animal products aren't cheap, so when people are in poverty, they don't eat as many of them. However, people tend to prefer animal products over plant-based alternatives, so as people's incomes rise, they tend to eat more animal products. And, as it happens, incomes are steadily rising around the globe. Unfortunately, this is very bad news for animals, as the increasing demand is being met by factory farming. As good as it is for people to get out of poverty, the cost in terms of animal suffering is enormous: for every person who rises into the global middle class, there are dozens—or perhaps even hundreds—of animals who pay the price. Given the Equal Consideration Principle, we have a strong reason to prevent this from happening. If our choice is between keeping people in poverty and having more factory farms, it would be better if we kept people in poverty.[16] The situation here is a bit like the one we'd face if we knew that if we helped people out of poverty in one country, they would immediately start torturing many more people in another country. All else equal, of course, pulling people out of poverty is good. *But if they would torture people with their increased income*, the price is too high. Likewise, if the global poor will start causing enormous animal suffering with their increased income—and if the Equal Consideration Principle is true—then poverty alleviation may be morally wrong. Indeed, poverty *maintenance* may be morally right.

5.2.4 Animal Citizenship

If animals' interests deserve equal consideration, then they probably deserve political recognition too. That might well mean granting animals citizenship.[17]

Remember: you don't need to be able to vote—or understand what citizenship is—to be a citizen. Children are citizens; so are those with severe cognitive disabilities. Still, these individuals have legal rights and they are recognized as members of the political community. Similarly, if animals' interests deserve equal consideration, then they should have legal rights and be recognized as members of the political community too. Citizenship, after all, is the way we ensure that the state recognizes its primary responsibilities: the state is for citizens first. But animals have been living here as long as anyone else. This is their homeland too. Moreover, they would benefit from citizenship—because it would give them legal

---

16. Plant 2019.
17. Donaldson and Kymlicka 2011.

representation—and they suffer because they aren't recognized in this way. So, it seems unjust to deny them this status.

Notice that the same line of reasoning will get you to property rights for animals. If animals' interests deserve equal consideration and if they have an interest in land, then they have some moral claim to it. Indeed, it seems to be a very strong claim insofar as animals' lives often literally depend on access to land. (Habitat loss is widely recognized as one of the main drivers of extinction—a point about species rather than individuals, but relevant to individuals too.) Moreover, if animals were actively using particular tracts of land long before humans came on the scene, and that land was simply taken away, then it seems like animals were treated unjustly: they were robbed of all the goods that come along with access to, and control of, territory.

You may have noticed another idea in the background here: namely, the idea that current animals can be owed things because past animals were treated badly. We often accept this when it comes to people. For instance, we often think that we owe Indigenous peoples reparations (which may come in the form of land rights or some other kind of compensation) due to past injustices. Likewise, we might argue, we can owe reparations to animals because we've systematically denied them citizenship, taken their land, and we've largely allowed our laws to ignore them. In any case, the basic thought here is that once we grant equal *moral* consideration to animals' interests, a wide range of *political* responsibilities are probably going to come along as well. The way to address those will probably be through dramatic legal reforms—including, but not limited to, making animals citizens.

6 Taking Stock

I've only hinted at the lines of reasoning that lead to these conclusions. Still, you can probably see how the arguments might be developed. Let's put them all together. If the Equal Consideration Principle is true, then:

1. We should prioritize relieving animal suffering given its severity and scope.
2. We should intervene in nature to help wild animals, perhaps by killing enormous numbers of them or by genetically engineering them.

3. Insect suffering is, in the aggregate, more important than human suffering.
4. We have good reason to let poor people stay poor if it saves a greater number of animals from extensive harm.
5. We should give animals various political rights, including citizenship and property rights, and we may owe them reparations.

I don't know what you think about these five conclusions, but I'll say this much: I don't think you'd be unreasonable to reject them. Indeed, here are some positions that seem very reasonable:

1. Given the choice between helping humans and animals who are suffering in comparable ways, it would usually be wrong to help the animals.
2. While there is nothing wrong with intervening in nature to correct anthropogenic impacts, we shouldn't try to alter the processes that naturally occur in ecosystems—including, of course, predation and considerable amounts of animal suffering.
3. No amount of insect suffering could ever be more important than human suffering.
4. We should do what we can to lift people out of extreme poverty, whatever the consequences for animals.
5. While the law ought to protect animal welfare, it should not recognize animals as citizens or grant them property rights. We do not owe them reparations.

I'm not saying that I believe all these things. For instance, I'm not sure about the second. I can get my head around the idea—and sometimes feel—that the world is a desperately tragic place, and the fact that life was created by the brutal process of natural selection is one of its most horrifying features. (Then again, I might be depressed!) So, I didn't highlight those five implications of the Equal Consideration Principle, or their alternatives, for autobiographical reasons. Instead, I'm trying to make it clear that the principle's implications are radical enough that I couldn't fault anyone for rejecting them. For many of us, those implications are dealbreakers. They threaten some very, very basic features of a common moral outlook. They challenge fundamental convictions about what justice requires. They toss aside standard views about the biggest moral problems in the world, replacing them with incredibly surprising alternatives. And if these implications *are* dealbreakers, then given their connection to the Equal Consideration Principle, it makes sense to reject the principle.

Of course, someone might object: "Hey! Those aren't *really* implications of the Equal Consideration Principle. In every case, we can find other assumptions that ought to be rejected so that we don't end up with such radical conclusions."

There are two problems with this response. First, this kind of reply becomes implausible as the number of radical implications adds up. If I just gave one example of a radical implication, then it would be fair to think that I'm mistaken about it. People make mistakes about what follows from what all the time! But the more examples I can give, the less plausible it is that the Equal Consideration Principle has totally boring implications.

Second, though I don't have time to show this, I'll just suggest that many of the challenges to these implications are going to be based on empirical disagreements. That is, they're going to be something like, "The Equal Consideration Principle doesn't imply that we should genetically engineer wild animals because that would actually lead to more suffering." (I'm not saying that's true; it's just the kind of thing someone might say.) However, this sort of move is totally unsatisfying. The right reply is: "So you're saying that the *only* reason we shouldn't genetically engineer wild animals is because it would cause more suffering? That's almost as bad! Moreover, if that's right, then as soon as we find a technological solution for that problem, we're back where we started."

In sum, if the Equal Consideration Principle is true, then some radical implications follow. It seems reasonable to reject the Equal Consideration Principle on that basis. But weren't we talking about veganism? What's the connection again?

7 Back to Veganism

I started my contribution to this debate by assuming that animals matter. As I said before, I believe they do. However, mattering is one thing; deserving equal consideration is another. If animals deserve equal consideration, then animal agriculture is probably the most pressing moral issue of our time. And if animal agriculture *is* the most pressing moral issue of our time, then it wouldn't just be *a* cause—one among the many that might attract some of your attention. Instead, it would be *the* cause. As a result, the objection we considered earlier—that if animals matter as much as people, it *just makes sense* that we ought to be vegan—seems pretty plausible.

To give a very charged analogy, it just makes sense that if the members of Group A are trying to wipe out the members of Group B, you should distance yourself from the members of Group A. Don't be associated *in any way* with people who are committing genocide. Yes, it may take some work to find the precise moral principle that explains why this is so. But it seems obvious that any problems along the way to finding it are problems to be solved— not reasons to conclude that, well, so much for the idea that you have that duty.

As I've just argued, though, it seems entirely reasonable to deny that the Equal Consideration Principle is true. One of the ways that we assess moral principles is by considering how well they fit with our considered moral judgments. Insofar as the Equal Consideration Principle conflicts deeply with our considered moral judgments, we should be less inclined to believe it. And it *does* conflict deeply with some of our considered moral judgments; it has radical implications indeed.

This doesn't imply, of course, that factory farming is trivial. I'm arguing that we can reject the Equal Consideration Principle, not that we can reject the view that animals matter. They *do* matter. Just not as much—or, at least, it can be reasonable to think that. And if they matter less, then it doesn't "just make sense" that we ought to be vegan. It isn't *crazy*, of course. There are good reasons to make the switch! But good reasons don't necessarily generate obligations. You've got good reasons to do lots of things.

Remember the big picture. Humans treat many animals badly, especially in factory farms. What are you morally required to do in response to that fact? According to many philosophers and animal advocates, the answer is that you ought to go vegan. We've considered and criticized two basic kinds of argument for that claim—one based on difference-making and another based on concerns about complicity. Of course, we haven't considered every possible argument for veganism, so we can't conclude that defenders of veganism haven't met their burden.

However, we can get a lot closer to that conclusion by trying to show that there probably isn't a better argument out there. One way to do that is by suggesting, as I did earlier (and very briefly), that the problems we've discussed don't *only* apply to those arguments for veganism. They probably apply more broadly. But the other and more important strategy is to challenge the assumption that drives many arguments for veganism, including the one we've already criticized: namely, the Equal Consideration Principle. If we don't owe animals' interests equal consideration, then it's a lot less plausible that, of all the morally important things you could do, responding to animal agriculture by being vegan is morally essential. So, though that still isn't enough to show that defenders of veganism haven't met their burden, it gets us in the ballpark, which—I hope—is good enough for present purposes.

All that said, we should spend some time on two objections. I'm trying to close the gap between "some arguments fail" and "the defenders of veganism haven't met their burden" by criticizing the Equal Consideration Principle. So, my criticism had better be good. What can be said against it?

The first objection is that we shouldn't trust the intuitions that led us to reject the Equal Consideration Principle. Those intuitions can be *debunked*. In other words, we can show why they aren't reliable. The second objection is that if we reject the Equal Consideration Principle, we'll have to say *other* very implausible things. So, we can't avoid radical conclusions by rejecting the Equal Consideration Principle; we can only avoid *some* radical conclusions. Once we appreciate this, it seems unreasonable to reject the Equal Consideration Principle simply because of its radical implications.

7.1 Debunking

The basic idea behind a debunking argument is that certain discoveries about the origins of our beliefs should affect whether we trust them. This is uncontroversial in other contexts. You're driving down the highway on a very hot day; it looks as though there's water on the road up ahead. Before you know about such optical illusions, you'd probably trust your eyes, believing that there is, in fact, water on the road up ahead. But after you learn about the illusion, you wouldn't. Instead of taking the way things *seem* (in this case) to be the way things *are*, you'd ignore the way things seem.

It's one thing to challenge the way things seem to us perceptually. But what about our ethical intuitions? Can those also be undermined by discovering how they're produced?

Yes. Consider C. P. Ellis, a member of the Ku Klux Klan who later became a civil rights activist (!). When he told his story toward the end of his life, he offered some insights into how his racist beliefs formed. Here's one glimpse into the process. Ellis grew up dirt poor, struggled to get ahead himself, and suffered setback after setback in life. Eventually, he had a heart attack while still quite young and, while unable to work, lost his business. He told the interviewer that after that last experience:

> I really began to get bitter. I didn't know who to blame. I tried to find somebody. I began to blame it on black people. I had to hate somebody. Hatin' America is hard to do because you can't see it to hate it. You gotta have somethin' to look at to hate. (Laughs.) The natural person for me to hate would be black people, because my father before me was a member of the Klan. As far as he was concerned, it was the savior of the white people. It was the only organization in the world that would take care of the white people. So I began to admire the Klan.[18]

Think about what Ellis is saying here. He understands that (1) he just needed someone to hate and (2) his hatred for black people was based on the fact that his father had hated black people. But based on the way he says it, and where he ends up, it's clear he understands that these weren't good reasons to hate black people. Yes, black people *seemed* awful to him at that time, but not based on a process worth trusting. Needing a target, and choosing one based on your dad's biases, isn't a reliable way to find out who deserves respect. In other words, Ellis is debunking his old beliefs: he's explaining how he formed them and acknowledging that this was a bad method.

Let's be clear: I am *not* saying that racist beliefs are just like the ones that conflict with the Equal Consideration Principle. Rather, I'm saying that *we can question how our beliefs were formed.* When we do, we sometimes discover that they weren't formed in a great way. When that happens, perhaps we shouldn't hang on to those beliefs anymore. So, if it turns out that the beliefs that conflict with the Equal Consideration Principle weren't formed in a great way, then perhaps we should abandon those beliefs. The Equal Consideration Principle wins.

---

18. Turkel 2005, 198.

My reply, essentially, is that it's going to be really hard to offer the debunking story that this objection requires. I have no idea how to explain away the beliefs that conflict with the Equal Consideration Principle without explaining away far too many of our moral beliefs. To see why, let's consider this question: What story can we tell about the origins of the beliefs that conflict with the Equal Consideration Principle? Insofar as we understand their backstory, it seems to be some very messy combination of the *general* story about how we came to have *any* moral beliefs and the wildly complicated history of human/animal relations. I don't know all the relevant parts, nor how to fit the parts I can identify into a single coherent narrative. Still, here are at least some of the things we would need to say:

> Over thousands upon thousands of years, human beings developed a range of psychological and social devices that made it possible to cooperate with other humans in increasingly large groups. Although we share with animals many of the capacities that made this possible, we have sophisticated versions of those capacities that are coordinated in the right way to produce a distinctive form of life. Indeed, it's so distinctive that people have come to think about humans as fundamentally different from animals—which isn't entirely true, but isn't entirely false either. The "fundamentally different" idea is even more tempting because, throughout so much of human history, most animals have been either threats or resources (or both), making it very tempting to view animals as "others" who need to be managed in one way or another (and, in our ancestors' defense, often did need to be managed if those ancestors wanted to survive). And, of course, viewing animals in these ways is made easier because animals don't look like us; they don't pass the intuitive "ingroup" test based on shared physiology. What's more, we often can't communicate with animals except in the most basic ways. We certainly can't deliberate with them or make agreements with them, and in many cases, we can only coerce them into behaving in the ways we want. And now, after generations of viewing animals as threats or resources, tremendous population growth, and an intense focus on intra- rather than interspecies relations (that is, on how humans relate to one another rather than on how they relate to animals), we both use and neglect animals in so many ways that it is difficult

to imagine a world in which their interests are given the consideration we give human interests. There is a stunning amount of momentum behind the status quo, some of which is motivated by deep moral concerns about the interests of, and justice for, human beings. As a result, it's almost impossible for most people to resist concluding that animals' interests are less important than people's interests, as so many of our moral judgments seem to assume exactly that.

I get the idea that, after you learn about the water-on-a-very-hot-road illusion, you shouldn't trust your eyes when it seems like there is water up ahead on a very hot road. Although I'm sure the physics is really complicated, the significance of it is fairly simple: a certain kind of situation reliably gives rise to a false impression; so, it would be a mistake to trust that impression. However, I don't know what to say about the story I just outlined. What kind of situation is it? What should we compare it to? How confident should we be that it's given rise to a false impression that animals' interests matter less than people's interests? I don't have good answers here.

To be clear: some of these factors don't seem to be morally wonderful. Isolated from the rest, we might observe that choosing ingroup members based on shared physiology doesn't seem justifiable. But when we put this complicated set of factors together, I have no idea whether that process—if it's even appropriate to call it a process—is unreliable. It's just too messy; there's too much going on. And as I've suggested, I don't see how we're going to come up with an analogy to help us sort through it. It isn't as though we can say: "Well look, here's this *other* case with very similar features and we agree that *there* the process is unreliable." No: there's obviously no simple parallel to be made. There is nothing else like our relationship with non-human animals, which makes it very difficult to show that it's an unreliable process.

For what it's worth, I don't think anyone has even tried to show that. Instead, people give one-off stories. When they try to debunk our intuitions about insects, they talk about how we have biases against small things that don't look like us. When they try to debunk our intuitions about not intervening in nature, they say that we have an optimistic bias that prevents us from recognizing how awful nature actually is. And so on. No one looks at all these beliefs—that we ought to help the poor even if that has negative implications for animals, that insect suffering can't outweigh human suffering, that animals should be citizens—as a package. But that's what we should do, since what's striking about them only emerges when we consider them all together. These beliefs should be examined together because of the consistent theme that humans matter more than animals. Indeed, there's a case to be made that humans are what they are because they see themselves as distinct and distinctly important. I'm not sure whether those elements can be removed from our worldview without rendering it unrecognizable.

This brings us to the second and more serious problem for the idea that we can debunk the intuitions that run counter to the Equal Consideration Principle. Once we consider those intuitions as a package, we quickly see that any story that debunks all these intuitions would have even *more* extreme implications. Intuitions like these form the backbone of our moral outlook. They amount to the idea that we may and should focus on human interests first—a view that's antithetical to the Equal Consideration Principle. If we give up that assumption, then it would be hard to explain why it's okay to build new housing for the homeless (which displaces wild animals), help people out of poverty (since they'll eat more animals), support medical research (which usually involves experimenting on animals), eat more plants than necessary (recalling that those plants were sprayed with insecticides), or any of the other countless ways we put humans first. If we think we aren't entitled to our intuitions about animals, then we aren't entitled to intuitions about all *sorts* of claims, since there are almost always links between them.

In sum, debunking arguments try to challenge our intuitions by way of their origins. But it isn't clear we can run a good debunking argument against the intuitions we used against the Equal Consideration Principle—we can't clearly identify a process or explain why it's unreliable—and in any case, it looks like a debunking argument will challenge too many of our moral beliefs to be plausible.

7.2 Radical Either Way

That's enough on the debunking argument. There is, however, a second objection to the idea that it's reasonable to reject the Equal Consideration Principle. To understand it, we need some background. One standard argument for the Equal Consideration Principle is that it explains what's wrong with racism, sexism, and xenophobic ideologies. Essentially, the idea is that what's wrong with racism is that the racist gives extra weight to the interests of the members of his race; or, equivalently, he discounts the interests of members of other races.[19] And since race isn't a morally relevant consideration, the racist acts wrongly. Likewise, of course, defenders of the Equal Consideration Principle want to say that far too many of us give extra weight to the interests of our own species; or, equivalently, we discount the interests of members of other species. Since species membership isn't a morally relevant consideration—membership in a particular biological category alone doesn't seem to be morally important—it's wrong for us to do this. We should give everyone's interests—black and white, male and female, human and non-human—equal consideration.

Now we're ready for the objection. The objection says that if we allow for species-based discrimination, then we'll have no story about why it's wrong to be racist, sexist, or xenophobic. We'll be stuck with the conclusion that we can privilege anyone's interests—or discount anyone's interests—on the basis of a morally arbitrary category. So, since we all agree that that kind of arbitrary discrimination would be wrong, we can't avoid radical conclusions by rejecting the Equal Consideration Principle. We can only avoid *some* radical conclusions. However, we'll be left with others, such as the conclusion that it's fine to say that the interests of two different people deserve different amounts of consideration based on their hair color, or where they happened to grow up, or whether they laugh at my jokes. The defender of the Equal Consideration Principle concludes that if we are going to have to be radical either way, better to be consistent (and accept the Equal Consideration Principle) rather than arbitrary (and reject it).

To that I say: sometimes, it's better to be arbitrary. That is, sometimes the reasons favoring incompatible ideas are good enough that we should hold on to them both. We aren't going to give up human equality. However, the consequences of the Equal Consideration Principle are unbelievable. So, we have to live with the tension.

Here's an analogy. Physics offers us two very powerful theories. On the one hand, there is general relativity, which offers an account

---

19.   Many people now define racism and sexism in structural terms rather than in terms of individuals' beliefs and attitudes. This argument predates that shift. However, nothing depends on the terminology, and we could make the same point either in structural terms or by talking directly about discriminatory beliefs and attitudes.

of gravity and all the objects influenced by it: from the expansion of the universe to the way satellites orbit around planets. On the other hand, there is quantum mechanics, which describes the workings of the strong nuclear force, which keeps the nuclei of atoms together; electromagnetic repulsion, which pushes similarly charged protons apart; and the weak nuclear force, which acts inside protons and neutrons. Unfortunately, these two theories aren't compatible: they describe reality as having fundamentally different features. Nevertheless, you won't find many physicists proposing that we abandon one or the other. Instead, one of the central puzzles of contemporary physics is how these two theories can be reconciled. The thought is that they are too well-confirmed to reject; in some way or other, they've both got to be true.

I want to propose something similar when it comes to our moral thinking about humans and animals. It's *obvious* that we should maintain a commitment to human equality. It's also obvious, at least to some of us, that we should reject the Equal Consideration Principle: the interests of animals don't deserve equal consideration, and in some cases, they deserve very little (e.g., mosquitos). To say otherwise would involve massive revisions to our moral outlook— revisions that no one can be faulted for regarding as horrifying. So, rather than conclude that we ought to reject one view or the other, we should accept that one of the central puzzles of contemporary ethics is to reconcile these two commitments: equality for people and inequality for animals. The thought, as before, is that they are too well-confirmed to reject; in some way or other, they've both got to be true.

Someone could say, of course, that we ought to value consistency *so much* in ethics that we shouldn't be satisfied with my proposal. Instead, we should just bite the bullet and accept uncomfortable revisions to our moral outlooks. I find this response totally implausible. First, *every philosopher I know* has problems in their theories; everyone has some puzzles they don't know how to address. No one actually values consistency as much as this response suggests. And second, I don't see why anyone *should* value it that much. The case of general relativity and quantum mechanics illustrates that there are other things that we can sensibly value more than consistency. In physics, it's the predictive power of those two theories—the fact that they get things right when we make observations. In the case of ethics, it's certain powerful, stable, and highly motivating intuitions—moral starting points that serve as the foundation for moral reasoning and engagement. If consistency asks us to give up too many of those, then we're better off being inconsistent.

Of course, some people think that we've already got a solution: we should accept their preferred theory about how humans are equal but animals aren't. I'll just report that I find those theories implausible. I think it's better to admit that we don't know how to reconcile these judgments than to accept third-rate attempts to achieve consistency. Humans are equal. Animals aren't. We don't know why—yet. And we can live with that.

8   The Big Picture, One Last Time

One last time, with feeling. Humans treat many animals badly, especially in factory farms. What are you morally required to do in response to that fact? One answer: go vegan. We've considered and criticized two basic kinds of argument for that claim—one based on difference-making and another based on concerns about complicity. Obviously, we haven't considered every possible argument for veganism, so we can't conclude that defenders of veganism haven't met their burden. However, we can get closer to that conclusion by trying to show that there probably isn't a better argument out there. I've done this by challenging an assumption that drives many arguments for veganism, including the one we've already criticized: namely, the Equal Consideration Principle.

The argument against the Equal Consideration Principle was based on its wildly counterintuitive implications. Someone might object that we shouldn't trust the intuitions that don't fit with the Equal Consideration Principle, either because they can be debunked or because we will have to accept some radical conclusions whether or not we accept that principle. I've argued that neither is true. There is no simple process that produced the intuitions that run counter to the Equal Consideration Principle; insofar as there is a process, it isn't clear that it's unreliable. Moreover, there's a real worry that we can't debunk some of our intuitions without debunking altogether too many of them. Finally, sometimes consistency is overrated. I have no unified theory about how moral reality works; I don't understand how to square human equality with animal inequality. But the price of consistency is too high—or, at least, I couldn't fault anyone for thinking as much.

Without the Equal Consideration Principle, it's going to be much harder to give a compelling argument for veganism. I'm not saying it's impossible; stranger things have happened. However, if we reject the Equal Consideration Principle, we can be a lot less worried that we've overlooked the best argument for veganism and, correspondingly, a lot more confident that the defenders of veganism haven't their burden. The real conclusion, then, is that if you have certain strong and stable intuitions about humans being morally special—ones you find yourself unable to abandon after serious reflection—then it can be reasonable for you to believe that the defenders of veganism have not met their burden, even if you haven't considered every last argument for veganism. As a result, it can be reasonable for you to believe that you have no moral duty to avoid purchasing and consuming animal products. Or much more simply and ignoring lots of complexities, you don't have to go vegan.

The argument I've offered isn't airtight. At almost every juncture, much more could and should be said. Moreover, I fully acknowledge that I'm arguing for the position that many people *want* to be true. Let's be honest: it would be terribly inconvenient if it were to turn out that you ought to stop eating animals, wearing leather, using products that have been tested on animals, and much else. So, there's a real risk that if you're a meat eater who agrees with what I've said, you're letting me get away with something. You aren't holding my feet to the fire the way you should.

It's also true that I've argued for a very weak conclusion. All I've tried to show is that it isn't *morally mandatory* to be vegan. That's compatible with your having very strong reasons to be vegan—the kinds of reasons that, if you weren't reading a book written by a professional philosopher, we would cite to explain why you really "ought" to go vegan—in the ordinary, "it would be really good if you did and I will be kind of irritated with you if you don't" sense of "ought."

At the same time, we should recognize that the best arguments for veganism rely on a moral principle that's incredibly radical. To put it mildly, its implications give me pause. Moreover, the most common arguments for veganism have serious problems. As I said at the beginning, I'm not here to defend much of what we do to animals. If I could wave a magic wand and change it, I would. Yes: animals matter and we should improve things for them. However, they don't matter as much as the Equal Consideration Principle implies. Yes: there are good reasons to go vegan. However, veganism isn't morally required; it's just a good thing to do. Or, at least, no one's shown that it's unreasonable to think otherwise.

First Round of Replies

Chapter 3

Reply to Bob Fischer's Opening Statement

Anja Jauernig

Contents

1 Introductory Comments and Plan

At the end of my opening statement, I highlighted as one noteworthy concrete practical consequence of my account of what we owe other animals that atrocities against animals, such as factory farming, morally wrong them and thus ought to be terminated. These practices conflict with the no-harm obligation—the obligation not to harm any living being, except in special circumstances—which is entailed by our obligation to show compassion to all beings with moral standing. But I did not have enough space to discuss an important question that arises at this juncture, namely, what each one of us ought to do specifically in the face of the moral impermissibility

DOI: 10.4324/9781003441823-6

of these atrocities. As a society, we ought to abolish them. But what exactly does this mean for each one of us individually?

This is the question on which Bob focuses in his opening statement. More particularly, he examines whether we are morally obligated to give up purchasing animal products that originated in factory farms. He concludes that we do not have such an obligation or, more precisely, that it is reasonable for us to believe that we do not have such an obligation. I disagree. The project for this reply is to explicate this disagreement and to argue that it is morally obligatory for each one of us to refrain from purchasing factory-farmed animal products. For ease of communication, instead of the mouthful "refrain from purchasing factory-farmed animal products" or "refrain from purchasing animal products that originated in factory farms," I will use the shorter "**abstain**." Furthermore, I will call the claim that we are morally obligated to abstain "**Abstinence**," and its denial, the claim that it is morally permissible for us not to abstain, "Not-Abstinence." In terms of this terminology, this reply aims to establish Abstinence.

Bob himself describes his overall conclusion in slightly weaker terms, as saying that it is reasonable for us to believe that we do not have a moral obligation to adopt a vegan diet. I will refer to the claim that we are morally obligated to adopt a vegan diet as "**Veganism**," and to the opposite claim as "Not-Veganism." I have two main reasons for focusing on Abstinence rather than Veganism in this reply. First, since Bob's arguments are primarily arguments for Not-Abstinence, and since Not-Abstinence is a stronger claim than Not-Veganism, one can agree with Not-Veganism, while rejecting Not-Abstinence and all of Bob's arguments for it. Purchasing and consuming factory-farmed animal products, on the one hand, and adopting a vegan diet, on the other hand, are not exhaustive options. Although the vast majority of meat, dairy, and eggs that are purchased by people in industrialized countries is produced in factory farms, some animal food products for sale originate elsewhere. A fraction of the market is supplied by organic or small family farms, and some meat is obtained by hunting wild animals. And there is also the seafood industry. Some industrialized seafood enterprises, such as bottom trawling, are not much better, from a moral point of view, than factory farming, since they too cause a lot of harm to animals. But there are also more traditional, less harmful fishing operations on a smaller scale. So, an alternative response to the moral wrongness of factory farming—instead of adopting a vegan diet—would be to purchase animal products exclusively from some of these other sources. Furthermore, one could also entirely refrain from purchasing animal products while still continuing to consume them. One option for doing so would be to restrict oneself to eating animals that one killed oneself by hunting or fishing. Or one could adopt what is called a "freegan" lifestyle, which takes advantage of the fact that a lot of animal products are regularly discarded as surplus, by supermarkets, restaurants, and private citizens. Freegans obtain their animal-based foods by recovering these discarded products from the trash. Finally, one could limit one's meat consumption to parts of animals that died of natural causes or through an accident. Accordingly, one can hold that the moral wrongness of factory farming is compatible with Not-Veganism, while insisting that it is incompatible with Not-Abstinence and rejecting all of Bob's arguments for Not-Abstinence.

To be sure, if Bob's arguments for Not-Abstinence were convincing, he would thereby have established Not-Veganism as well. For if it is morally permissible to purchase factory-farmed animal products, arguably it is also morally permissible to consume factory-farmed animal products. And if it is morally permissible to consume factory-farmed animal products, then a vegan diet is not morally obligatory. But since Bob's case for Not-Veganism hinges on his arguments for Not-Abstinence, the latter claim is what we should focus on in our debate. It is a further question whether we are obligated to adopt a vegan diet, a question that arises even if Bob's case for Not-Abstinence is unsuccessful—which, indeed, it is, or so I will argue.

My second reason for focusing on Abstinence rather than Veganism is pragmatic. As explicated in my opening statement, I endorse Veganism or, more precisely, I endorse the claim that we are morally obligated to adopt a benign vegan diet, a diet that consists of synthetically produced foods and parts of plants that have been cultivated and harvested in a cautious, harm-minimizing way, possibly supplemented by parts of animals that died of natural causes or through an accident. This kind of diet is our best bet to fulfill the no-harm obligation while still meeting our nutritional needs. But I certainly concur that some methods for obtaining animal food products are morally worse than others on account of causing more harm and embodying a greater failure of compassion, and that factory farming ranks very high on the "bad" list. Moreover, it is hard to deny that, given the current norms and customs of our society, convincing people to become vegan is still a rather hard sell. So, for the purpose of both helping our moral progress along and minimizing harm to animals, it is a prudent strategy to start by trying to convince people that they ought to stop purchasing factory-farmed animal products, rather than risking to antagonize them and lose their ear completely by lecturing them about giving up animal products altogether. It would already be a significant step forward on the road of moral progress and a huge improvement in overall animal flourishing if people who now primarily rely on factory farms for their animal-based foods were to switch to relying on organic farms or small fisheries or to hunting and fishing for themselves.[1] Once this milestone has been reached, we can then turn to the more ambitious goal of converting everybody to a vegan diet.

For reasons of space, I cannot discuss all of the interesting issues raised by Bob's rich essay and thus must be ruthlessly selective. This reply has two main parts. In the first part, I call into question Bob's general argumentative strategy of regarding his own Not-Abstinence position in the debate about Abstinence as the default and of assigning the burden of proof to his opponents. After voicing general skepticism about the appropriateness of this kind of burden-of-proof-assigning maneuver in a moral debate, I argue that, *pace* Bob, the default in the present debate is Abstinence. So, if we are to play the game of sticking someone with the burden of proof at all, then Bob must be stuck with it, not me.

In the second part, I defend what Bob calls the Anti-Complicity Argument against his objections, an argument that relies on the moral premise that we are morally obligated not to be complicit in moral wrongdoing. My reason for selecting this argument for closer inspection is that it, or at least an argument very close to it, is the only argument for Abstinence considered by Bob that I endorse. (I am doubtful about the truth of the moral premises of the other arguments that he examines.) The Anti-Complicity Argument is not my favorite argument for Abstinence, though. My favorite argument relies on the moral premise that in circumstances where it is the collective responsibility of the members of a given society to rectify or ameliorate a morally bad situation, every member is morally obligated to do her fair share in achieving the morally

---

1. This would have to go hand in hand with a serious reduction in how much meat and other animal products people consume since these other sources offer a much more limited supply of these items compared to factory farms.

mandated improvement. It is our collective responsibility to end factory farming. For most of us, abstaining is part of what doing our fair share in ending factory farming requires. Accordingly, we ought to abstain. But since this essay is supposed to be a reply to Bob's opening statement and a careful discussion of my favorite argument would lead us too far afield, I will focus on defending and fortifying the Anti-Complicity Argument, which will give us plenty of instructive material to talk about.

2   Burdens of Proof and Default Positions

At the beginning of his opening statement, Bob tells us that the way in which he is going to argue for Not-Abstinence is by showing that his opponents in the debate have not met their burden of proof, since their arguments fail to establish that it would be unreasonable to believe Not-Abstinence. This assumes that (1) in a debate about a purported moral obligation ("**moral debate**" for short from now on), assigning the burden of proof to one of the involved parties is an appropriate argumentative strategy, and (2) in the present debate, Not-Abstinence is the default position, which one is justified to adopt without providing any arguments for it. Bob makes clear that he indeed assumes as much: "In a moral debate, the person insisting that you have a moral obligation has the burden of proof ... In the context of this debate, I'm the defense attorney. I don't have to prove that you can keep living the way you'd like; that's the default position. I only need to show that your critic hasn't met his burden. If not, then he hasn't shown that you've got a certain responsibility" (p. 76). As I see it, both of these assumptions are questionable.

2.1   Is Burden-of-Proof-Assigning an Appropriate Strategy in a Moral Debate?

We all should want to live a morally decent life and care about making moral progress. The attitude expressed in the passage from Bob just quoted is at odds with these moral aspirations. It is an attitude of seeing moral obligations as an inconvenient burden and an obstacle to living one's life as one would like to live it, and of complacently presuming that the way one is accustomed to live is just fine. But with that kind of mindset, it will be rather difficult to live up to the demands of morality, and moral progress will be very

hard to come by. It seems more conducive to these ends to incorporate the goal of fulfilling as many of one's moral obligations as
possible in one's conception of the life that one would like to live
and to presume that the way one is accustomed to live is probably
not morally ideal yet. We all should be eager to figure out what
our moral obligations are and anxious about possibly having overlooked some of them so far.

In order to make headway in the important project of identifying
our moral obligations, moral debates are to be welcomed, and all
parties to these debates are to stand ready to mount the strongest
arguments at their disposal in support of their own position. We
should want the position to win that has the most convincing arguments behind it and thus is most likely to be true, not the one that
is most convenient. Nobody should try to skirt his responsibility to
offer arguments for his view by declaring it as the default. So, evalu-
ated in light of our moral aspirations, the strategy of assigning the
burden of proof to one's opponent strikes me as inappropriate in
a moral debate, especially if employed by the party who holds that
the purported obligation in question is not actually one.

2.2   Default Positions

I am generally skeptical about the appropriateness of burden-of-
proof-assigning in a moral debate, but I agree that in every such
debate there is a default position. And a good thing it is. Often,
we are forced to make a choice about how to act without having
had time to carefully think about what is morally required of us
in that situation. We also do not have a guarantee that all of our
moral debates will end conclusively, even if we have sufficient time
to carry them out before we must decide what to do. It might well
be that, even after a patient evaluation of all arguments on both
sides, none of the positions under discussion will have emerged as
clearly more plausible. And, in contrast to debates about theoretical matters, in a practical context, we usually cannot indefinitely
refrain from choosing a side, since not acting tends not to be an
option (not least because not doing anything is a way of acting too).

So, then, what is the default position in our present debate about
Abstinence, which we can adopt provisionally if time for thorough
reflection is scarce or in the eventuality that our debate remains
inconclusive? Bob compares a moral debate to a legal case where
the prosecutor has to establish beyond a reasonable doubt that the

defendant is guilty. And since Not-Abstinence corresponds to the presumption of innocence, he assumes that it is the default in our debate. But if we think more closely about why, in the legal case, the presumption of innocence is the default and the prosecutor has the burden of proof, it becomes clear that, in the moral case, matters stand differently. More specifically, it becomes clear that, in the debate about Abstinence, the default is Abstinence. So, if anybody must bear the burden of proof in this debate, it must be borne by Bob and the Not-Abstinence party, rather than the other way around. Let us take a closer look.

2.2.1 Default Positions in the Legal Context

It is not very difficult to reconstruct a likely explanation for the default status of the presumption of innocence in the legal case. From the point of view of justice, it would be best if all and only guilty defendants were convicted. But since we do not have a crystal ball that reliably informs us about who is guilty and who is innocent, there is some uncertainty attached to all convictions. Accordingly, our legal practices must take this uncertainty into account and be designed in such a way as to yield the best outcome from the point of view of justice given that we cannot be completely certain about a defendant's guilt or innocence. We want to make sure that, if we err in our verdict, we err on the side that is better from the point of view of justice. This means that the crucial question that underlies the determination of the default position in the legal case is which outcome is better from the point of view of justice, all else being equal: (a) an innocent defendant is found guilty, or (b) a guilty defendant is found innocent.

We do not want to get sidetracked by a detailed analysis of the justice-relevant costs and benefits of the two outcomes compared to one another, that is, of all the bads and goods associated with the two outcomes that are relevant from the point of view of justice. But a moment's reflection makes clear that the net cost of outcome (a) is larger than the net cost of outcome (b). For there is one very large justice-relevant cost of (a) that dominates the calculation, namely, that the innocent defendant suffers undeserved harm through the erroneous verdict. So, while neither outcome is optimal, outcome (b) is better than outcome (a) from the point of view of justice, all else being equal. Consequently, if we are to err, we should err on the side of (b). And the way to ensure this is by presuming as the default position that the defendant is innocent. Going with this presumption as the default guards us against incurring the very large justice-relevant cost of inflicting undeserved harm on a person by convicting her despite her innocence. Arguably, this is the main underlying reason why, in the legal case, the presumption of innocence is the default and the burden of proof falls on the prosecutor.

2.2.2   Default Positions in the Moral Context

A similar line of reasoning can be pursued in the moral case but with rather different results. From the point of view of morality, it would be best if all and only those purported obligations that in fact are obligations were regarded by us as obligations. But since we do not have a crystal ball that reliably informs us about what our moral obligations are, there is some uncertainty attached to all judgments about what is morally required of us. Accordingly, our moral deliberations must take this uncertainty into account and be designed in such a way as to yield the best outcome from the point of view of morality given that we cannot be completely certain about whether a purported obligation actually is one. We want to make sure that, if we err in our judgments about moral obligations, we err on the side that is better from the point of view of morality. This means that the crucial question that underlies the determination of the default position in a moral debate is which outcome is better from the point of view of morality, all else being equal: (i) we regard a purported obligation as an obligation even though it is not, or (ii) we do not regard a purported obligation as an obligation even though it is.

This question is a bit more difficult to answer than the analogous question in the legal case. In fact, I am far from certain that a general answer can be given that covers all possible purported obligations that might be debated. For the morally relevant costs and benefits of (i) and (ii), that is, the goods and bads associated with (i) and (ii) that are relevant from the point of view of morality, depend on the content of the obligation and the details of the situation. One general observation can be made, though: outcome (ii) comes with a morally relevant cost for which there is no analogue in the case of outcome (i). At least, this observation is defensible if we assume, as I think we should, that all participants in a moral debate properly so-called admit that the purported obligation has a chance of actually being one or is a reasonable candidate for being one and thus agree that what the purported obligation demands of us is morally permissible.[2] The special morally relevant cost of outcome (ii) derives from the following facts: the mistaken belief that a purported obligation is not an obligation makes it more likely for us to violate it and thus commit a moral wrong, and moral wrongdoing is very costly from a moral point of view. I will call costs of this kind "**moral-wrongness costs**." In contrast to outcome (ii), outcome (i) does not engender any morally wrong actions and thus does not come with a moral-wrongness cost. The mistaken belief that a purported obligation is an obligation also makes a certain course of action more likely for us, namely, doing what the purported obligation demands. But since, by assumption, there is nothing wrong with doing what the purported obligation demands, outcome (i) does not have any morally relevant cost that is analogous to the cost of outcome (ii) just considered. So, without any further information about the specifics of a given case, it thus seems plausible to assume as a default guess that outcome (ii) is more costly from a moral point of view than outcome (i). Accordingly, if we insist on a general rule of thumb that tells us which position in a moral debate is the default, the rule should be that the default is the position that asserts that we have the purported obligation.[3]

---

2. Unless there is consensus on that score, there will not be a real debate. If there is some initial doubt about whether the purported obligation is a reasonable candidate for being one, the person who claims that it is an obligation must present a preliminary argument to remove the doubt. This preliminary argument could be compared to the prosecutor's preliminary presentation of his case in front of a grand jury in order to obtain an indictment. With respect to our present debate, note that, while Bob denies that we are morally obligated to abstain, he agrees (I take it) that abstaining is morally permissible and that there is at least some chance that abstaining is morally obligatory.

3. It is important to be clear that this kind of cost-benefit analysis to determine which position should be the default in a moral debate is to be distinguished from a cost-benefit analysis to determine which one of several options in a decision situation has the greatest utility and thus should be pursued. For the purpose of the latter determination, the costs and benefits of the different options must be multiplied by the options' probabilities. But for the purpose of determining the default position in a moral debate, it would be a serious mistake to try to figure out how likely it is that the purported obligation is or is not an actual obligation and take these probabilities into account. Figuring this out is what the debate is for. The point of determining a default is precisely to identify which position is preferable before or independently of any arguments about whether and with what likelihood we actually have the purported obligation. (To be sure, it might be that some probabilities must be taken into account in the determination of the morally relevant costs and benefits of the different possible outcomes of a moral debate; but that is yet another use of probabilities.)

2.2.3   The Default Position in the Debate about Abstinence

But let us not worry too much about general rules of thumb. Let us focus on the specific case at hand, that is, on our debate about Abstinence. The crucial question that underlies the determination of which position is the default in this debate is which outcome is better from the point of view of morality, all else being equal: (A-i) we regard it as morally obligatory to abstain even though it is morally permissible not to abstain, or (A-ii) we regard it as morally permissible not to abstain even though it is morally obligatory to abstain.

In order to answer this question, we must compare the morally relevant costs and benefits of the two outcomes. These costs and benefits differ for different groups of people. For people who are committed to abstaining regardless of what morality demands, it makes not much of a difference whether they are in scenario (A-i) or (A-ii). The same goes for people who are committed to not abstaining regardless of what morality demands. Whether (A-i) or (A-ii) is the case does make a significant difference, however, for people who like to consume animal products and who care about morality. I will call them "moral meat-lovers" for short.

Starting with (A-i), one could argue that a morally relevant cost derives from the following facts: for a moral meat-lover to mistakenly believe that he is obligated to abstain makes it likely for him to abstain; abstaining makes it likely for him to miss out on some gustatory pleasure from eating animal products that he could have otherwise experienced since his abstinence makes it much less convenient and more expensive to obtain these products; and missing out on some gustatory pleasure is a morally relevant cost. Turning to the plus side, one could argue that, at least for a non-negligible contingent of moral meat-lovers, namely, meat-lovers who tend to overindulge in these products, a morally relevant benefit derives from the following facts: for a moral meat-lover to mistakenly believe that he is obligated to abstain makes it likely for him to abstain; abstaining makes it likely for him not to overindulge in animal products since overindulgence usually depends on convenient and cheap access to these products; not overindulging in animal products is good for his health; and being healthy is a morally relevant benefit.

Moving to outcome (A-ii), there are no morally relevant benefits to speak of but there is at least one morally relevant cost, namely, a moral-wrongness cost. This cost derives from the following facts: for a moral meat-lover to mistakenly believe that he is not obligated to abstain makes it very likely for him not to abstain; not abstaining is morally wrong; and moral wrongdoing is morally very costly. By contrast, there is nothing wrong about abstaining, which is why (A-i) does not have an analogous moral-wrongness cost. (One could also argue that the harmful impact of factory farming on the environment translates into another morally relevant cost of (A-ii). But since this assumes that individual animal product purchases make a difference to the production quantities of factory farms, which is precisely what Bob disputes, I am willing to overlook this cost for the present calculation.)

I do not have much hope that one could succeed in measuring the various mentioned costs and benefits with respect to a common standard or in precisely capturing the indicated likelihoods in terms of numbers. Nevertheless, I think it is fair to say, based on this summary of costs and benefits, that outcome (A-ii) is clearly more costly from a moral point of view than outcome (A-i). Just focusing on the costs of both options, as I see it, missing out on a gustatory pleasure, no matter how great the pleasure, is never worse, in a morally relevant way, than committing a moral wrong, even if the moral wrong is on the "less bad" end of the spectrum of moral wrongs. Moreover, given the ubiquity and affordability of factory-farmed animal products, it is all but guaranteed that moral meat-lovers will purchase and consume these products if they believe that it is morally permissible for them to do so. Accordingly, even before taking the health-related benefit of (A-i) into account (and without insisting on including the environmental cost of (A-ii)), it is quite safe to say that the morally relevant net cost of outcome (A-ii) is larger than the morally relevant net cost of outcome (A-i).

Also note that, in our discussion so far, we have granted that all of the mentioned costs and benefits are indeed morally relevant. One could reject this assumption and argue that, in contrast to health and fulfilling one's moral obligations, gustatory pleasure is not a morally relevant good at all, which means that missing out on some gustatory pleasure is not bad from a moral point of view either. In that case, it would be even more obvious that, from the perspective of morality, (A-ii) is more costly than (A-i).

The moral of the story is that, in our debate about Abstinence, while neither outcome is optimal, (A-i) is much better than (A-ii) from the point of view of morality, all else being equal. That is, from the point of view of morality, all else being equal, it would be much better if we ended up in a situation where we regard it as morally obligatory to abstain even though it is morally permissible not to abstain than if we ended up in a situation where we regard it as morally permissible not to abstain even though it is morally obligatory to abstain. Consequently, if we are to err, we ought to err on the side of (A-i). And the way to ensure this is by presuming as the default position in our debate that we have an obligation to abstain. Going with this presumption as the default guards us against incurring the very large morally relevant cost of making it likely for the moral meat-lovers among us to act in ways that are morally wrong. This is why, in our debate about Abstinence, Abstinence is the default.

2.3 Implications for the Debate about Abstinence

The result that, in the debate about Abstinence, Abstinence is the default, has three important consequences. First, if Bob wants to insist on assigning the burden of proof to somebody in this debate, he should assume it himself, rather than trying to pin it on me.

Second, in the debate so far, Bob has confined himself to criticizing various possible arguments in support of Abstinence but has not presented a single positive argument in support of his own Not-Abstinence position yet. So, if we were to apply the burden-of-proof-assigning strategy, the current standings in the debate would be that I am clearly in the lead, simply in virtue of advocating the default position.

Third, if our debate were to end inconclusively such that, after carefully evaluating all of the examined arguments, neither Abstinence nor Not-Abstinence will have emerged as clearly more plausible, we ought to adopt the position that we do have a moral obligation to abstain. This way of proceeding is an instance of a generally strongly advisable strategy in all moral deliberations that we already encountered in my opening statement, namely, the strategy of erring on the side of caution in cases of uncertainty, given the high cost of moral wrongdoing. Going above and beyond what is morally required of us might be inconvenient or burdensome. But falling short of what is morally required of us is a costly moral failure, which we ought to avoid if possible.

3 The Anti-Complicity Argument Reconsidered

3.1 The Basic and the Revised Anti-Complicity Argument

Bob considers several arguments for Abstinence and tries to establish that all of them fail. One of these arguments is the Anti-Complicity Argument. In this second part of my reply, I will take a closer look at the Anti-Complicity Argument (section 3.2) and show that Bob's objections to it are not convincing (section 3.3) or can be circumvented by slightly revising the argument (section 3.4).

The basic version of the Anti-Complicity Argument goes like this.

Basic Anti-Complicity Argument:

1. We are morally obligated not to be complicit in an action or practice that is unjust. (Moral premise.)
2. Not abstaining makes us complicit in factory farming. (Empirical premise.)
3. Factory farming is unjust. (Additional premise.)
4. We are morally obligated to abstain. (Abstinence; from 1, 2, and 3.)[4]

Bob grants for the sake of the argument that factory farming is unjust. His criticism of the Anti-Complicity Argument is focused on the moral premise. His main objection to the moral premise of the basic version of the argument is that, due to its considerable demandingness, it conflicts with our intuitions about what can reasonably be required of us and thus must be false.

As a possible response to this objection on behalf of proponents of the Anti-Complicity Argument, Bob then considers a revised version of the Anti-Complicity Argument, in which the original moral premise is replaced with the claim that we are morally obligated not to be directly complicit in an action or practice that is extremely unjust. Bob argues that the revised moral premise is false as well. On his view, there are some cases in which being directly complicit in extreme injustice is morally permissible. For complicity comes in degrees, and sometimes the degree of the complicity in question is quite small, and its moral badness can be offset.

---

4. Bob formulates this argument slightly differently but this is a mere difference in presentation, not content.

3.2   The Refined Anti-Complicity Argument

I like the Anti-Complicity Argument and am prepared to defend it against Bob's objections. But before we can examine these objections in detail, one cosmetic change and a few conceptual clarifications with respect to the argument are required so that I can fully endorse it.

The cosmetic change that I want to propose concerns the moral premise. I agree that factory farming is morally wrong but I am reluctant to describe the flavor of its moral wrongness as a kind of injustice, at least not in the absence of a chance to say more about what it means for an action or practice to be unjust. On my view, the primary reason why factory farming is morally wrong is because it violates the no-harm obligation. Inflicting undeserved harm may be described as a form of acting unjustly but it would be desirable to avoid having to get into this discussion here. So, I propose to circumvent this potential difficulty by formulating the moral premise in more general terms as saying that we are morally obligated not to be complicit in an action or practice that is morally wrong. For ease of communication, I will call such an action/practice "**impermissible action/practice**" and the resulting argument the "Refined Anti-Complicity Argument."

> Refined Anti-Complicity Argument:
>
> 1.   We are morally obligated not to be complicit in an impermissible action or practice, i.e., an action or practice that is morally wrong. (Moral premise.)
> 2.   Not abstaining makes us complicit in factory farming. (Empirical premise.)
> 3.   Factory farming is morally wrong. (Additional premise.)
> 4.   We are morally obligated to abstain. (Abstinence; from 1, 2, and 3.)

The conceptual clarifications I have in mind concern the notion of complicity in play. First of all, it would be very useful to have a more explicit characterization on the table of what it means to be complicit in the relevant sense. This is how complicity is to be understood for the purposes of the Refined Anti-Complicity Argument:

> X is **complicit** in a practice or action W if, and only if, (a) X voluntarily performs an action S that supports W, and (b) X has no legitimate excuse for not knowing that S supports W or what W is.

The qualification that the supporting action must be voluntary takes account of the fact that regarding somebody as complicit in a practice that he is coerced to support against his will would be unreasonable. (In the following, I will assume that all actions under discussion are voluntary. I also take it that all voluntary actions are intentional.) Condition (b) is included to acknowledge that, while in general we ought to know what we are doing, there can be situations in which this is not the case through no fault of our own. In a situation like this, it would be unreasonable to ascribe complicity to the ignorant party. Suppose you bought a factory-farmed piece of chicken that is clearly labeled as such. Your purchase makes you complicit in the impermissible practice of factory farming, even if you did not look at the label and even if you have no idea what factory farms are. If you pay money for something, you ought to make a reasonable effort to inform yourself about what it is that you are paying for and who profits from the payment. But now suppose that you bought a factory-farmed piece of chicken that is labeled as having been synthetically produced in a lab, you read the label, and you had no reason to suspect fraud. In that case, it would be implausible to say that your purchase makes you complicit in the impermissible practice of factory farming, even though your purchase does support it.

Another clarification concerns Bob's characterization of complicity as having degrees, which I find somewhat unhelpful and misleading. Talk about degrees of complicity could be taken to suggest that all cases of being complicit can be ordered with respect to being more, less, or equal on a general complicity scale, which, however, seems doubtful to me. To be sure, supporting a practice/action can take many forms—instigating it, actively participating, expressing approval, contributing funds or materials, fundraising on its behalf, recruiting further participants, and so on—and some of these ways of supporting amount to stronger forms of support than others. But I prefer to capture this by acknowledging that there are different *kinds* of complicity that differ with respect to the way in which the practice in question is supported, rather than saying that there are different degrees of complicity.

I am also happy to acknowledge that different kinds of complicity in an impermissible practice can differ with respect to their degree of moral badness, as Bob repeatedly emphasizes. But it should be noted that this is not directly relevant for the question at the center of our debate about Abstinence, which is whether being complicit in an impermissible practice is morally wrong. That not all kinds of murder are equally morally bad does not make a difference for the question of whether all kinds of murder are morally wrong. Murder is morally wrong, regardless of what kind of murder it is. Similarly, that not all kinds of complicity in an impermissible practice are equally morally bad does not make a difference for the question of whether all kinds of complicity in an impermissible practice are morally wrong. Complicity in an impermissible practice is morally wrong, regardless of what kind of complicity it is, or so I will argue.

3.3   In Defense of the Refined Anti-Complicity Argument

The cosmetic change and conceptual clarifications just considered do not alter the substance of the Anti-Complicity Argument. This means that Bob's objections, *mutatis mutandis*, apply to the moral premise of the refined version of the argument as well. So, are these objections convincing? I do not think so.

3.3.1   Objection I: Overdemandingness

The first objection, tailored to the moral premise of the Refined Anti-Complicity Argument, is that most people do not think that we are obligated to avoid complicity in each and every impermissible practice, since that would be asking too much. Accordingly, the moral premise of the Refined Anti-Complicity Argument is false.

In response, even if Bob's guess about people's thoughts were true, it would not show that complicity in some impermissible practices is morally permissible. Avoiding complicity in impermissible practices across the board is demanding and requires serious vigilance. So, it would be psychologically understandable if people were attracted to the thought that this challenging task is not morally required of them. However, wishing something to be the case out of laziness or inconvenience-avoidance does not make it so. As I already said in my opening statement, morality may well be a demanding business, like it or not.

But I am also rather skeptical about the claim that most people do not think that we are obligated to avoid complicity in each and every impermissible practice. To be sure, a lot of people (myself included) end up being complicit in some impermissible practices. But it seems plausible to me that this happens, not because these people regard their complicity as morally unproblematic in these cases, but because they are thoughtless or lack relevant information or falsely believe that the practice is permissible or judge (correctly or incorrectly) that being complicit in this case is only a very slight moral transgression, which they are willing to commit for the sake of some other benefit, or because their complicity is as good as unavoidable given the circumstances in which they find themselves. To use one of Bob's examples for purposes of illustration, I venture to say that most people who know that the cocoa in a certain kind of chocolate is harvested by children or slaves and who agree that the practice of using children or slaves as cheap laborers is impermissible, would also agree upon reflection that they ought not to buy the chocolate. Conversely, most people who do buy this kind of chocolate only do so because they are generally unreflective or unaware of how the cocoa is harvested or falsely believe that using children or slaves as cheap laborers is morally permissible or that buying this kind of chocolate is only a small moral failure that is worth committing for the benefit of enjoying a tasty treat at a discount price.

It should be explicitly acknowledged that, for many people living in industrialized countries, avoiding complicity in each and every impermissible practice is not only very demanding but close to unattainable at present. Even if we could successfully sort out which companies to boycott on account of their moral infractions against other people, many of us cannot entirely avoid relying on the provision of certain essential goods and services by big corporations and large multi-national conglomerates that wreak havoc on the environment and many animals. A special manifestation of this unfortunate situation is that a benign vegan diet is currently not available to the vast majority of people in industrialized nations, as already noted in my opening statement. As I said there, this kind of tragic predicament—that we presently have no choice but to be complicit in the relevant impermissible practices unless we radically change our lives by opting out of living in ordinary civilized society or even accept starvation—can plausibly be seen as a mitigating circumstance that reduces our blameworthiness for our complicity. But, on my view, it does not render the complicity morally permissible. Indeed, the predicament brings with it a further kind of moral obligation, namely, to work toward changing our culture and political-economic system in such a way that we all are able to do what is morally required of us, including not being complicit in impermissible practices.

3.3.2   Objection II: Counterexamples and Mitigating Factors

The second objection is that there are counterexamples to the moral premise of the Refined Anti-Complicity Argument. More specifically, there are cases in which complicity in an impermissible practice is morally permissible due to the presence of mitigating factors. These mitigating factors are the following three: (i) the supporting action that renders the agent complicit does not make a difference to the practice ("Influence"), (ii) although the agent knowingly and voluntarily supports the practice, he does not intend to support it ("Intention"), and (ii) the agent combines his supporting action that makes him complicit with another action so that the complicity's moral badness is offset ("Offsetting").

3.3.2.1   The Main Counterexample: Sad Sally

Bob uses the case of Sad Sally to illustrate his claim that sometimes complicity in an impermissible practice is morally permissible on account of the presence of the indicated mitigating factors. Sally is complicit in factory farming since she purchases factory-farmed products. But, according to Bob, Sally's influence on the moral wrong done on factory farms is negligible due to the very small probability that her individual purchases make a difference to the production quantities of those farms. She also does not intend to support the injustice, or so Bob says, since, although she knows what is happening on factory farms, she hates it and does not want to support it. She only does so because consuming animal products is important to her due to the way she was raised and because she believes that her choices as a consumer do not make any difference to the production quantities. Moreover, we can assume that Sally donates to a farm sanctuary and thereby helps some farm animals in order to offset the moral badness of her complicity. Since the mitigating factors of Intention, Influence, and Offsetting are all present in the case of Sad Sally, Sally's complicity in the practice of factory farming is morally permissible, according to Bob. If Bob is right about that, the case of Sad Sally is a counterexample to the moral premise of the Refined Anti-Complicity Argument.

3.3.2.1.1   REPLY—STEP I: SAD SALLY IS NO BETTER THAN DIABOLICAL DOLLY

In his opening statement, Bob highlights at several places that, for the purposes of his critical discussion of the arguments for

Abstinence in the first part of his opening statement, which include the Anti-Complicity Argument, he grants that animals and humans morally matter equally. "I've *assumed* that animals matter as much as people, and I've argued that *even given that assumption*, there are problems with the arguments for veganism" (p. 101). I want to start my response to Bob's second objection by pointing out that, if we assume that animals morally matter as much as humans, then it is particularly easy to see that, *pace* Bob, Sally's complicity in factory farming is not morally permissible.

Consider the case of Diabolical Dolly, which is exactly like the case of Sad Sally, except that the creatures in the factory farms whose body parts Dolly purchases are not animals but people whose race differs from Dolly's and that, instead of donating to an animal charity, she donates to a charity that supports people with the relevant racial background. Dolly is complicit in factory farming humans since she purchases factory-farmed human products. But her influence on the moral wrong done on these farms is negligible, due to the very small probability that her individual purchases make a difference to the farms' production quantities. Like Sally, Dolly knows what is happening on the farms; she hates it and does not want to support it. However, again just like Sally, she believes that her choices as a consumer do not make any difference to the production quantities, and since some human products are important to her because of the way she was raised, she buys them. As in the case of Sad Sally, the mitigating factors of Intention, Influence, and Offsetting are all present in the case of Diabolical Dolly.

On the assumption that animals morally matter as much as humans, if Sally's complicity in factory farming animals is morally permissible, then Dolly's complicity in factory farming humans is morally permissible as well. The problem is that it will be fairly difficult to find anyone who agrees with that result. Of course, Dolly's complicity is morally wrong! Being complicit in factory farming humans is morally impermissible, even if one's complicity does not make a difference to the production quantities of these farms, one does not intend to support this kind of farming (in Bob's sense of "intend"), and one makes regular generous donations in an attempt to offset the moral badness of one's complicity.

So, something has to give. Either Sally's complicity in factory farming animals is morally wrong too or animals do not morally matter as much as people. Faced with the choice of giving up on his main objection to the Anti-Complicity Argument altogether or on his claim that this objection works even if it is granted that animals and humans morally matter equally, I expect that Bob will want to take the latter route.

3.3.2.1.2   REPLY—STEP II: SAD SALLY IS NO BETTER THAN SPINELESS STEVE

So, is Bob's objection decisive if we assume that animals morally matter less than humans? Merely admitting that the objection depends on this assumption will not save it. Bob still has to explain why Dolly's complicity in factory farming humans is morally impermissible even though all of the indicated mitigating factors (Influence, Intention, and Offsetting) are in place.

The obvious move would be to say that not all kinds of complicity in an impermissible practice are morally permissible when these mitigating factors are present but only those kinds of complicity where the degree of moral badness of the practice remains below a certain threshold. Call this kind of threshold "permissibility threshold." In other words, there is a fourth mitigating factor, namely, the comparatively small degree of moral badness of the impermissible practice in question. Since, as we are now assuming, humans morally matter more than animals, factory farming humans is morally much worse than factory farming animals. Since the degree of moral badness of factory farming animals falls below the permissibility threshold, so the argument goes, Sally's complicity in it is morally permissible. By contrast, since the degree of moral badness of factory farming humans exceeds the permissibility threshold, Dolly's complicity in it is morally impermissible. (From now on, by "factory farming" without any further qualifications I should again be understood to mean "factory farming animals.")

This move is problematic. For starters, as reported above, the moral premise of Bob's Revised Anti-Complicity Argument, to which the case of Sad Sally is supposed to be a counterexample, explicitly specifies that we are morally obligated not to be directly complicit in an action or practice that is *extremely* unjust. In formulating the moral premise in this way and in regarding the case of Sad Sally as a counterexample to it, Bob is thus conceding that factory farming is extremely unjust and thus extremely morally bad. So, in order to be able to avail himself of the indicated move to explain why Dolly's complicity is morally impermissible while Sally's complicity is morally permissible Bob must take one of two options. The first option is to backpedal and admit that the case of Sad Sally is not a counterexample to the moral premise of the Revised Anti-Complicity Argument after all but merely to the moral premise of the Basic Anti-Complicity Argument. This would allow him to endorse the claim that factory farming, although quite bad, is not extremely morally bad, which is why Sally's complicity, in contrast to Dolly's, is morally permissible. The second option is to assert that, even though factory farming is extremely morally bad, its degree of moral badness still does not exceed the permissibility threshold. Only complicity in impermissible practices that are worse than extremely morally bad is impermissible if the mitigating factors are present.

As I see it, both options ultimately succumb to the same problem. They both rely on the claim that the degree of moral badness of factory farming lies below the permissibility threshold. But this claim is very implausible, even if we assume that humans morally matter more than animals. How so?

It is hard to imagine that anybody who is sane and not in the grip of a prejudice or misguided theory and who takes the trouble to really look at what is going on in factory farms could come away with the judgment that the degree of moral badness of factory farming, although fairly or even extremely great, does not reach the level at which complicity in it à la Sally would count as morally impermissible. Just attentively watch one of those undercover videos and ask yourself: in your considered opinion, is it morally OK to be complicit in *that*? My expectation is that most of you will respond with a version of "hell no," whether the three mitigating factors are present or not.

The same point can be made more forcefully with the help of another case that is modeled on Sad Sally, the case of Spineless Steve. Suppose there is a club devoted to perfecting the art of puppy torturing, called the Puppy Nazis. Steve's friends and family are all enthusiastic supporters of the Puppy Nazis. Steve himself does not want to encourage puppy torture; in fact, he hates it. But because it is important to him not to lose the respect of his family and friends, he joins them in paying a monthly membership fee to the club. If Steve thought that individual membership fees did make a difference to the torturing activities of the club, he would stop his payments immediately. But since he believes—correctly, we may assume—that his payments do not make a difference, he continues to send the Puppy Nazis his monthly contributions. (The club has a large endowment and a lot of members so that individual membership fees do not influence the club's programming.) In order to make up for his complicity in puppy torturing, Steve occasionally donates money to an animal welfare organization devoted to helping dogs.

Like the case of Diabolical Dolly, the case of Spineless Steve exactly mimics the structure of the case of Sad Sally, including that all of the mitigating factors of Influence, Intention, and Offsetting are present. Note that, like Sally, Steve also gets something out of his complicity. Sally gets gustatory pleasure and convenience; Steve gets the continued respect of his family and friends. The difference compared to the case of Diabolical Dolly is that, while factory farming humans is morally worse than factory farming animals—or so we are assuming for the sake of the argument—torturing puppies is not morally worse than factory farming cows, pigs, and chickens. After all, what happens on factory farms is a form of torture. And since cows, pigs, and chickens are quite similar to puppies with respect to their psychological capacities, it would be completely arbitrary and thus indefensible to hold that puppies morally matter more than cows, pigs, and chickens. So, since on Bob's view (after the suggested move to save his second objection to the Anti-Complicity Argument) the degree of moral badness of factory farming is not great enough for Sally's complicity in it to be morally objectionable, he is committed to the assessment that the degree of moral badness of puppy torturing is also not great enough for Steve's complicity in it to be morally objectionable.

Again, the problem is that it will be fairly difficult to find anyone who agrees with that assessment. Of course, Steve's complicity is morally wrong! Being complicit in torturing puppies is morally impermissible, even if one's complicity does not make a difference to any concrete torturing activities, one does not intend to support puppy torturing (in Bob's sense of "intend"), and one makes regular generous donations in an attempt to offset the moral badness of one's complicity.

The case of Spineless Steve is structurally exactly like the case of Sad Sally. So, given that Steve's complicity in torturing puppies is morally impermissible, Sally's complicity in factory farming is impermissible as well. If there is a threshold of permissibility, the degree of moral badness of factory farming exceeds it. The lesson is that the case of Sad Sally is not a counterexample to the moral premise of the Refined Anti-Complicity Argument *even if we assume that humans matter more than animals.* Bob's second objection to the Refined Anti-Complicity Argument fails as well, just like the first one.

3.3.2.2   Mitigating Factors, Intention

We could further bolster this result by subjecting the allegedly mitigating factors of Influence, Intention, and Offsetting to scrutiny and
showing for each one of them that it is not in fact mitigating, that
is, that its presence does not render complicity in an impermissible
practice morally permissible if it would have been impermissible
otherwise. We do not have space to take a closer look at all three
factors, but, for illustration, we will briefly examine Intention, with
respect to which it is most obvious that it does not play such a
mitigating role.

The claim that lack of intention to support an impermissible
practice (à la Sally) reduces the moral badness of one's complicity
is simply implausible. To start with a conceptual point, it seems
plausible to me to think that, if one voluntarily and thus intentionally performs an action of which one knows that it has a certain
consequence, then one also intends the consequence, regardless of
whether one wants the consequence—where "want" here and in
the following is to be understood in the somewhat strained sense
in which Sally, in Bob's example, does not want to support factory
farming. Case in point, if one voluntarily purchases factory-farmed
products and is aware that those purchases support factory farms,
then one also intends to support factory farming. So, on my view,
it is conceptually impossible to be complicit in an impermissible
practice without intending to support it. But let us not get too hung
up on the word "intend." Bob's main point, I take it, is that Sally's
not wanting to support factory farming reduces the moral badness
of her complicity, where "not wanting" is to be understood in the
sense of "not endorsing" or "not approving of" or "being emotionally opposed to" or something like that. But even understood like
that, the claim in question is highly suspect.

Suppose Bill kills his brother by chopping his head off and tries
to defend himself by saying that he did not want to kill him but
merely wanted to see what he looked like without a head. I wager
that most people will not buy that this circumstance reduces the
moral badness of Bill's murder compared to the moral badness of
a murder by somebody who wanted to kill his victim—unless they
regard Bill's remark as evidence that he is literally insane. Since it
is no secret that chopping somebody's head off will kill him, Bill
voluntarily killed his brother; and that is all that matters in this
context. Or suppose that Lilly tells a deliberate lie to her best friend.

When she gets caught, she tries to appease the friend by saying that she did not want to lie to him but only did it because it was more convenient for her than telling the truth. Again, I have a strong hunch that the friend will not be convinced that Lilly's not wanting to lie makes the lie any less morally bad. Lilly voluntarily lied to him; period. Similarly, that Sally and Steve do not want to support torturing animals does not reduce the moral badness of their complicity in animal torture compared to the corresponding complicity of somebody who does want to support it, like Meathead Mike in Bob's example or Steve's family and friends in mine. Sally and Steve voluntarily support torturing animals; end of story. By the way, I also do not think that they are "less complicit" compared to these others. But even if they were, that would not change the fact that their complicity is not less morally bad.

In fact, I am inclined to think that there is something seriously psychologically screwed up about supporting factory farming or puppy torturing when one hates it. And if we assume that Sally and Steve regard these forms of animal torture not only as hateful but as morally impermissible, their complicity in these practices is not only psychologically suspect but also might be regarded as morally *worse* than the corresponding complicity in these practices by people who want to support them. Sally's and Steve's support of animal torture is in direct tension with their moral convictions, which, one might argue, is itself morally problematic since we all ought to strive for moral integrity.

These considerations make it clear that the degree of moral badness of one's complicity in an impermissible practice is not reduced if one does not intend to support the practice (in Bob's sense of "intend"). But this also means that one's lack of intention to support an impermissible practice cannot render one's complicity in the practice morally permissible if it is impermissible otherwise. (If it rendered the complicity permissible, it would reduce its degree of moral badness.) In other words, the foregoing considerations explain why Intention is not a mitigating factor in the way Bob claims it to be.

3.4 The Ultimate Anti-Complicity Argument

I have a suspicion that, even after the foregoing defense of the Refined Anti-Complicity Argument, some opponents of the argument will continue to insist that its moral premise is too strong and that cases of complicity in an impermissible practice where the mitigating factors of Influence, Intention, and Offsetting are present are counterexamples to it after all. These stubborn opponents are forced to admit that supporting puppy torture à la Steve is also morally permissible. But they may well be prepared to bite the bullet, unsavory as it is. So, for the benefit of these stubborn opponents, I will propose a further refinement to the moral premise of the argument, which will take the wind out of the sails of the alleged counterexamples, so to speak. I will call the resulting argument the "Ultimate Anti-Complicity Argument." While the Ultimate Anti-Complicity Argument does not demonstrate that Abstinence is true, it establishes that we ought to assume that Abstinence is true, which comes down to the same bottom line, namely, that we ought to abstain. If I ought to assume that I ought to do X, then I ought to do X.

Influence is clearly the most important mitigating factor discussed by Bob, not least because the other two factors seem to presuppose it. In arguing for the claim that offsetting is an option in the case of Sally's complicity in factory farming, he explicitly relies on the assumption that her abstaining would not make any difference to what is happening on the farms. (See p. 97.) And in trying to make plausible that Sally does not intend to support factory farms, he puts heavy emphasis on the claim that, if she thought that her purchases did make a difference, she would stop making them immediately. (See pp. 96–97.) So, I think it is fair to say that, in the eyes of opponents of the Anti-Complicity Argument such as Bob, in order for one's complicity in an impermissible practice to be morally permissible, it is necessary that one's support of the practice does not make a difference to the degree of its moral badness. For ease of communication, I will refer to the kind of complicity in a practice with respect to which one's support makes a difference to the practice's degree of moral badness or goodness "**influential complicity**," and will say of somebody whose complicity is of this kind that he is "influentially complicit."

The moral premise of the Refined Anti-Complicity Argument states that we are morally obligated not to be complicit in an action or practice that is morally wrong. For the Ultimate Anti-Complicity Argument, I propose to replace this premise with the claim that we are morally obligated not to be *influentially* complicit in an action or practice that is morally wrong. The alleged counterexamples to the earlier moral premise are all cases of non-influential complicity since the mitigating factor of Influence is present. Accordingly, they are not counterexamples to the updated moral premise, even if the complicity featured in them were morally permissible.

On first glance, this might seem like a pyrrhic victory. If Bob is right that buying factory-farmed products makes one only non-influentially complicit in factory farming, the updated moral premise does not even apply to this case. So, how are we supposed to get to the desired conclusion that we ought to abstain? In order to answer this question, we need to revisit an assumption that we granted in our previous discussion, namely, that complicity in factory farming through one's animal product purchases is of the non-influential kind. Closer inspection reveals that there are at least two kinds of scenarios in which purchasing factory-farmed animal products makes one influentially complicit in factory farming.

To Bob's credit, he acknowledges that our individual purchases of factory-farmed animal products could make a difference to the production quantities of those farms. An individual purchase would make a difference if it were made in what one might call a "**threshold scenario**," in which it triggers an adjustment in the supply chain that affects the production quantity of some factory farm.

Relatedly, there is a claim underlying much of Bob's discussion in the first part of his opening statement that can be rejected. This claim is that abstaining would make a difference to the production quantities of factory farms only if individual acts of abstaining were *complete* and *direct* causes for the adjustment of those quantities. Think of a production manager of a factory farm reducing the number of chicken thighs to be produced by one in response to receiving the information that a certain store did not sell a particular chicken thigh. The indicated claim can be rejected because, arguably, our abstinence can make a difference to the production quantities of factory farms by way of *partially* or *indirectly* causing an adjustment of those quantities. If a large number of people were to significantly reduce the volume of their factory-farmed animal product purchases, this would certainly make a difference to the production quantities. To see this, just imagine the extreme case in which nobody purchases any factory-farmed animal products anymore at all. Surely, this would force factory farms to go out of business before long. But this means that an individual person's abstinence can be a partial cause of an adjustment in the production quantities of factory farms in virtue of being part of a larger pattern of abstinence that brings about the adjustment. And it also means that an individual person's abstinence can be an indirect cause of an adjustment in the production quantities in virtue of being at least partly responsible for getting a large number of people to frequently abstain. Your example of abstaining, especially if practiced as a rule or if supplemented with an explanation of your reasons for abstaining, may well inspire some of your friends and family members to abstain as well, either occasionally or also as a rule, whose example, in turn, may well inspire some of their friends and family to abstain, and so on. Over time, this process could lead to a large number of frequently abstaining people and thereby make a difference to the production quantities of factory farms. The first step in most moral revolutions consists in somebody taking a stand. I will call a situation in which one's abstaining would be a partial or indirect cause for an adjustment in the production quantity of a factory farm a "revolutionary scenario."

Against the background of these considerations, we can see that it is not true in general that the updated moral premise of the Ultimate Anti-Complicity Argument does not apply to the case of complicity in factory farming through one's animal product purchases. In threshold or revolutionary scenarios, purchasing factory-farmed animal products makes one influentially complicit in factory farming since refraining from the purchase would have made a difference to the production quantities. The updated moral premise thus applies to cases of complicity in factory farming in these scenarios and declares it to be morally impermissible. If Sally is in a threshold or revolutionary scenario, her complicity in factory farming through purchases of factory-farmed animal products is morally impermissible since, in those scenarios, the mitigating factor of Influence is not present after all.

This result does not yet yield the desired conclusion that we ought to abstain, though. There is one more complication to consider. The complication is that, for any particular purchase, the likelihood that we are in a threshold or revolutionary scenario is not very large. On the other hand, this does not mean that we can simply ignore this possibility. *For all we know*, we could be in one of these scenarios. And here the by now familiar principle becomes centrally relevant again, according to which, in cases of uncertainty in moral deliberations, if we are to err, we ought to err on the side of caution, given the high cost of moral wrongdoing. In this case, the side of caution is to assume that we are in a threshold or revolutionary scenario and thus have the moral obligation to refrain from our purchase. In a situation where there is even a tiny chance that we have a moral obligation to do X, and all that speaks for not doing X is that this would afford us some small amount of pleasure, the side of caution is to do X since it guards us against incurring the large cost of committing a moral wrong. More concretely, using Bob's example, the question facing somebody who is contemplating the purchase of a factory-farmed chicken sandwich is whether the gustatory pleasure of eating the sandwich is worth the risk of violating the moral obligation not to be influentially complicit in an impermissible practice. To my mind, the answer is clearly no. No gustatory pleasure of a chicken sandwich can possibly make up for the cost of failing to do what is morally required, even if the risk of this failure is fairly low.

Putting all of this together, here is the Ultimate Anti-Complicity Argument.

Ultimate Anti-Complicity Argument:

1. We are morally obligated not to be influentially complicit in an action or practice that is morally wrong. (Moral premise.)
2. If we are in a threshold or revolutionary scenario, not abstaining makes us influentially complicit in factory farming. (Empirical premise.)
3. Factory farming is morally wrong. (Additional premise.)
4. If we are in a threshold or revolutionary scenario, we are morally obligated to abstain. (Intermediary conclusion; from 1, 2, and 3.)
5. For any particular candidate purchase of a factory-farmed animal product, we do not know whether we are in a threshold or revolutionary scenario but there is some chance that we are. (Additional empirical premise.)
6. For any particular candidate purchase of a factory-farmed animal product, we do not know whether we are morally obligated to refrain from making the purchase but there is some chance that we are so obligated. (From 4 and 5.)
7. Given the high cost of moral wrongdoing, in cases of uncertainty in moral deliberations, if we are to err, we ought to err on the side of caution. (General moral principle.)

8. For any particular candidate purchase of a factory-farmed animal product, we ought to assume that we are morally obligated to refrain from making it. (From 6 and 7.)

9. We are morally obligated to abstain. (From 8.)

The Ultimate Anti-Complicity Argument is immune to Bob's second objection to the Refined Anti-Complicity Argument. Bob's counterexamples to the moral premise of the Refined Anti-Complicity Argument are not counterexamples to the moral premise of the Ultimate Anti-Complicity Argument. Since Bob's first objection to the Anti-Complicity Argument is also unconvincing, absent any further objections there is thus at least one successful argument for Abstinence. So, even if Abstinence were not the default position in our debate, we would be justified in our conclusion that each one of us is morally obligated to refrain from purchasing factory-farmed animal products. Given that Abstinence is the default, as argued in the first part of this reply, this conclusion is overdetermined and more than secure.

As a final comment, I want to highlight that neither the refined nor the ultimate version of the Anti-Complicity Argument relies on the assumption that animals and humans morally matter equally. To be sure, both versions assume that animals have moral standing and morally matter to some extent—an assumption with which Bob claims to agree. But this assumption is compatible with the claim that humans morally matter more than animals. This is important to emphasize because Bob spends the second part of his opening statement arguing against this assumption since, on his view, "if there are problems with the main arguments for veganism [read: Abstinence] even when we grant a big assumption about the moral importance of animals [namely, that animals morally matter as much as humans], and that assumption turns out not to be true, it seems a lot less likely that we're going to find a good argument for veganism somewhere else" (p. 102). I am not convinced that this line of reasoning is cogent. But for now, I merely want to stress that since the Anti-Complicity Argument, in the refined but certainly the ultimate version, is both successful and does not depend on the assumption that animals morally matter as much as humans, the entire second part of Bob's opening statement, interesting as it may be, does not cause any kind of trouble for my case for Abstinence, even if everything that he says there were true (which is debatable).

Factory farming is morally wrong and thus ought to be terminated. There are various ways in which each one of us can contribute to bringing the end of factory farming about, including engaging in political activism, voting for candidates who support introducing stricter animal protection laws, and donating to animal welfare and animal rights organizations, to name just a few. Doing any of these things would be morally praiseworthy. But there is another kind of action in support of ending factory farming that is morally obligatory for each one us, namely, to abstain, that is, not to purchase any factory-farmed animal products. Among other things, being influentially complicit in factory farming is morally impermissible, and purchasing factory-farmed animal products makes us liable to being thus complicit. No chicken sandwich is worth the price of possibly violating a moral obligation. Moreover, in the debate about whether or not we ought to abstain, Abstinence is the default position. Accordingly, even if Bob were to provide an argument for Not-Abstinence (which he has not done) and the debate were to wind up inconclusively, at the end of the day, we should still endorse Abstinence.

Chapter 4

Reply to Anja Jauernig's Opening Statement

Bob Fischer

Contents

1 Introduction

Now that we're into it, I want to begin my first reply by saying how grateful I am that we're having this exchange. Not 25 years ago, a debate volume on what we owe to animals would have been quite different. The person defending the "radical" view probably wouldn't even consider arguing that we have such extensive duties to non-human animals, taking every opportunity to moderate their claims to sound more reasonable to the average ear. ("Yes, *factory* farming is a problem, but maybe there's room for *humane* farming ...") And the person taking the "standard" or "common sense" position would be much less animal-friendly than I am. They

DOI: 10.4324/9781003441823-7

would probably be some sort of contractualist or natural law theorist (terms you don't need to know if you don't know them already), arguing via one framework or the other that animals don't matter in and of themselves. They might even defend factory farming as an efficient—if imperfect—way to satisfy important human interests.

The baseline has shifted. Anja and I agree that animals matter. She and I agree that factory farming is a serious problem that we ought, collectively, to address via the most effective means available. We agree that so much ordinary thinking about animals is confused, that human beings treat animals badly in countless ways in countless contexts, and that progress is both practically possible and morally necessary. We have our disagreements, of course, to which we'll soon come. But outside the classroom, our disagreements are probably less significant than the areas where we see eye to eye. So, while I don't want to minimize the gap between Anja's views and my own, I do want to highlight our commonalities. I'm glad to be part of a conversation where so much is shared.

Nevertheless, we do need to spend some time on our differences. Perhaps most notably, Anja thinks we should accept Status Egalitarianism, according to which there is no hierarchy of moral considerability. This is basically equivalent to the view I described in my opening statement as the Equal Consideration Principle:

> *The Principle of Equal Consideration of Interests* (or the "Equal Consideration Principle," for short). To the degree that interests are similar, they deserve equal consideration in our moral deliberations regardless of whose interests they are.

She also thinks we should accept some additional claims that make Status Egalitarianism more radical still. For instance, she accepts the Good Criterion:

> *The Good Criterion for Moral Standing* (or the Good Criterion, for short): X has moral standing if, and only if, X is capable of flourishing, which, in turn, is the case if, and only if, X has a good for which it strives.

The upshot of the Good Criterion is that all living things—including plants—have equal moral status. And on top of that, Anja rejects the main strategies for moderating Status Egalitarianism's implications. For instance, she doesn't think that humans have more to lose in death. So, she can't use the relative badness of death to explain why, all else equal, it's worse to let humans die than to let animals die. In fact, she doesn't even think that many welfare comparisons make sense. (Recall her example about whether thinking is better for a human than running is for a tiger.) If we can't make such comparisons, then we can't say that it's more important to satisfy some human interests because they're stronger than animals' interests. Put these add-ons together—the Good Criterion, death not being worse for humans, and skepticism about welfare comparisons—and you have an extreme view indeed. If you were worried about the consequences of the Equal Consideration Principle, you should be worried about the consequences of Anja's brand of Status Egalitarianism, as her view is practically designed to get those results. Indeed, you should be more worried, as she thinks we owe things to plants too!

This is the point at which you'd expect me to say, "And that's why we should accept Human Exceptionalism." But here's the thing. Though I'm inclined toward Human Exceptionalism—which says that there's a hierarchy of moral considerability that favors human beings—the inclination isn't that strong. And that's because I have much stronger convictions about practical rather than theoretical questions. For instance, I think that if we have to choose between saving you, dear reader, and saving an animal, we should save you. That's where I start, not where I finish. So, I think the task is to come up with a theory that has that implication. If Status Egalitarianism can deliver that result, then at least on that score, anyway, I'm fine with Status Egalitarianism. If it can't, then I'll accept Human Exceptionalism.

You might object to this approach to ethics. We'll talk about that in a minute. (See section 2.) For present purposes, though, I share this to explain what I'm going to do in this reply. First—and perhaps surprisingly—I'm going to argue that you can accept Status Egalitarianism *without* being nearly as radical as Anja. We can defend at least some priority for many people without Human Exceptionalism. Since I think it's more important to get that priority than to defend any particular normative theory, I'm glad to try to make Status Egalitarianism more human-friendly. That's going to be the main work of section 3. In section 4, however, I'll argue that Status Egalitarianism will only take us so far. If we want true human equality—without radical implications regarding our duties to animals—we probably need to accept Human Exceptionalism.

So, I'll try to reply to Anja's criticisms of Human Exceptionalism, arguing that it can be perfectly reasonable to accept the view.

2   Starting with Practical Conclusions

We'll soon turn to the work of making Status Egalitarianism more human-friendly. Before we get there, I promised you a few words about the idea of starting our theorizing with certain practical conclusions. My approach is vulnerable to an obvious objection, which is that I'm getting things entirely backward: we should start with *principles* and see where they lead—not with practical conclusions that we try to rationalize. Our practical conclusions could be the products of all sorts of biases, and—sadly—often are. It's wiser to figure out which principles seem most likely to be true and then just accept whatever follows from them.

As you might imagine, I'm not convinced. First, I don't agree that it's just rationalizing. Granted, starting with practical conclusions *can* be rationalizing, but it can also be a kind of moral seriousness. On my view, our ethical system has to be livable; we have to respect it and see ourselves as bound by it. If you tell me that according to your moral theory, we should flip a coin when faced with the choice between saving the lives of human beings and saving the lives of chickens or sharks or beavers, then I'd say that your moral theory isn't one I can consider. It rejects something so foundational that it isn't among the options on the table. In saying this, I'm not being facetious or flippant. I'm not trying to find a theory that says things I like to hear, one that happens to fit with my whims. Instead, I'm trying to find a theory that fits with the starting points that, on reflection, I regard as non-negotiable. You can't ask people to believe theories that have what are, to them, unbelievable implications. And I can't believe a theory that doesn't prioritize human beings in these kinds of situations.

(To be clear, Anja did *not* say that we should flip a coin when faced with the choice between saving the lives of human beings and saving the lives of chickens or sharks or beavers. Instead, she said that there are some considerations that can tip the scales toward saving humans. But *only* in those very special circumstances, *only* when all else is truly equal. And most of the time, all else *isn't* truly equal. Normal circumstances tend to favor animals. This is because our choices are almost always between helping small numbers of humans and helping large numbers of animals. So, the animals win.)

Second, the point about bias is fair enough. We have to guard against that. But I've already suggested how we can. I'm trying to find a theory that fits with the starting points that I regard as non-negotiable *on reflection*. That is, we really do have to ask ourselves whether what *seems* like a fixed point, *is* a fixed point. If we imagine our moral beliefs as the parts of a building, we have to consider whether we're really talking about beliefs that are foundational—on which the whole superstructure depends—or whether we're talking about beliefs that are just window dressings, easily swapped out without any impact elsewhere. There is no failsafe method for doing this; we can certainly get it wrong. We can be stubborn and morally inflexible when we should be open-minded and willing to change. But those problems are unavoidable in intellectual work. We just have to do our best.

(Someone might want a recipe for doing this reflection. I don't have one. I do think, though, there are ways we can put pressure on ourselves. For instance, we can try to assess whether—and if so, why—we'd feel any guilt, shame, or embarrassment if we were to act in ways that conflict with that practical conclusion. We can consider whether we'd be prepared to criticize others if they were to assess the situations differently. We can ask whether we'd be willing to teach our children that a particular practical conclusion is true. And so on.)

The third thing to say is that we should test methods by their results. Philosophers are highly creative people who love consistency. Partly for that reason, they love starting with principles, as it's much easier to make principles consistent than it is to reconcile our many complex and conflicting judgments about practical questions. But the problem is that philosophers often go off the rails. When you turn them loose on a concept, they'll do their best to make it consistent whatever the consequences—including losing touch with the original concept. This sort of thing happens all the time. Philosophers start theorizing about an ordinary notion—*truth, material object, time, duty, free will*—and they keep theorizing about it until it's unrecognizable; then, they accuse those who won't accept their analysis of being arbitrary or morally backward or what have you. But if someone offers a conception of moral obligation that's too far from the ordinary one, then either they've failed or they've given us reason to stop caring about moral obligation—not a reason to submit to their preferred conception.

That last point sums up my deepest worry about starting with principles. The people who do it risk turning ethics into a kind of consistency game that ignores what's important in our lives, the very things that give us reason to care about morality in the first place. If we start coming up with approaches to ethics that almost no one is interested in living out, approaches that leave us completely cold when we consider the portrait they paint of the moral landscape, then I think we've lost our way. Those are alien moralities, inhumane moralities—not anything that could be the scaffolding for the communities in which we act and by which we're sustained.

The upshot is that while I understand why someone might want to start with principles rather than practical conclusions, I think it's a risky idea. I certainly wouldn't recommend it. Again, I'm trying to find a moral theory that fits with the starting points that, on reflection, I regard as non-negotiable. On my view, if a theory starts questioning whether we should save people over pigs, something's gone wrong. With that in mind, let's see if we can make Status Egalitarianism a bit more friendly to humans. After that, we'll try to defend Human Exceptionalism against Anja's criticisms.

In this section, I've explained why I think it's okay to start our moral theorizing with non-negotiable practical conclusions. Starting with the moral intuitions that we aren't willing to abandon isn't simply rationalizing; it's a key requirement of building a livable moral system. (At the same time, *seemingly* non-negotiable starting points need to be scrutinized carefully; we shouldn't give equal weight to every intuition we have; otherwise, we won't root out any of our biases.) On my view, if we don't take certain practical conclusions as starting points, we'll risk developing a consistent but unbelievable moral system—which, I think, misses the point of doing ethics.

3   Salvaging Status Egalitarianism

As I mentioned earlier, Anja makes Status Egalitarianism quite extreme. The aim of this section is to try to reel Status Egalitarianism back toward the center. Are there theses we can add to it such that it can respect many of our non-negotiable commitments? I think so—or, at least, it can do a better job than we would have thought initially. Let's see how.

3.1 The Interest Profile Approach

To get a feel for what I have in mind, let's recall that Anja distinguishes three ways of understanding Human Exceptionalism (not Status Egalitarianism):

1. The "interest profile" approach
2. The "higher moral status$_1$" approach, which is based on the relative weight of individuals' interests
3. The "higher moral status$_2$" approach, which is based on the relative value of individuals

We'll come back to the second and third approaches later on. For now, let's consider the interest profile approach, which starts with a mundane observation: humans and animals have many different interests. I have an interest in having a driver's license; I don't have an interest in laying my eggs in the waste of other creatures. Dung beetles, by contrast, don't have an interest in the former and do have an interest in the latter.

The next step is to say: if you have a *richer* interest profile, then you have higher moral status. The third step is to defend a view about what makes an interest profile "richer" than another. And if you can complete these steps in a plausible way, then—it seems— you've got an account of higher moral status.

Anja has doubts about this strategy. She writes:

> The interest-profile conception is unhelpful because (a) it renders moral status an idle cog in that it does not add anything to the description of the interests of a being, and (b) on its assumption, it turns out to be trivially true that not all beings with moral standing have the same moral status since, obviously, not all beings with moral standing have the same interest profile. Similarly, since it is fairly uncontroversial that humans have a richer interest profile than animals and plants, on the proposed conception, human exceptionalism turns out to be a disappointingly weak and toothless view, with which pretty much everybody agrees as a matter of course and which is thus not worth making a big deal about.

On one level, Anja is absolutely correct. The interest profile approach is *not* really an account of higher moral status, as it concedes that relevantly similar interests deserve equal weight in our deliberations, regardless of whose interests they are. So, if the interest profile approach is supposed to be a way of understanding Human Exceptionalism, then it's true that it makes moral status into an idle cog. However, that's a feature rather than a bug. The interest profile approach is supposed to deliver the result that we should prioritize human interests *even though they don't have higher moral status*. Why? Because humans can have *stronger* interests than non-humans, even if their interests are of the same kind. For instance, perhaps both humans and non-humans can be in pain, but humans' pain is more intense, meaning that we have greater reason to alleviate it. In other words, while we might have thought that many human and non-human interests are similar in *all* relevant respects, differences in strength can distinguish them, and so it can be appropriate to prioritize human interests.

That's why I can't completely agree with what Anja says in the passage above. Although it may be trivially true that all living beings have different interest profiles, it's an open question whether that's "a disappointingly weak and toothless view." To get that outcome, we need to add a corollary to the interest profile approach. To appreciate the issue here, let's consider two possibilities: the *addition* hypothesis and the *compression* hypothesis.

Here's the way the addition hypothesis works. Individual #1 has three interests, resulting in a certain capacity for wellbeing—that is, how well things can go for that individual in principle. Individual #2 has five interests. However, Individual #2 has greater capacity for wellbeing than Individual #1. When Individual #2 has her interests fulfilled, they make the same contribution to her wellbeing that the fulfillment of Individual #1's interests make to his. And because Individual #2 has more interests, she has greater capacity for wellbeing.

Ind. #1

Ind. #2

However, while things could work this way, we know there are other possibilities. The compression hypothesis, by contrast, goes as follows. Individual #1 has three interests, resulting in a certain capacity for wellbeing. Individual #2 has five interests. However,

Individual #2 has *the same capacity for wellbeing*. It just turns out when Individual #2 has her interests fulfilled, the fulfillment of each one makes a smaller contribution to her total wellbeing.

Now, when people use the interest profile approach to motivate prioritizing humans, they usually say that humans have *higher-level interests*—in building political communities, making art, practicing their religious traditions, etc.—that animals don't have. So, these people argue, the higher-level interests should be "tacked on" to the basic interests that humans share with animals, effectively increasing the total amount of wellbeing that's at stake in humans relative to non-humans. In other words, they assume that we should accept the addition hypothesis over the compression hypothesis.

But once we distinguish these possibilities, it isn't clear why we should assume that any higher-level interests should be "tacked on" to the basic interests that humans share with animals. Someone might say that we should "tack them on" precisely because they're "higher-level" interests. But this seems speciesist. Digging burrows matters as much to groundhogs as—and perhaps more than—making music matters to humans. Why say that the one matters more than the other—unless we assume a distinctively human perspective?

With all this in mind, it looks like we shouldn't infer anything from the mere fact that humans have more interests than do animals, as the fulfillment of human interests may just make smaller proportional impacts on total wellbeing. Indeed, we might say that if people assume the addition hypothesis, they're just begging the question—they're assuming what needs to be established. That's why it's tempting to conclude that the interest profile approach is trivial.

However, there's a third hypothesis to consider: namely, the *difference in strength* hypothesis. Now suppose that Individual #1 and Individual #2 have three interests. However, Individual #2's interests are *stronger* than Individual #1's—which could be true even if the content of the interests is the same. (That is, both can be about avoiding bodily damage, and yet Individual #2's interest in avoiding pain can be stronger than Individual #1's, perhaps because Individual #2 suffers more due to the same damage.) Yet again, then, Individual #2 has a greater capacity for wellbeing than Individual #1, though without having any additional interests.

Ind. #1

Ind. #2

The "begging the question" criticism doesn't apply to the difference in strength hypothesis. The difference in strength hypothesis doesn't appeal to the number of interests; it doesn't appeal to any speciesist assumptions about music mattering more than digging burrows. It just says that some beings can have stronger interests than others, and so the satisfaction of those interests is more important.

This seems plausible. Animals differ with respect to their evolutionary history, neurophysiology, and neurobiology; this seems to have led to significant variation in their cognitive capabilities. (To give just one example, humans have some 86 *billion* neurons; a brown rat has roughly 200 million; a honeybee, one million.) Given this variation, it would be surprising if there weren't significant differences in their experiential lives. And in principle, those differences could ground big differences in the strength of their interests, so that *ostensibly* similar interests in fact *aren't* similar—perhaps because some species may be able to experience much more intense highs and lows than others. If it turns out that such differences are linked to the possession of sophisticated cognitive capacities, then it could well be more important to satisfy many human interests over the interests of non-human animals.

Plainly, there are lots of complicated empirical and conceptual issues here. It would take us too far afield to defend this view in any detail. So, I just want to point out the following. If the interests of humans are *significantly* stronger than those of non-humans, then we have a way to get something a bit like Human Exceptionalism within the confines of Status Egalitarianism. This is because, in principle, it would work out that many humans' interests are so much stronger than the interests of many animals that, when we give them equal consideration, the human interests almost always win—even when we're considering just one human and multiple animals.

In short, then, we may be able to concede to Anja that Status Egalitarianism is true while defending much more intuitive conclusions about the kinds of cases mentioned earlier, such as the choice between saving either one human or two pigs. Since I care more about such conclusions than the theory that gets us to them, I can live with that outcome.

Granted, though, I haven't actually defended the interest profile approach and the expansion hypothesis. Moreover, there are no guarantees that, when we work out the details, we'll get all the practical conclusions we want. So, it seems prudent not to pin all our hopes to the interest profile approach. Instead, let's explore an entirely different way of reaching the kinds of non-negotiable conclusions that I mentioned earlier—namely, challenging all the add-ons that lead Anja to such radical conclusions, which include the Good Criterion, her view that death isn't worse for humans, and her skepticism about welfare comparisons. If we can resist those outcomes, then yet again, we may be able to get more palatable conclusions without having to argue about Status Egalitarianism itself.

3.2 The Good Criterion

The first hurdle is Anja's Good Criterion. The radicalness of Status Egalitarianism is greatly affected by the criterion for moral standing that you pair with it. If you accept Human Centrism, according to which only humans have moral standing, then Status Egalitarianism isn't radical at all—it just implies what we all believe, namely, that all humans matter equally. (Of course, it also implies that no animal has moral standing, which many of us *don't* believe. So, I'm not recommending Human Centrism.) If you accept the Sentience Criterion, which says that all and only sentient beings have moral standing, then Status Egalitarianism becomes a more dramatic thesis. And if you accept the Good Criterion, as Anja does, then Status Egalitarianism becomes extreme.

Remember: we aren't debating *whether* animals have moral standing; Anja and I agree that they do. Anja and I only disagree about *why* animals have moral standing. I favor the Sentience Criterion, whereas Anja favors the Good Criterion. That view, again, goes like this:

> *Good Criterion for Moral Standing* (or the Good Criterion, for short): X has moral standing if, and only if, X is capable of flourishing, which, in turn, is the case if, and only if, X has a good for which it strives.

As I've suggested, the Good Criterion makes Status Egalitarianism a more radical thesis. In my opening statement, I talked about all the wild consequences if we accept equal consideration for *animals*. Anja wants to extend Status Egalitarianism even further, as she thinks that *all living things* have *equal* moral status. Each alga in each stream, each bacterium growing in yesterday's leftovers, each mosquito, each elephant, and each human—their interests all matter equally. It's hard to *over*state how radical Status Egalitarianism is when it's paired with the Good Criterion. For instance, they may imply that it's wrong to use antibiotics—since those are, of course, designed to kill bacterial infections, and if the infection wouldn't kill you, then bacteria's basic interest in existing may trump your less basic interest in being healthier a bit more quickly. Or consider that where I live, it's practically impossible to avoid running over worms after it rains—they're everywhere on the street. If Status Egalitarianism and the Good Criterion are true, then each worm's interest in continuing to live is *just as weighty as yours*, making a post-rain trip to the grocery store a *very* high-stakes proposition. If we accept Anja's views, the changes to our moral outlook will be off the charts.

As you might imagine, I think those are good reasons to reject the Good Criterion. Of course, that won't convince Anja, given her skepticism about relying on intuitions like these. But there is an independent problem that doesn't rely on such intuitions.

As Anja discussed in her opening statement, criteria of moral standing tell us which things matter intrinsically. Typically, they do that by way of a (partial) theory of wellbeing—a theory about what makes this go well and badly for each individual. For instance, the Sentience Criterion for moral standing says that things matter intrinsically if they can experience pleasures and pains. Why are pleasures and pains supposed to be relevant to moral standing? They're supposed to be relevant because they affect wellbeing: the lives of sentient beings go better and worse depending on how many pleasures and pains they experience.

So, while the Good Criterion is a criterion of moral standing rather than wellbeing, it strongly suggests a theory of wellbeing. According to the suggested theory:

> Good Criterion of wellbeing: Y is good for X just in case Y is part of (or otherwise appropriately related to) the good for which X strives.

Seems reasonable enough. But remember that Anja thinks plants have moral standing. So, she needs to interpret the "striving" in a way that doesn't involve individuals setting conscious goals for themselves. She can't say: "The good for which X strives is whatever X consciously values"—as plants don't consciously value anything. What can she say instead?

Her proposal goes like this:

> ... the good of a being is to be understood teleologically as determined by what Aristotle calls the being's characteristic function or essential activity ... More specifically, the good of a being consists in performing its characteristic function, its essential activity, well or excellently. When that happens, the being flourishes.

According to Anja, then, "striving" isn't a conscious activity; it's just a thing doing what it's supposed to do—its function or "essential activity."

Where do these functions come from? Historically, one influential story has been that God sets the good for each being—the end for which they strive. But I doubt that Anja wants to appeal to divine intentions here. She could appeal to species-specific natures, but it isn't clear that species *have* natures. Biologists tend to think that there are lots of different species concepts that allow us to carve up biological reality differently, none of which is privileged over the others. And in any case, even if we do grant that species have natures, it's easy to generate cases where what's good for *typical* members of a species doesn't seem to matter for others. (It might be part of river otters' natures to hunt, but if they have all their needs met by humans and seem perfectly happy *not* hunting, then what, exactly, are they missing?) So, she may be stuck with the ends set by the evolutionary process, since that's the way biologists explain how anything in nature can have a purpose or function. In other words, Anja might have to say that the good for which beings strive is the propagation of their genes, which is generally achieved through survival and reproduction.

Unfortunately, though, this seems to lead to deeply implausible results. What's good for propagating your genes may not be good for *you*. Some female praying mantises eat male praying mantises as they mate. This seems to be good for gene propagation while being bad for male praying mantises. Likewise, there is some evidence of phenoptosis in nature—that is, organisms being genetically programmed to die. It isn't that difficult to imagine such a mechanism arising: it could prevent organisms who are past reproductive age from hanging around and consuming resources that their descendants need. That's good for the descendants but bad for the beings who are programmed to die.[1]

Anja may have a way out of this problem that I'm not seeing. But from where I sit, the best way out is to reject the Good Criterion. And if we do, then we can make Status Egalitarianism significantly less radical and—in my view—much more plausible.

Still, that's only going to take us so far. As I argued in my opening statement, the combination of Status Egalitarianism and the Sentience Criterion can have some hugely counterintuitive consequences. Those could be moderated with some additional assumptions, though Anja rejects them. Let's find out whether we can defend them.

3.3   Do Humans Have More to Lose? Can We Compare Welfare Across Species?

If death is worse for humans than it is for animals, then in situations where we have to choose between sacrificing a human and an animal, we have a principled reason for preferring the human. And if we can compare welfare across species, then we can say, for instance, that humans being able to acquire knowledge is better for them than freedom is for mice. And if we can say that, then we have a principled justification for some actions that might otherwise be objectionable, such as keeping animals in captivity for research purposes. Anja, of course, denies both that death is worse for humans and that we can compare welfare across species. Let's remind ourselves why and try to respond to her criticisms.

These claims come up when Anja discusses the main *objection* to Status Egalitarianism. She actually says that she'd like to be able to rely on them, as they'd make Status Egalitarianism easier to defend;

---

1. It's worth noting that if Anja is right that the best alternative to Human Centrism is the Good Criterion, and the Good Criterion has some serious problems, then that's a point in favor of Human Centrism. And if Human Centrism *were* true—which I'm not saying it is!—then we would get Human Exceptionalism for free. After all, if humans are the *only* beings with moral standing, then it follows automatically that human beings are at the top of the hierarchy of moral considerability.

instead, though, she argues against them. (We should give her credit for not taking any easy outs.) This means that there's a sense in which I'm helping her, but as I said before, I think what matters is protecting some degree of human priority for practical purposes, not the philosophical framework that gets us there. If we can get there via Status Egalitarianism, all the better for that view.

You probably remember the main objection that Anja considers to Status Egalitarianism: namely, the lifeboat case. I'm not going to talk about the details of that case; they don't matter for our purposes. The crucial aspect of it is that you're forced to choose between saving either a human or a dog; you can't save both. The Human Exceptionalist says you ought to save the human, and presumably, many find this intuitive. Anja could agree if she thought she could say that humans have more to lose in death. But as we've said, she doesn't think she can.

Let's consider her challenges to the "humans have more to lose" claim—the idea that it's somehow worse for humans to die than for animals to die, at least all else equal—which is supposed to explain why you should save the human over the dog in the forced choice situation. Against that claim, Anja makes three independent points (so this is a list rather than an argument):

1. Some humans don't have more to lose—for instance, individuals with severe cognitive disabilities—and yet we may still have the intuition that the human should be saved.
2. We overestimate how much humans benefit from their lives.
3. We can't compare the flourishing of the members of different species—their flourishing is *incommensurable*.

I think we can defend the "humans have more to lose" claim against these objections. We can deal with the first two fairly quickly. The third, however, will take a bit of time. Given its importance, though, it's worth the investment.

3.3.1   Some Humans Don't Have More to Lose

Anja's point here is that some humans don't seem to have more to lose than some animals, but the intuition favoring humans persists. So, the claim that humans have more to lose isn't really explaining the intuition.

The first thing to say is that we should distinguish between two senses of "explains" here. The first sense of "explains" is roughly equivalent to *predicts*: the claim explains the intuition, in this sense, if it helps you predict when people will have it. The second sense of "explains" is roughly equivalent to *provides the grounds of*: the claim explains the intuition, in this sense, if it reveals what makes the intuition true.

Now, it doesn't matter whether the claim that humans have more to lose *predicts* our intuition about this case, in the sense that we only have the intuition when the claim is true. Instead, what matters is whether the claim *provides the grounds* of the intuition. And in some cases, it seems to. Let's suppose we're talking about infants, who are, while still infants, less cognitively sophisticated than dogs. Still, the intuition that *those* humans have more to lose remains plausible. They have rich lives ahead of them! So, at least in cases involving infants, as long as we can reply to Anja's second objection, we can say that we should save infants over dogs because infants have better, richer futures ahead of them than dogs.

Moreover, in cases where humans *don't* seem to have more to lose—think, for instance, of humans in permanent vegetative states—then it may be true that we shouldn't save the human. After all, many people think of their loved ones as "already gone" when they're in that state, so the conclusion isn't so counterintuitive: maybe Status Egalitarianism just gets the right result without any supplementation.

Finally, let's note that even if the "humans have more to lose" hypothesis can't provide the grounds for all our intuitions, it may still provide the grounds for many of them. And that's good enough. It doesn't need to be a silver bullet, offering the foundations for all our intuitions about all cases. (To be clear, Anja doesn't think otherwise: she never claims that the "humans have more to lose" hypothesis is the only possible way to defend saving the human over the dog, and she herself suggests another possible route, at least in a limited range of cases.) So, once we distinguish cases and calibrate our expectations for the "humans have more to lose" hypothesis, it seems to me that Anja's first criticism has limited force.

3.3.2   Humans Don't Benefit That Much from Their Lives

Anja's second objection to the "humans have more to lose" claim is that the lives of humans typically may not benefit them more than the lives of animals benefit animals. After all, our sophisticated cognitive capacities seem to make us miserable a good portion of the time!

I feel the force of this challenge. However, there is a famous reply from J. S. Mill, a nineteenth-century philosopher and social reformer. He wrote:

> It is indisputable that the being whose capacities of enjoyment are low, has the greatest chance of having them fully satisfied; and a highly endowed being will always feel that any happiness which he can look for, as the world is constituted, is imperfect.[2]

Translation: if you're a simple soul who wants simple pleasures—feeling full, sleeping late, the sun on your back—you've got a good shot at getting what you want. But if you're a more sophisticated individual, you're likely to notice all the shortcomings in the things you work for. So, there's a cost to having these more sophisticated capacities. As the author of Ecclesiastes put it, "For with much wisdom comes much sorrow; the more knowledge, the more grief" (Eccles. 1:18). But Mill thinks that there's a silver lining:

> But [the more sophisticated individual] can learn to bear [the world's] imperfections, if they are at all bearable; and they will not make him envy the being who is indeed unconscious of the imperfections, but only because he feels not at all the good which those imperfections qualify. It is better to be a human being dissatisfied than a pig satisfied; better to be Socrates dissatisfied than a fool satisfied. And if the fool, or the pig, are a different opinion, it is because they only know their own side of the question. The other party to the comparison knows both sides.[3]

Translation: the simple soul doesn't realize what he's missing. True, he doesn't see the imperfections, but as a result, he doesn't appreciate the goodness of the things that are imperfect. And all things considered, it's better to have access to the best the world has to offer.

There are many important implications if Mill is correct, but one of them is about how we ought to assess how good different lives

---

2. Mill 1863, chapter 2.
3. Mill 1863, chapter 2.

are for those who lead them. Here's the idea. I like to go for a walk in the evening; my dog does too. If we compare how happy I am about the walk and how happy he is, he certainly seems happier. Anja wants to infer from this that my dog is better off—or, at least, that we aren't entitled to believe that I'm better off in such circumstances. Mill denies this. He thinks we shouldn't be comparing how happy I appear to be in that moment with how happy my dog appears to be. Instead, we should be asking whether I'd *trade places* with my dog. And the answer, Mill thinks, is that I wouldn't—and shouldn't. However happy a dog may be in some particular moment, that happiness isn't valuable enough to make it worth giving up a human's kind of life. And if that's right, Mill insists, then my life is better for me than my dog's is for him.

Of course, you might not share the intuition. Maybe you think you'd swap places with a dog in a heartbeat! In all honesty, there are moments when I've thought the same. There's something appealing about the idea of a life that isn't shaped by all the fears and pressures that humans face. But what's appealing, I think, is mostly the absence of those fears and pressures—not the life of the dog. What I want is to know that I'll always have enough money to keep a roof over my children's heads, not to lose my ability to understand what money is. I want to be confident that my children will inherit a world containing polar bears and river dolphins, not to lose my ability to understand the sixth mass extinction. And as the latter example suggests, I value my cognitive abilities despite their costs. I think it's worth knowing hard truths even though they're hard, even though they create fears and anxieties I'd like to avoid. I suspect, therefore, that there's something to Mill's "trading places" test. If so—and if we agree that we shouldn't trade places—then it's plausible that the lives of humans typically benefit them more than the lives of animals benefit animals. So, I think we can resist Anja's second objection to the "humans have more to lose" claim.

3.3.3 Incommensurability

All that said, Anja actually rejects a crucial assumption behind the first two objections. Both depend on the idea that we can make sense of *interspecies wellbeing comparisons*—judgments about how things are going for salmon relative to chimps or lobsters relative to warthogs. If we can't make such judgments, then we can't say, for instance, that human suffering is generally worse than chicken suffering, as that would provide support for the claim that, all else equal, a human's interest in pain relief is stronger than a chicken's interest in pain relief.

Why is Anja skeptical of interspecies wellbeing comparisons? Here's what she says:

> I contend that the flourishing of members of different species generally cannot be compared. I believe that cases of interspecies comparability of goods/bads are quite rare—if, indeed, they exist at all. (Our intuitions about these cases may well be misleading.) When asked whether it is better for a human to be able to think for as much as she wants (assuming that thinking is an integral part of the characteristic function of human beings) than it is for a tiger to be able to run for as much as he wants (assuming that running is an integral part of the characteristic function of tigers), most of us will draw a blank. Trying to compare the good of thinking for humans and the good of running for tigers is like trying to compare apples and oranges. And the same goes for a great many other goods/bads for humans and other animals. Only very few, if any, of the goods/bads for members of different species can be compared with respect to being better, worse, or equal. And since the flourishing of a being is determined by all of the goods/bads for it in its life, this means that the flourishing of members of different species generally cannot be compared either.

There's a lot going on in this passage, so before we dive into it, we should pause to introduce some terminology.

If A and B are *incommensurable*, then you can't rank them on a cardinal scale. In other words, there are no specific *units* of better and worse. *The Sword in the Stone* is a much better Disney movie than, say, *The Lion King 2*—which, sadly, a small child once made me watch. However, it might not be a specific *amount* better, such that it makes sense to say that *The Sword in the Stone* is 7.4 units of Disney-movie-goodness better than *The Lion King 2*.

Notice, then, that A and B can be incommensurable while still being *comparable*. A and B are comparable just in case they can be ordinally ranked relative to one another—which in many contexts means "First, Second, Third, etc.," but here just means better and worse. (We don't need the categories of "best" and "worst" to have comparability.) I've suggested that Disney movies are comparable: they can be ordinally ranked (A is better than B) even if they can't be cardinally ranked (A has 5 units of goodness; B has 10; so, B is twice as good as A).

Anja is open—though not fully committed—to comparability in at least some cases. (She writes: "For example, it seems intuitively obvious not only that the suffering endured by a chicken on an average day in a factory farm is very bad as far as chicken suffering goes, and that my suffering from a mild headache for five minutes is not very bad as far as human suffering goes, but also that the suffering of the chicken in the factory farm is much worse than my suffering from the mild headache.") However, she resists a *general* commitment to comparability—recall the human thinking/tiger running case—and she's opposed to commensurability across the board. In other words: limited ordinal ranking, no cardinal measures.

Let's start with her claim that we can't compare the wellbeing impacts of humans thinking for humans and tigers running for tigers. For what it's worth, I don't share the intuition. This isn't to suggest that I have some clear sense of which is better. Rather, I think they're comparable because I think that additional information could help me decide. Most obviously, I could learn that tigers don't like running that much—or don't satisfy many of their desires by running—compared to the amount of pleasure and the number of desires that humans satisfy by thinking. I could also learn that either running or thinking differ in whether they are instrumentally or intrinsically valuable. Maybe running is only instrumentally good for tigers (they only do it to catch prey) but thinking is both instrumentally and intrinsically good for humans (it's an activity that's valuable in itself). I could also learn about differences in the relative instrumental values of thinking and running. Perhaps thinking opens humans up to a much wider range of goods. In each case, the information would affect my view about the relative value of thinking and running for the members of each species. And if it ought to affect my assessment of their relative value, then they must be comparable. (Note that this also gives us a plausible story about why there might be the *appearance* of incomparability: we don't have a bunch of information that's relevant to making judgment calls.)

I also think there are serious costs of giving up comparability. Recall Anja's example about chickens on factory farms: as that case suggests, we want to be able to compare wellbeing impacts *when arguing on animals' behalf*. For instance, here's a simple way to set back human wellbeing: have people eat foods they don't like—which, for many people, includes the standard protein sources in vegan diets (tofu, beans, etc.). Many animal advocates have argued that any such impact on humans' wellbeing is trivial when compared to the impacts that factory farms have on animals' wellbeing. But if we deny that we can make interspecies wellbeing comparisons, we lose the ability to make that claim.

Similarly, if we want to do the most good we can, we have to make difficult choices that require interspecies welfare comparisons. If you've only got so much money to spend on lobbying, what's more important? Trying to end the use of gestation crates for sows or trying to expand the sizes of the cages that hold layer hens? This, of course, leads us to ask whether intense confinement is worse for pigs than it is for chickens. That latter question seems to be both perfectly well-formed and very important; it's one we hope that animal welfare science can help us answer. But if we can't make interspecies welfare comparisons, then it's a mistake to ask it.

Finally, Anja might want to rely on interspecies wellbeing comparisons to explain why humans don't have to let themselves starve to death. Remember: she says we may cause "a minimal amount of harm" to keep ourselves alive. But why, exactly? One plausible explanation is that the impacts of starvation on humans' wellbeing are huge relative to the tiny harms associated with harvesting fruit from plants. (Indeed, this kind of claim might even be important if we think of things in terms of rights. Perhaps it's generally true that you don't have a right to something if it would give you trivial benefits relative to the costs that your having it would impose on others. If that's right, then plants have no right to keep their fruits to themselves.)

It seems to me, therefore, that we shouldn't accept what Anja says about incomparability. But getting comparability leaves us a long way from commensurability. And ultimately, commensurability—having a way to measure welfare—is what would be most useful. If we want to be able to make reasonably precise judgments about when humans' interests do and *don't* outweigh animals' interests, we need to be able to quantify welfare. We need a cardinal scale.

For what it's worth, I think that with enough time and effort, we might be able to come up with a cardinal scale for wellbeing. It certainly seems as though humans and animals have overall welfare states—that we can say how they're doing on the whole, even if only roughly. And if "how someone's doing on the whole" depends on more basic states that are themselves measurable—such as how much pain they're in or how satisfied they are—then eventually, we should be able to measure those states. We already can, at least to some degree, in humans, where we've made significant progress in the science of wellbeing. Admittedly, our knowledge of other species is relatively impoverished. The science of sentience—that is, the study of how some organisms produce conscious states that have either a positive or negative feel to them—is still very young. But before sciences develop, it's easy to think that they never will, that certain questions will forever remain unanswerable. When sciences do develop, though, seemingly-intractable problems have a way of disappearing.

However, it doesn't matter whether I'm right about all this. Comparability is enough, even if more would be beneficial. I think we can conclude, therefore, that Anja's criticisms of the "humans have more to lose" hypothesis don't work. So, we can say both that death is worse for humans than it is for animals and, at least in principle, that humans being able to acquire knowledge is better for them than freedom is for mice. This gives us a principled, non-arbitrary way of arguing that even if Status Egalitarianism is true, we can prefer humans in a wide range of cases. We can have a more modest, less radical Status Egalitarianism.

In this section, I've tried to make Status Egalitarianism fit better with the idea that we should prioritize humans in many tradeoff cases. First, we can accept the interest profile approach. The interest profile approach says that humans should often be prioritized because they have stronger interests. Second, we can make Status Egalitarianism less radical by pairing it with the Sentience Criterion—in contrast to Anja's preferred Good Criterion. This spares us from having to include plants in our moral deliberations. Third, we can defend the claims that humans have more to lose in death, that humans benefit from their lives, and that interspecies wellbeing comparisons are possible. Together, these claims allow us to explain why it's usually worse for humans to die than for animals to die.

4 Human Exceptionalism

Still, I have my doubts that Status Egalitarianism is going to accommodate all my non-negotiables. For instance, if we want to help Status Egalitarianism avoid the radical consequences we've discussed, we need to add the kinds of assumptions we've discussed—ones based, essentially, on the idea that beings with certain sophisticated cognitive capacities have stronger interests (in not dying, in being free from pain, etc.) than those without them. But if we make that move, then Status Egalitarianism famously struggles to explain why *all* humans could have equally strong interests. Just think of infants and those with severe cognitive disabilities—individuals who don't yet or won't ever have those sophisticated cognitive capacities. Status Egalitarianism still implies that they deserve equal moral consideration. However, if we take on the idea that beings with certain sophisticated cognitive capacities have stronger interests than those without them, then the interests of infants and those with severe cognitive disabilities will rarely be as strong as those of normal human adults. So, despite having equality in principle, we get hierarchy *de facto*.

This reveals that we've been a bit too casual up to this point. I've been arguing that Status Egalitarianism is compatible with prioritizing *humans* over animals in many cases, but that isn't quite right. It's more accurate to say that, in many cases, Status Egalitarianism is compatible with prioritizing *beings with certain sophisticated cognitive capacities* over those without them—which roughly tracks the human/non-human divide, but only very roughly. Neurotypical adult humans generally have these cognitive capacities; many younger humans and neurodiverse humans have them too. However, very young children don't, nor do some people with severe cognitive disabilities. They're also absent in the comatose, in late-stage Alzheimer's patients, and some others who are the victims of either injury or disease.

For many of us, though, *human* equality—not just equality among beings with certain sophisticated cognitive capacities—is non-negotiable. We don't want an ethical theory that downgrades those with cognitive disabilities. To be clear, Anja doesn't either: that's one reason why she doesn't take on the assumptions that make Status Egalitarianism less radical with respect to animals. So, what I've said so far in this section isn't meant as a criticism of anything she's said.

Instead, I'm trying to point out that we have to choose between:

1. Anja's brand of Status Egalitarianism—which rejects the importance of sophisticated cognitive abilities, and therefore has many radical implications regarding our duties to animals;
2. Status Egalitarianism combined with a commitment to the importance of sophisticated cognitive abilities—which doesn't have as many radical implications regarding our duties to animals, but introduces a *de facto* hierarchy among humans; and
3. Human Exceptionalism—which avoids many radical implications regarding our duties to animals and does not require introducing a hierarchy among humans, albeit at the (current) price of not having a neat explanation for the significance of the human/animal divide.

Anja, of course, goes for the first option. Many philosophers have decided that the price of true human equality is too high—namely, not having a neat explanation for the significance of the human/animal divide—so they accept the second option. I go for the third.

You'll recall, though, that Anja has some objections to Human Exceptionalism. First, she says that it's incoherent: she thinks we can't even formulate the view properly. Second, she says that it's speciesist. Third, she's skeptical of the intuitions that motivate Human Exceptionalism. Let's tackle these problems in turn.

4.1   Is Human Exceptionalism Incoherent?

We've already discussed one way of making sense of Human Exceptionalism that isn't really a form of Human Exceptionalism—namely, the interest profile approach. You'll recall, though, that Anja offered two other possible interpretations of Human Exceptionalism:

1. The "higher moral status$_1$" approach, which is based on the relative weight of individuals' interests
2. The "higher moral status$_2$" approach, which is based on the relative value of individuals

Let's consider her objections to each one.

Anja defines the "higher moral status$_1$" approach this way: "A has higher moral status$_1$ than B if, and only if, there is at least one interest of A that has more weight than a similar interest of B, and there is no interest of B that has more weight than a similar interest of A." Since she rejects most interspecies wellbeing comparisons, she thinks it's usually confused to say that an interest of A has more weight than a similar interest of B. And since she thinks that animals' interests are sometimes weightier than humans' interests—recall the human headache/chicken-on-a-factory-farm example—it follows from her definition that humans don't have higher moral status$_1$ than animals.

Of course, since I don't reject most interspecies wellbeing comparisons, I don't think it's usually confused to say that an interest of A has more weight than a similar interest of B. And although I'm inclined to think that even the weakest human interests outweigh the interests of some animals—like earthworms—I don't think I have to defend that view. That's because there's a weaker version of the "higher moral status$_1$" approach that's good enough for my purposes. Suppose that things work like this:

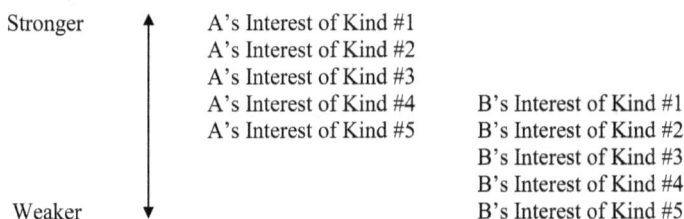

Stronger		A's Interest of Kind #1	
		A's Interest of Kind #2	
		A's Interest of Kind #3	
		A's Interest of Kind #4	B's Interest of Kind #1
		A's Interest of Kind #5	B's Interest of Kind #2
			B's Interest of Kind #3
			B's Interest of Kind #4
Weaker			B's Interest of Kind #5

The central claim I want to make here is that A has higher moral status than B even though one of B's interests—namely, B's Interest of Kind #1—outweighs A's Interest of Kind #5. If most of A's interests outweigh most of B's interests even when they're of the same kind, it seems fair to describe that as A's having a higher moral status. This is basically the way I think things work with humans and animals. A human's interest in survival is weightier than a deer's interest in survival. But a deer's interest in being free from pain is weightier than a human's interest in recreation. So if you need to kill a deer to survive, you may: your interest in survival outweighs the deer's interest in survival. If you want to kill a deer because you enjoy hanging antlers on your wall, you shouldn't: your interest in that particular recreational activity is outweighed by the deer's interest in survival. I don't see what's incoherent about this, at least as long as we grant that we can make interspecies wellbeing comparisons.

Let's now turn to Anja's second way of cashing out Human Exceptionalism: the "higher moral status$_2$" approach, which says that "A has higher moral status$_2$ than B if, and only if, A's intrinsic value is greater than B's intrinsic value." Against the second view, she objects that all individuals with moral standing have a *dignity* rather than a *price*, with basically just means that they have a distinctive kind of incomparable value. But as Anja recognizes, that isn't an argument for thinking that it's *impossible* to say that some beings have more intrinsic value than others. Instead, it's an explanation for why Anja can't say that some beings have more intrinsic value than others. And from my perspective, that view has implications that no one can be faulted for rejecting: you, dear reader, matter more than a dandelion or a house fly. If that means we have to give up the idea of dignity—in the technical, all-beings-with-moral-standing-have-this-special-sort-of-incomparable-value sense of "dignity"—then so be it.

The upshot: whichever way we decide to formulate Human Exceptionalism, I think we can come up with a coherent understanding of the view.

4.2   Is Human Exceptionalism Speciesist?

This brings us to Anja's second criticism of Human Exceptionalism: namely, that it's speciesist. But now that we've replied to all these objections, we can see that speciesism isn't an independent objection. A hierarchy isn't speciesist if there's some basis for it. And while I haven't shown that there is some *particular* basis for the hierarchy that Human Exceptionalism posits, I have made the case both that it's reasonable to believe that there is such a hierarchy and that the objections to it aren't successful. So, if we had no reason to believe in a hierarchy, then it would be speciesist to posit one. But whether we have such a reason is precisely what we're debating. At this stage, you know which side I'm on.

4.3   What's Wrong with the Intuitions That Favor Human Exceptionalism?

Anja's final objection to Human Exceptionalism isn't listed as such. However, it's in her opening statement nonetheless and it goes to the heart of my case for Human Exceptionalism. So, it may be one of the deepest points of disagreement between us. The objection is to some of the intuitions that support Human Exceptionalism. Her strategy is to try to undercut those intuitions—to show that we shouldn't trust them. She writes:

> The mainstream culture of industrialized nations tends to be human exceptionalist if not human centrist, and most of us are brought up and educated by human exceptionalists if not human centrists. It is thus no surprise at all that most people believe that they would save the human over the dog, and have the intuition that they ought to do so. The prevalence of this reaction and intuition cannot be counted as evidence for the truth of the claim that one ought to save the human being over the dog, let alone for the truth of human exceptionalism.

As you know, I think that if we reject intuitions to the effect that we should save people over dogs, then we end up having to make pervasive and radical changes to our moral outlook. In my view, we should be very careful before heading down that path. I think it's a recipe for ending up with a moral view that we don't have any reason to believe.

Let me explain by adapting what a famous philosopher said in a very different context:

> Ethics aims to *improve* our common sense theory of our obligations, which means that we're going to change it. But we're still trying to improve *that theory*, which requires leaving it recognizable as the same theory we had before. It's pointless to build a theory, however nicely systematized it might be, that it would be unreasonable to believe. And a theory can't earn credence—it can't become worth believing—just by being elegantly simple and perfectly consistent. So, what credence it can't earn, it must inherit from the theory with which we began. In other words, a worthwhile theory must be credible, and a credible theory can't disagree with too much of what we thought before. And much of what we thought before was just common sense.

In my view, Anja wants us to give up far too many of the beliefs that ground the ethical project, the ones that motivate it and provide us with some reason to hope we can make progress. She wants us to adopt a theory of our obligations that's simple and consistent, but is so far from where we started that we can't believe it. *That's* why we should be Human Exceptionalists instead of Status Egalitarians.

And just to be clear: the philosopher I'm paraphrasing above—David Lewis—believed some things that many people regard as completely out of this world. So I am *not* arguing for preserving every bias and prejudice, every xenophobic impulse, every dimension of patriarchy, racial oppression, and animal exploitation. Far from it! As I said at the outset, Anja and I agree that animals matter; we agree that factory farming is a serious problem that we ought, collectively, to address via the most effective means available; we agree that so much ordinary thinking about animals is confused, that human beings treat animals badly in countless ways in countless contexts, and that progress is both practically possible and morally necessary. I want things to change for animals and I want our *thinking* about animals to change. But wanting change is one thing; wanting Species Egalitarianism is another. We can have the former without the latter. And the latter is a bridge too far.

Having said all this, we can see that Anja's argument either misses its target or proves too much. Her goal is to undercut the intuitions that support Human Exceptionalism. So, she wants to make an inference from *this intuition is inculcated by the dominant culture* to *the prevalence of this intuition has no evidential value*. But we weren't appealing to the *prevalence* of intuitions that support Human Exceptionalism—that is, we weren't appealing to how common they are in the general population. We were appealing to their *strength*, to how true certain claims seem to be to us.

You might think that Anja can make a quick revision here: she can instead make an inference from *this intuition is inculcated by the dominant culture* to *this intuition has no evidential value*. But now we have the "proves too much" problem, as we could make basically the same inference to criticize the idea that humans matter equally. The mainstream culture of industrialized nations tends to value the lives of normal adult human beings equally, and it is thus no surprise that most people believe that they should not endorse a criterion of moral status that would provide less-than-equal status to any normal adult human being. So, if we make this revised inference, we should conclude that this reaction can't be counted as evidence for the truth of the claim that one ought to reject criteria of moral status that do not give equal weight to normal adult human beings.

Indeed, we could go further: we could point out that many of us *benefit* from the idea that normal adult humans deserve equal moral weight, and so have self-interested reasons to preserve that idea. So again, we should be skeptical that our intuition in favor of equality provides any evidence for it. And in both cases, the right response is that that's wildly implausible. Sure, our intuitions never guarantee that any moral conclusion is true, but they provide some evidence, even if we happen to live in a culture where that intuition is widely shared.

It seems, then, that we can reply to Anja's skepticism about the intuitions that support Human Exceptionalism.

In Section 3, I tried to make Status Egalitarianism less radical. In this section, I began by pointing out that even if we manage to accomplish that, the view isn't perfect. That's because our strategy for making Status Egalitarianism more human-friendly was to create a hierarchy based on cognitive sophistication. However, this hierarchy also differentiates humans from one another, leading to unacceptable conclusions about infants and those with certain disabilities. To avoid this problem, I defend Human Exceptionalism against Anja's critiques, I argue that Human Exceptionalism is coherent as long as we can make interspecies wellbeing comparisons—which, I think, we can. I also argue that we can set aside the charge of speciesism as long as we can respond to all the other objections to Human Exceptionalism and that it can be reasonable to rely on the intuitions that favor Human Exceptionalism.

5   Conclusion

Let's take stock. At the beginning, I said that I had two goals. First, I wanted to show that we can defend at least some priority for many people without Human Exceptionalism. So, I tried to make Status Egalitarianism more human-friendly. Second, I wanted to reply to Anja's criticisms of Human Exceptionalism since, as I argued, Status Egalitarianism won't give us true human equality without radical implications regarding our duties to animals.

In pursuit of that first goal, I showed how we can salvage some of the additional hypotheses that Anja rejects. Status Egalitarianism isn't as radical if we reject the Good Criterion, suppose that death is worse for humans than for animals, and argue that we can make some interspecies wellbeing comparisons.

Of course, this leaves us with a view where beings with more sophisticated cognitive capacities have stronger interests than those without them. For many of us, that's untenable. So, we have reason to accept Human Exceptionalism. Moreover, we can reply to Anja's criticisms of it: it isn't incoherent, it isn't necessarily speciesist, and the intuitions behind it can't be quickly undercut.

But let's not make too much of this conclusion. Nothing I've said implies that you can do what you want to animals. In fact, I think quite the opposite is true. We don't need the resources of Species Egalitarianism to argue for major change on animals' behalf. We can look to much more ordinary ideas—about what's compassionate, sustainable, and fair—to get deep and powerful critiques of the status quo. Most obviously, factory farming is neither compassionate, sustainable, nor fair to many of the humans and animals involved in the supply chain. Researchers perform painful experiments on animals that won't have any appreciable human benefits; that isn't compassionate. Destroying the habitat on which wild animals depend isn't sustainable: even if people don't care about those wild animals, they are systematically destroying the ecosystems from which we all benefit.

I could give many other examples, but these should suffice to show that our values—our perfectly ordinary, common values— challenge standard operating procedures in agriculture, in research facilities, and in the wild. We can be Human Exceptionalists *and* recognize that we owe non-human animals much better than the status quo. And on both counts, that's what I think we should do.

Second Round of Replies

Chapter 5

Second Reply to Bob Fischer

Anja Jauernig

Contents

Many intriguing questions have come up in our debate so far
that would merit further discussion. Two of these questions have
emerged as lying at the heart of the disagreement between Bob and
me. The first is the practical question of the moral permissibility
of purchasing factory-farmed products, which I discussed in my
first reply. The second is the theoretical question of which view of
the moral status of humans compared to non-humans is preferable, the kind of humans-first view advocated by Bob or the kind
of status egalitarianism advocated by me. This is the question on
which I will focus in my second reply. I will start by reinforcing my
case against Bob's view and then respond to Bob's main objections
against mine.

DOI: 10.4324/9781003441823-9

I   Humans-First à la Bob Revisited: Human Exceptionalism and Human Prioritism

According to human exceptionalism, there is a hierarchy of moral considerability among beings with moral standing, and human beings are at the very top in that they have higher moral status, or morally matter more, than all other beings. Bob claims to be endorsing human exceptionalism, and a large part of his first reply is ostensibly devoted to responding to my objections against this view. These objections, you will recall, are the formulation objection and the speciesism objection. The formulation objection says that the prospects for providing a more explicit formulation of human exceptionalism by spelling out what it means for a being to have higher moral status than another such that this formulation (i) captures the thought that humans morally matter more than all non-humans, and (ii) is both meaningful and defensible, are rather bleak. The speciesism objection says that since speciesism, just like racism and sexism, is morally wrong, and human exceptionalism is a form of speciesism, human exceptionalism is morally wrong as well.

Upon closer examination of Bob's discussion in the sections in which he allegedly defends human exceptionalism, it transpires, however, that something else is going on there. What he is actually doing, deliberately or inadvertently, is recommending a different, albeit related, view, which is not speciesist and can be given an acceptable explicit formulation, or so Bob claims. I will call this view "human prioritism."

> **Human prioritism:** There is a hierarchy of beings with moral standing, and human beings are at the very top in that their interests generally have greater magnitude than the interests of all other beings, even if the interests in question are of the same type.

It would have been welcome if Bob had explicitly flagged this switch of allegiance from human exceptionalism to human prioritism in the relevant sections so as not to invite the charge of confusion, obfuscation, or false advertisement. But, in itself, such a switch of loyalty is certainly permissible. The problem is that there are powerful objections to human prioritism too, Bob explicitly acknowledges at least one of them, and his way of dealing with it is to switch his allegiance back to human exceptionalism! That is, Bob seems to be oscillating between human exceptionalism and human prioritism, depending on which objections he is trying to rebut. But, of course, this kind of oscillation does not weaken any of the objections in the least. Human exceptionalism and human prioritism are each beset by fatal problems, which means that neither position is tenable. Switching back and forth between them is thus not a viable defense strategy. Let us take a closer look.

1.1 The Formulation Objection Revisited

1.1.1 Human Prioritism and the Interest Profile Approach

Human prioritism makes its initial appearance in section 3.1 of Bob's first reply, in which he focuses on what, following Bob, we may call the "interest-profile approach" to providing a more explicit formulation of human exceptionalism. This approach utilizes the interest-profile conception of higher moral status, according to which A has higher moral status than B if, and only if, A has a richer interest profile than B. In my opening statement, I quickly dismissed the interest-profile approach mainly because the interest-profile conception does not capture the thought that a being with higher moral status morally matters more, which, however, is essential for any acceptable conception of higher moral status.

Bob begins by pointing out that there are different ways in which one could cash out what it means for a being to have a richer interest profile than another and that, on some of them, such as the "compression hypothesis," it is not even plausible to say that having a richer interest profile amounts to enjoying some kind of priority or privileged position. So far, I am in complete agreement. It is correct that there are different possible conceptions of what it means to have a richer interest profile. And it is also correct that several of these conceptions are complete non-starters if the goal is to provide a more explicit formulation of human exceptionalism.

Bob apparently takes himself to be scoring a point against me with his next move. The first step of this move is to sketch another conception of what it means for A to have a richer interest profile than B, the "difference-in-strength hypothesis," according to which the interests of A are generally stronger than the interests of B, or, in the terminology introduced in my opening statement, according to which the interests of A generally have greater magnitude than the interests of B.[1] The second step is to point out that, on this conception, the claim that a being with a richer interest profile enjoys some kind of priority is both plausible and not speciesist. (See p. 166.)

To start with a quibble, I do not think that having generally stronger interests can reasonably be described as a form of having a *richer* interest profile. That is just not what the word "rich" means. But, for the sake of the argument, let us set this quibble aside. Another worry is that, on my view, the goods/bads for members of different species are generally not comparable, which means that the magnitudes (or strengths, in Bob's terminology) of the corresponding interests are generally not comparable either, as explicated in section 3.2 of my opening statement. If I am correct about that, the interest-profile conception of what it means for a being to have higher moral status cashed out according to the difference-in-strength hypothesis turns out not to make any sense. But this means, in turn, that the difference-in-strength hypothesis is of no help in saving the interest-profile approach from my formulation objection. Since Bob rejects the relevant incomparability claim (in section 3.3.3 of his first reply), for the sake of the argument, I am willing to set this worry aside as well.[2]

I agree that, on the assumption that the difference-in-strength hypothesis is meaningful, the claim that a being with a richer interest profile, in the sense of having generally stronger interests, enjoys a kind of priority or privileged position is also meaningful, plausible, and not speciesist. However, I do not agree that this finding amounts to a successful defense of human exceptionalism against my objections, which is how Bob presents it. Bob's response does not answer my objections for the simple reason that the view that is captured by the formulation that results from understanding "higher moral status" according to the interest-profile conception cashed out according to the difference-in-strength hypothesis is *not* human exceptionalism. The resulting formulation is that humans

---

1. It would be useful to spell out more explicitly what it means for the interests of A to be "generally" stronger, or to "generally" have greater magnitude, than the interests of B. One option would be to say that it means that a large proportion of the interests of A (say, more than 90%) have greater magnitude than all or a large proportion of the interests of B.

2. For reasons of space, I cannot revisit the discussion about incomparability here. I will leave it to our readers to decide whose views on this matter strike them as more plausible.

stand at the top of a hierarchy in the sense that their interests are generally stronger than the interests of all non-humans. The defining tenet of human exceptionalism, however, is that humans stand at the top of a hierarchy of *moral considerability* in the sense of *morally mattering more* than all non-humans. Whatever priority A can be said to have over B on account of its interests being generally stronger than the interests of B, it is not a priority of morally mattering more. If all interests of both A and B are appreciated and given appropriate consideration, then A and B are given equal consideration and treated as morally mattering equally, even if A's interests are generally stronger than B's interests.

Somewhat confusingly, despite his pose of arguing against me, Bob explicitly admits that having a richer interest profile is not a form of having higher moral status in the relevant sense.[3] That is, he admits that the interest-profile approach does not deliver an acceptable formulation of human exceptionalism, on account of not capturing the thought that humans morally matter more than all non-humans—which was my main point exactly and why I quickly set the approach aside in my opening statement. Bob also highlights, though, that, on the difference-in-strength hypothesis, the interest-profile approach does deliver a meaningful formulation of "something a bit like Human Exceptionalism within the confines of Status Egalitarianism" (p. 166). This view is human prioritism. While human prioritism does not ascribe higher moral status to humans, it is a bit like human exceptionalism because, as Bob explains, "in principle, it would work out that many humans' interests are so much stronger than the interests of many animals that, when we give them equal consideration, the human interests almost always win—even when we're considering just one human and multiple animals" (p. 166).

Even though section 3.1 of Bob's first reply is written as if he were responding to my objections to human exceptionalism, what is really going on there is something else. Human prioritism is introduced into the conversation and shown not to be speciesist and to be explicitly characterizable in a meaningful and defensible way—provided that we grant that the magnitudes of interests of members of different species are generally comparable. Human exceptionalism, however, does not benefit from Bob's considerations in any

---

3. See his first reply, pp. 163–164.

way, regardless of whether the relevant interspecies comparisons are possible or not. My objections to human exceptionalism stand, including my formulation objection with respect to the interest-profile approach.[4]

1.1.2 Human Prioritism and the Similar-Interest Approach

In section 4.1 of Bob's first reply, we get further evidence that Bob's allegiance to human exceptionalism might be waning, at least temporarily, in favor of a waxing allegiance to human prioritism. In this section, he ostensibly attempts to respond to my formulation objection with respect to what we might call the "similar-interest approach" to providing a more explicit formulation of human exceptionalism. This approach utilizes a conception of higher moral status on which A has higher moral status$_1$ than B if, and only if, there is at least one interest of A that has more weight than a similar interest of B, and there is no interest of B that has more weight than a similar interest of A.

In my opening statement, I argued that the similar-interest approach fails since the spelled-out formulation of human exceptionalism yielded by it is either not meaningful or indefensible on account of rendering human exceptionalism necessarily false. There is no need to recapitulate this argument here, except to say that it centrally rests on my view that the magnitudes of interests of members of different species are generally incomparable. As just reported, Bob disagrees with this incomparability claim. So, he could have restricted his response to my objection to reinforcing his view that interspecies comparisons of the magnitudes of interests are generally possible. Somewhat surprisingly, that is not what he does. His response appears to consist in an underhanded switch of allegiance similar to what we just found in our examination of his response to the formulation objection with respect to the interest-profile approach. Despite explicitly stating at the beginning of section 4.1 that he will be talking about human exceptionalism and not about the exceptionalism-like view that he introduced in connection with the discussion of the interest-profile approach (a.k.a.

---

4. We will revisit the speciesism objection in more detail in section 1.2 below, where we will address Bob's responses that he makes to it in section 4.2 of his first reply and in his opening statement.

human prioritism), Bob seems to wind up advertising human prioritism yet again.

A central element of Bob's response to my objection is the figure on p. 181, which depicts a comparison of various kinds of interests of A with the same kinds of interests of B, where each interest of A is stronger than the same kind of interest of B, but B has two interests, of kind #1 and kind #2, that are stronger than two interests of A, namely, the interests of kind #4 and kind #5. Here is Bob: "The central claim I want to make here is that A has higher moral status than B even though one of B's interests—namely, B's Interest of Kind #1—outweighs A's Interest of Kind #5. If most of A's interests outweigh most of B's interests even when they're of the same kind, it seems fair to describe that as A's having a higher moral status. This is basically the way I think things work with humans and animals. A human's interest in survival is weightier than a deer's interest in survival. But a deer's interest in being free from pain is weightier than a human's interest in recreation ... I don't see what's incoherent about this, at least as long as we grant that we can make interspecies wellbeing comparisons" (p. 181). This response is puzzling for several reasons.

First, the crux of my formulation objection with respect to the similar-interest approach is the denial of the claim that we can generally make interspecies wellbeing comparisons. So, obviously, if we were to grant that we can make such comparisons, my objection would collapse. But we do not have to construct any special scenario such as the one depicted by Bob to see this.

Second, the second clause in my characterization of higher moral status$_1$ does not say that for A to have higher moral status than B it is required that B has no interest that outweighs any interest of A. Rather, it says that it is required that B has no interest that outweighs a *similar* interest of A. In the situation depicted by Bob, no interest of B outweighs a similar interest of A (at least not on my understanding of 'similar interest'). It thus is not a counterexample to my characterization of higher moral status$_1$. Having said that, it is fair to note that there are other possible characterizations of higher moral status in the general category of similar-interest approaches that are weaker than my characterization of higher moral status$_1$, characterizations that allow that B has some interests that outweigh similar interests of A. For example, one could say that A has higher moral status$_{1b}$ than B if, and only if, A and B have some similar interests, and the number of interests of A that outweigh similar interests of B is larger than the number of interests of B that outweigh similar interests of A. In my opening statement, I elected not to discuss any other versions of the similar-interest approach, partly because it would have required working through several attendant complications for which there was no room, but mostly because it would not have changed the overall dialectic. If any formulation of human exceptionalism that depends on the notion of a similar interest falls prey to my objection, then all such formulations fall prey to it.

Third, it is a bit unclear what exactly Bob means by the "strength" and "kind" of an interest. To recall, in my terminology, similar interests are interests that are of the same type and have the same magnitude, and the weights of interests are to be understood as coefficients by which the magnitudes of interests are to be multiplied. If we were to give greater weight to an interest of A than to a similar interest of B, we would be giving A greater moral consideration. Bob seems to agree with this way of thinking about similar interests and unequal moral consideration, at least in substance if not in terminology. For example, in his opening statement, he illustrates the Equal Consideration Principle (ECP), according to which similar interests deserve equal consideration in our moral deliberations regardless of whose interests they are, with the following example: "If a pig and a child are experiencing roughly the same level of hunger, then at least as far as their hunger goes, we have no reason to prioritize the child over the pig. Humans don't get special consideration simply because they are humans" (p. 102). In this example, the type of interest at issue is avoidance of suffering on account of lack of food, and the magnitude of the interest corresponds to the "level" of hunger. Since the magnitude and the type of interest are the same for the child and the pig, their interests are similar. And so, if, despite this similarity, we were to prioritize the child over the pig by giving greater weight to its interest in our moral deliberations, we would be violating the ECP.

Now, using my terminology, there are basically two ways in which one could understand what Bob means by the "kind" and "strength" of an interest respectively. According to reading (A), he means something different by "kind" from what I mean by "type," understanding it to be determined by the type *and* the magnitude of an interest (in my sense), and he conceives of the strength of an interest as determined by multiplying the magnitude and the weight of an interest (in my sense). In this case, interests of the same kind$_{Bob}$ would be what I call similar interests, and similar interests could have different strength, depending on their weight. For example, if

A in the figure on p. 181 is the child and B the pig from the previous example, A's interest of $kind_{Bob}$ #3 could be the child's interest in not suffering hunger of level X, and B's interest of $kind_{Bob}$ #3 could be the pig's interest in not suffering hunger of level X. While these interests are similar, the child's interest has greater weight and thus is stronger than the similar interest of the pig. If this were how "kind" and "strength" are to be understood, the situation depicted in the figure would be a straightforward illustration of what it means to have higher moral $status_1$. The child has higher moral $status_1$ than the pig since it has several interests that outweigh similar interests of the pig, while the pig has no interests that outweigh similar interests of the child. The problem with this reading is that Bob presents the situation that is depicted in the figure as being at odds with the conception of higher moral $status_1$ and thus quite clearly does not intend it as an illustration of it.

According to reading (B), Bob means by "kind" what I mean by "type," and by "strength" what I mean by "magnitude." If this were how "kind" and "strength" are to be understood, there would be no similar interests in the situation depicted by the figure on p. 181. For in order for two interests to be similar, they must not only be of the same type but also have the same magnitude. For example, A's interest of kind #1 could be the child's interest in survival, and B's interest of kind #1 could be the pig's interest in survival. These interests are of the same type but the child's interest in survival has greater magnitude/strength than the pig's interest in survival, maybe because the child has more to lose by dying than the pig. (I do not believe that it makes sense to say that the child has more to lose but Bob does.) In that case, the situation depicted in the figure would be an illustration of the interest-profile conception of what it means for a being to have higher moral status cashed out according to the difference-in-strength hypothesis and, more generally, of human prioritism. The problem with this reading is that (i) my objection to which Bob's figure and the accompanying argument are supposed to be a response is directed against the similar-interest approach, not the interest-profile approach, and (ii) we are supposed to be talking about human exceptionalism and a hierarchy of moral considerability, not human prioritism and some other kind of hierarchy that is grounded in different magnitudes of interests.

For all of these reasons, it is not obvious what to make of the figure on p. 181 and the accompanying argument. There are two main interpretative options. Interpretation (1): Reading (A) of what Bob means by "kind" and "strength" is correct. Bob intended to make the modest and with respect to the overall dialectic largely irrelevant point that there are other versions of the similar-interest approach available in addition to the one that utilizes the conception of higher moral status$_1$, versions that are equally vulnerable to my formulation objection. But he got muddled and botched the example. Interpretation (2): Reading (B) of what Bob means by "kind" and "strength" is correct. Bob is not really responding to my formulation objection to human exceptionalism with respect to the similar-interest approach. Rather, he inadvertently or surreptitiously reverted to the interest-profile approach and is defending the meaningful and defensible formulability of a different position, namely, human prioritism—even though he explicitly said at the beginning of the section that he would set human prioritism aside.

Section 4.1 of Bob's first reply is written as if he were responding to my formulation objection to human exceptionalism with respect to the similar-interest approach, but that is not really what is happening there. Regardless of which of the two indicated interpretations is correct, human exceptionalism does not profit from Bob's considerations in any way. If interpretation (1) is correct, no humans-first view is defended in this section at all. If interpretation (2) is correct, instead of defending human exceptionalism, Bob is holding up human prioritism as an example of a view that can be formulated in a meaningful and defensible way—if we grant that the magnitudes of interests of members of different species are generally comparable. I am inclined to regard interpretation (2) as correct. It is more charitable than interpretation (1), and its reading of what is meant by "strength" of an interest coheres better with Bob's use of this term in the rest of his reply (including section 3.1 that we discussed earlier where by "strength" he quite clearly means what I mean by "magnitude"). That is, in my ultimate assessment, what is presented in section 4.1 as a defense of human exceptionalism turns out to be, yet again, an unacknowledged switch from human exceptionalism to human prioritism. But no actual defense of human exceptionalism is offered. My formulation objection to it still stands, including the formulation objection with respect to the similar-interest approach.

1.2   Human Prioritism and the Speciesism Objection

The same unsettling slide from ostensibly defending human exceptionalism to recommending human prioritism is in evidence in Bob's response to the speciesism objection in section 4.2 of his first reply. Human exceptionalism still has to contend with this objection even if an acceptable spelled-out formulation of it could be provided (which I continue to doubt, as just rehearsed).

Bob's response to the speciesism objection in his first reply is quite short: "Now that we've replied to all these objections [that is, the objections to the different approaches to providing a more explicit formulation of human exceptionalism; AJ], we can see that speciesism isn't an independent objection. A hierarchy isn't speciesist if there's some basis for it. And while I haven't shown that there is some particular basis for the hierarchy that human exceptionalism posits, I have made the case both that it's reasonable to believe that there is such a hierarchy and that the objections to it aren't successful" (p. 182).

This response is a good response only if we replace the term "human exceptionalism" in it with the term "human prioritism." In his previous discussion, Bob has shown that, on the assumption that interspecies comparisons of magnitudes of interests are generally possible, it is possible for there to be a kind of hierarchy in which humans occupy a privileged position compared to all other beings with moral standing on account of the generally greater magnitude of their interests. Since this kind of hierarchy is grounded in the different magnitudes of the involved interests, asserting its existence is not a morally objectionable form of discrimination on the basis of species membership. But the described hierarchy is not a hierarchy of moral considerability, of higher and lower moral status, of morally mattering more or less. That is, it is not the kind of hierarchy asserted in human exceptionalism. Rather, it is the kind of hierarchy asserted in human prioritism. The hierarchy that is asserted in human exceptionalism is not grounded in the different magnitudes of the involved interests. Rather, it is grounded in the greater weight of human interests compared to similar interests of non-humans, weights that, as I argued, are arbitrarily introduced for the sole purpose of giving an unfair boost to the interests of members of the human species. In short, Bob defends himself against the speciesism objection by switching his allegiance to human prioritism. But, for all he has said in his first reply, the speciesism objection to human exceptionalism still stands.

To be fair, Bob's first reply is not the only place where he takes on the speciesism objection. He also addresses it in his opening statement. A slightly different way of presenting the speciesism objection couches it in the form of an inconsistency challenge. If X regards discrimination on the basis of gender or race as morally impermissible, then X is committed, on pain of inconsistency, to regard discrimination on the basis of species membership as morally impermissible too given that species membership is as morally irrelevant as race and gender. This means that anybody who rejects racism and sexism as morally impermissible is committed, on pain of inconsistency, to rejecting human exceptionalism as well given that it is a form of speciesism. In other words, one can endorse human exceptionalism and reject racism and sexism at the same time only if one is willing to be inconsistent. Bob's brave response is to agree with this line of reasoning and opt for being inconsistent. "Sometimes the reasons favoring incompatible ideas are good enough that we should hold on to them both" (p. 120). In the present case, the incompatible ideas are that all humans are equal in the sense of morally mattering equally ("human equality"), on the one hand, and that human and non-human animals are not equal in the sense of not morally mattering equally ("animal inequality"), on the other hand. In an effort to make this sizable bullet more palatable, Bob offers an analogy with how physicists (allegedly) handle the incompatibility of the general theory of relativity and quantum mechanics. "The thought is that they are too well-confirmed to reject; in some way or other, they've both got to be true" (p. 121).

Granted, consistency is not the be-all and end-all of philosophical theorizing, at least not in those areas of philosophy that aim to uncover substantive truths. But, contrary to what Bob alleges, one does not have to suffer from some kind of consistency fetish to regard consistency as a necessary condition for the truth and acceptability of a view. If a view is consistent, it could still be false; but if a view is inconsistent, it is certainly false. Incidentally, all physicists of whom I am aware also agree with that assessment. The general theory of relativity and quantum mechanics cannot both be true, precisely because they are incompatible. Physicists continue to use these theories for the time being, not because "they've both got to be true," but simply because they are useful prediction tools, and nobody has come up with a better alternative yet.

In the face of the speciesism objection, proponents of human exceptionalism have two, and only two, options: (1) provide a consistent theory that accounts for both human equality and animal inequality, just like contemporary physicists are engaged in trying to find a consistent theory that accounts for both gravity and quantum phenomena, or (2) change their minds and reject human equality or animal inequality. The most popular strategies for accomplishing the task set in option (1) are versions of the two strategies for showing that human centrism is not a morally objectionable form of speciesism that I examined in my opening statement. Tailored to the case at hand, the strategies are to argue that all humans have the same moral status compared to each other but higher moral status than all non-humans because (a) all and only humans have certain sophisticated psychological capacities that are morally relevant, or (b) all and only humans are part of human society and thus stand in various social relations to one another, which are especially morally important. Both of these proposals fail for the reasons detailed in my opening statement. This leaves option (2). Since Bob agrees that human equality is non-negotiable, he thus should reject animal inequality and, with it, human exceptionalism. And, as we have seen, in several sections of his first reply, he seems prepared to do just that by way of defecting to human prioritism.

1.3 Objections to Human Prioritism

Human prioritism is not affected by the speciesism objection but it has its share of problems. First, as already noted, if the goods/bads for members of different species and, with them, the magnitudes of their interests are generally incomparable, then the formulation of human prioritism is meaningless, just like the formulation of human exceptionalism on the similar-interest approach.

Second, whether human prioritism is true depends on contingent, empirical facts about how the magnitudes of the interests of different kinds of beings happen to be related to one another. For the truth of human prioritism, the claim that the interests of humans generally have greater magnitude than the interests of all non-humans must not only be meaningful; it must correspond to what is actually the case. But it may well turn out that matters stand differently. Perhaps there are no beings at all in the actual world whose interests are generally stronger than the interests of all other kinds of beings. As Bob himself points out, there are many other possible ways in which the magnitudes of the interests of different kinds of beings could be related to one another apart from the way reflected in the difference-in-strength hypothesis. Or maybe there are beings whose interests are generally stronger than the interests of all other kinds of beings but these beings are cockroaches, not humans. In that case, while human prioritism would remain a possibility, cockroach prioritism would be actually true. All of this shows that it is quite a risky move for somebody like Bob to translate his seemingly unshakable humans-first intuitions into an endorsement of human prioritism. The only view that captures the relevant kind of humans-first intuitions and is not liable to potentially turning out to be false for contingent, empirical reasons is human exceptionalism. Maybe that is also part of the reason why Bob apparently pivots back to advocating human exceptionalism in section 4.3 of his first reply—after favoring human prioritism in sections 4.1 and 4.2, as we just saw.

Indeed, adopting human prioritism is a risky move for Bob for yet another reason. Even if human prioritism were true, it could turn out that, as a matter of fact, the interests of humans are generally *overwhelmingly* stronger than the interests of animals. For example, it could turn out that the magnitude of the human interest in recreation by hunting dwarfs the magnitude of the interest of animals in survival, or that the magnitude of the human interest in enjoying the special kind of gustatory pleasure caused by meat swamps the magnitude of the interest of animals in not suffering. In that case, somebody with Bob's moral-theoretical commitments, which seem to be largely utilitarian, would lose all basis for opposing such practices as hunting for recreation or factory farming, which, however, he claims to want to oppose.[5]

Third and most importantly, human prioritism has practical implications that most people will find unacceptable. If human interests generally have greater magnitudes than the interests of all other beings with moral standing, there must be some difference between these two groups that accounts for this fact. The most obvious candidate difference is that humans have certain sophisticated psychological capacities that all other beings lack. This is also the explanation favored by Bob (see his first reply,

---

5. It also seems quite difficult to come up with a principled opposition to these kinds of practices in a human exceptionalist framework, at least for anybody with utilitarian leanings. Maybe that is the reason why Bob does not offer any positive arguments to the effect that we ought to change how we treat animals even though he insists that change is needed on moral grounds.

p. 166). So, more precisely stated, the main tenet of human prioritism is that beings with certain sophisticated psychological capacities stand at the top of a hierarchy of beings with moral standing
in that their interests generally have greater magnitude than the
interests of all other beings. The familiar problem with this kind
of account is that, as a matter of fact, not *all* humans possess
the relevant sophisticated psychological capacities. If we prioritize beings whose interests generally have greater magnitude, and
beings whose interests generally have greater magnitude are beings
with sophisticated psychological capacities, we will be prioritizing
a certain sub-set of humans over both animals and humans who
lack these capacities, such as humans with severe cognitive disabilities. A proponent of human prioritism who, like Bob, thinks
that it is morally permissible to keep mice in captivity for research
purposes (see section 3.3 of his first reply) would thus be committed to saying that it is equally morally permissible to keep certain kinds of humans in captivity for research purposes provided
their psychological capacities are not more sophisticated than
the psychological capacities of mice. Most people will find this
implication unacceptable.[6] Strikingly, Bob explicitly acknowledges
this problem with human prioritism in the opening paragraphs
of section 4 of his first reply and pinpoints it as the main reason why he ostensibly rejects human prioritism in favor of human
exceptionalism—only to revert to human prioritism in sections 4.1
and 4.2, as documented above.

In sum, Bob seems to be oscillating between human exceptionalism and human prioritism depending on which objection he is
considering at the moment. Since switching to another view in the
face of an objection does not amount to a defense of the original
view, Bob's discussion does nothing to rehabilitate either human
exceptionalism or human prioritism. Both of these positions are
subject to fatal objections. So, regardless of whether Bob eventually settles on human prioritism or human exceptionalism, or
ends up oscillating between them forever, his humans-first view is
untenable.

---

6. Note that the reason why most people will find this implication unacceptable is
not that it asks something challenging of them or requires them to sacrifice some
of their own interests. The implication will simply strike most people as morally
appalling.

2   Status Egalitarianism à la Anja Revisited: All Organisms Are Equal

2.1   Another Look at the Good Criterion

Recall the good criterion for moral standing, according to which X has moral standing if, and only if, X is capable of flourishing, which, in turn, is the case if, and only if, X has a good for which it strives. Bob rejects this criterion largely for two reasons. First, the criterion has "radical" practical consequences when combined with status egalitarianism. Second, Bob thinks that the good for which a being strives cannot be properly understood other than as the propagation of its genes, which, however, conflicts with the "criterion of wellbeing" that, according to Bob, is "strongly suggested" by the good criterion, namely, that "Y is good for X just in case Y is part of (or otherwise appropriately related to) the good for which X strives" (p. 168). In the present sub-section, I will focus on the second objection. The objection of "radicalness" is the topic of the final sub-section.

Bob is right that the good criterion is closely connected to a certain theory of wellbeing, or flourishing, as I prefer to say, and it is useful to begin by recalling this connection. My basic proposal for how to demarcate the class of beings with moral standing is to say that X has moral standing if, and only if, X is capable of flourishing. Call this the "flourishing criterion" for moral standing. Beings who are capable of flourishing are beings for whom something can be good or bad, as a result of which they deserve moral consideration. The good criterion is my attempt at making the flourishing criterion more explicit by adding a clause that spells out what it takes for a being to be capable of flourishing, namely, that it has a good for which it strives. Given this set-up, it is obvious from the start that the good of a being must be understood in such a way that a being's successful pursuit of it positively contributes to the being's flourishing. Accordingly, it is evident right away that the relevant good cannot be identified with the propagation of a being's genes. For, as Bob's examples illustrate, in many cases, success in propagating its genes negatively impacts a being's flourishing.

So, how should the good of a being be understood? And why do I think it is promising to spell out what it takes for a being to flourish in terms of it having a good for which it strives? As I see it, there are three non-negotiable features of flourishing that any satisfactory theory of flourishing must respect. First, flourishing is not restricted to human beings or sentient beings; all living organisms can flourish to a greater or lesser extent. Second, even in the case of sentient beings, it would be problematic to regard their flourish-ing as solely dependent on how much pleasure and pain there is in their lives, as is illustrated by the thought experiment of the experi-ence machine (see my opening statement, pp. 32–33). Third, what is good for a being and thus its flourishing centrally depend on what kind of being it is and, more specifically, on what kind of capacities it has. The good criterion is the result of combining the flourishing criterion with a theory of flourishing, namely, (roughly) Aristotle's, that successfully accommodates these three non-negotiable features. According to the suggested Aristotelian theory, a being flourishes insofar and to the extent that it succeeds at realizing its good, where the latter is determined by (what Aristotle calls) its characteristic function or essential activity. The characteristic function of a being is tied to what kind of being it is, including what capacities it has, and crucially includes the maintenance of its own existence.

Now, there is no shame in admitting that, in order to mount a full-fledged defense of the sketched Aristotelian theory of flourish-ing, more would have to be said than what I was able to say in my opening statement or will be able to say here.[7] At the same time, Bob's brief remarks are also not sufficient to show that the indicated theory must be rejected. So, it seems fair to say that a final decision about the theory's ultimate defensibility must be deferred until a later time. For now, I will restrict myself to making two additional observations.

First, I want to comment briefly on Bob's case of the otter, call him "Otto," which he brings up as a counterexample to the claim that all members of a species share the same kind of good.[8] In contrast to typical otters in the wild, Otto does not have any opportunity for hunting but has all of his other needs met by humans and seems "perfectly happy *not* hunting" (p. 169). So, even though Otto is an

---

7. Fortunately, many people have done excellent work in this general area, which I recommend to the interested reader. See Hursthouse 1999; Foot 2001; Nussbaum 2006; and Korsgaard 2018.

8. Note that I am actually not committed to the claim that all members of a species share the same kind of good but only to the weaker claim that all beings who have the same characteristic function share the same kind of good. It is certainly true that all able members of a species have the same characteristic function and, thus, share the same kind of good. But since the characteristic function of a being also depends on its capacities, there can be disabled members of a species that have a somewhat different kind of good on account of lacking some of the capacities that all able members of the species possess. However, since the otter example can also be presented as a potential counterexample to the weaker claim to which I am committed, we can ignore this slight wrinkle.

(able) otter, he does not have the same kind of good as typical otters in the wild, Bob suggests, since their good includes hunting, while Otto's good does not. This example is instructive since it provides a nice illustration of how Bob's and my conception of flourishing differ. As I see it, the example rests on an implausible understanding of flourishing, an understanding that is at odds with the second and third non-negotiable features of flourishing indicated above. On my view, the capacity for hunting is a capacity whose exercise is good for any (able) otter, including Otto, just as autonomy is a capacity whose exercise is good for any (able) human. If I did not have any opportunity for acting autonomously, I would be missing out on an important human good. Similarly, by not having any opportunity for hunting, Otto is missing out on an important otter good. Crucially, this would hold even if both our lives were not any less pleasurable as a result of missing out in these ways, and we were "perfectly happy" in the sense Bob seems to have in mind when describing Otto's situation. (Able) humans who do not act autonomously and (able) otters who do not hunt flourish less than (able) humans and otters who do these things, respectively, all else being equal.

Second, I want to highlight that, even if, upon further consideration, it turned out that the Aristotelian theory of flourishing on which the good criterion rests is untenable, this would not require any changes in my overall argument. As I said, the sole function of bringing up the sketched Aristotelian theory was to offer a further explanation of what it takes for a being to be capable of flourishing in order to make the flourishing criterion more explicit. But my overall argument does not depend on the Aristotelian theory. If Bob turned out to be correct that the good criterion must be rejected because of the Aristotelianism implied by it, I could happily fall back on the flourishing criterion and leave it to our readers to fill in their own favorite theory of flourishing, provided that it respects the three non-negotiable features of flourishing listed above. My basic account of which beings have moral standing and on what grounds would remain unaffected, "radical" as it is.

2.2 Let's be Radical

Bob's mantra throughout his discussion is that views on which all animals or even all organisms are equal in the sense of morally mattering equally are *radical*, a circumstance that he evidently holds against them. Indeed, it seems fair to say that this complaint about radicalness is his main objection against my view.[9] Bob does not explicitly tell us what "radical" is supposed to mean in this context. But, based on his various remarks, it appears that a radical view for him is a view that has concrete practical consequences about what we ought to do that conflict with moral judgments that intuitively seem true to most people "on reflection."[10] He substantiates the charge that status egalitarian views like mine are radical in this sense by arguing that they have concrete practical implications that conflict with moral judgments expressing human exceptionalist convictions that enjoy the relevant intuitive support. More specifically, he derives these counterintuitive consequences from the Equal Consideration Principle (ECP)—which, as noted, says that similar interests deserve equal consideration in our moral deliberations regardless of whose interests they are—and the claim that all sentient beings have moral standing and thus must be taken into account in our moral deliberations. The practical consequences derived by Bob fall into two main categories. Most of them are obligations to help of some kind, for example, the obligation to re-allocate massive amounts of resources from helping humans to helping wild animals or the obligation to save two pigs over one human in a lifeboat situation. A few of them are obligations not to harm of some kind, for example, the obligation not to drive to the supermarket during heavy rainfall if one knows that a lot of vulnerable worms are bound to be on the street.

In response, the first point to make is that the kind of status egalitarianism that I endorse by itself does not entail any of the counterintuitive practical consequences highlighted by Bob. To start with a clarification, while I am committed to the claim that all sentient beings have moral standing, I do not take myself to be committed to the Equal Consideration Principle as understood by Bob. Bob presents human exceptionalism and the ECP as exhaustive options (opening statement, pp. 101–103) and claims that status egalitarianism "is basically equivalent to the view that I described

---

9. The objection that my view has practical consequences that are overly demanding, which could also be leveled against it, is related but different. Since space is tight and I have addressed worries about overdemandingness in my opening statement already, I will not devote any discussion to this objection here.

10. See his opening statement, sections 5–7, and his first reply, pp. 160–161.

in my opening statement as the Equal Consideration Principle" (first reply, p. 158). But this equivalence claim is questionable. If I am right that the magnitudes of interests of members of different species are generally incomparable, it follows that talk about similar interests and thus the ECP only makes sense with respect to interests of members of the same species. But if the scope of the ECP is thus restricted, it is not basically equivalent to status egalitarianism. For the latter says that there is no hierarchy of moral considerability among beings with moral standing in general, not just within a given species. Since Bob's derivations of the counterintuitive practical consequences rely on the ECP, understood as applying to the interests of members of different species, they can be resisted by anybody who, like me, rejects the claim that the magnitudes of interests of members of different species are generally comparable.

More generally and more importantly, *no* account of moral standing and status by itself has any concrete practical consequences. All such accounts only tell us what kind of beings have moral standing and whether there is a hierarchy of moral considerability among beings with moral standing. For example, my account says that all beings with a good for which they strive (which includes all sentient beings) have moral standing and that there is no hierarchy of moral considerability among beings with moral standing. In order to deduce any concrete practical consequences from claims such as these, we need to rely on various additional substantive assumptions, most importantly, assumptions about what our moral obligations are. But this means that there are other ways of resisting Bob's counterintuitive conclusions apart from rejecting the ECP (as understood by him) or the claim that all sentient beings have moral standing. We could reject one or more of these additional assumptions. For example, take Bob's inferences to the practical consequences that we ought to re-allocate massive amounts of resources from helping humans to helping animals and that, in a lifeboat situation, we ought to save two pigs over one human. For these inferences, Bob relies not only on the ECP, understood as applying to the interests of members of different species, and the claim that all sentient beings have moral standing but also, at least implicitly, on the following two assumptions: (i) we ought to maximize flourishing or interest satisfaction, as prescribed by utilitarianism; and (ii) the goods/bads for different beings can straightforwardly be aggregated so that, say, a situation where two beings have a headache of strength S is twice as bad as a situation where only one being has a headache of strength S. But both of these additional assumptions can be questioned. (For the record, I reject both of them.) This also means that, even if interspecies comparisons of magnitudes of goods/bads and interests were generally possible, and the ECP could properly be claimed to be basically equivalent to status egalitarianism, we would still not be forced to give up on either status egalitarianism or the view that all sentient beings have moral standing. All of Bob's derivations depend on several further assumptions that could be called into question instead.

There is an obvious rejoinder of which Bob could avail himself at this point. After admitting that his derivations of various counterintuitive practical consequences are insufficient to show that my version of status egalitarianism commits me to the same consequences, he could insist that my version of status egalitarianism plus certain additional assumptions about our moral obligations that I do endorse lead to some of the same or at least equally counterintuitive practical consequences. Accordingly, the ultimate verdict that my overall view should be rejected on account of being radical still stands.

It is correct that the overall view sketched in my opening statement comprises not only an account of moral standing and status but also a rudimentary moral theory, including claims about what our moral obligations are. It is also correct that my overall view has some concrete practical consequences that, I assume, many people will find counterintuitive. But the conclusion that the view should thus be rejected on account of being radical is still not convincing. I will wrap up my reply by explaining why I am not convinced.

It is useful to start by reiterating that my overall view is not a fountain of concrete practical consequences to begin with, in particular not in the "obligations to help" category. At least, this is fair to say if by "concrete practical consequences" we mean consequences that can be figured out from a theoretical "armchair" perspective merely by thinking through the implications of various general principles. As explicated in my opening statement, I regard quasi-mechanical calculations based on abstract universal principles that spit out specific directives for what we ought to do as being a far cry from the ideal of moral deliberation. Being a good moral deliberator means appreciating and appropriately responding to the many complex moral reasons at play when we confront particular beings with moral standing in concrete situations.[11] As far as general claims about our moral obligations are concerned, I am committed to the assertion that we owe all beings with moral standing compassion, which entails, minimally, that we appreciate and are moved by two basic moral reasons, namely, the very weighty reason not to harm them and the reason to help them in need. These two reasons are the most important moral reasons provided by beings with moral standing that stay invariant across different situations. But they are not the only moral reasons that can make demands on us. Other possible moral reasons include reasons connected to special loyalties we might have, for instance, to family members, friends, pets, or fellow citizens; reasons arising from promises we have made or special commitments we have undertaken; or reasons stemming from the social roles that we occupy, to name but a few. How much weight we accord to the different reasons in a given situation, and how we combine them to arrive at an overall assessment of what we have most reason to do from a moral point of view, are, to a large extent, judgment calls that we all must make on our own, for which we cannot rely on any universal principles, and for which we must accept responsibility. As one might put it, the derivation of concrete practical consequences from our basic obligation to show compassion to all beings with moral standing is itself largely a practical matter. These consequences only emerge as a result of our compassionate practical deliberations in concrete circumstances. This is why my view cannot pride itself on issuing a great wealth of concrete practical consequences that are available from a theoretical "armchair" perspective.

More specifically, as already explicated in my opening statement, since the reason to help in need is an only moderately weighty pro tanto reason, it does not translate into a general moral principle to the effect that we ought to help every being with moral standing in need, nor does it underwrite any specific practical directives about how much of our resources we ought to allocate to helping other beings, or how we ought to distribute these resources between different kinds of beings. We are obligated to help as many beings with moral standing as much as we can without disregarding or

---

11. For this reason, Bob's complaint about people who are led to radical views by "starting from principles" and "turning ethics into a kind of consistency game" (pp. 161–162) also misfires completely if it is intended as a criticism of me.

failing to be properly moved by any other relevant moral reasons. But which beings to help and by how much are difficult questions that we all must figure out for ourselves in accordance with our concrete circumstances. This also means, in particular, that I am not committed to the counterintuitive practical consequences in the "obligations to help" category that Bob identifies. My overall view does not imply that we ought to re-allocate massive amounts of resources from helping humans to helping wild animals, nor that, in general, we ought to save two pigs over one human in a lifeboat situation.

Now, as also explicated in my opening statement, since the reason not to harm, although equally pro tanto, has extremely great weight and can be overridden or outweighed only in special circumstances, it is possible to formulate a general moral principle on its basis. This principle is (what I have called) the no-harm obligation, according to which we are obligated not to harm any being with moral standing, except in special circumstances. And this no-harm obligation does have a number of concrete practical consequences. Some of these consequences are pretty much universally accepted, such as that we ought not to torture our pets for entertainment; and some of them are rapidly gaining ground these days, especially with people from younger generations, such as that we ought to abolish factory farming. But the no-harm obligation also has some consequences that probably will strike many or even most people as counterintuitive, such as that, except in special circumstances, we ought not to drive to the supermarket in heavy rain if we know that a lot of vulnerable worms are bound to be on the street, or that we ought to adopt a benign vegan diet. So, the crucial question is whether the fact that my view has some counterintuitive concrete practical consequences in the "obligations not to harm" category is a good enough reason to reject it. As I see it, the answer is clearly no, for mainly two reasons, both of which have come up before, at least indirectly.

First, why should it be a problem for my view that some of its practical consequences clash with moral judgments expressing human exceptionalist commitments that seem intuitively true to most people? This would be a problem only if the fact that such moral judgments seem intuitively true to most people is evidence for their actual truth. While I do not believe that intuitions have no place in moral theory at all, I continue to think that, in discussions about whether members of one particular group are to be privileged in some desirable way compared to members of other groups, intuitions to the effect that members of one's own group deserve the privilege should not be given much evidentiary weight. For it is rather likely that the semblance of truth of these intuitions is grounded in one's wish for them to be true, which, however, is compatible with their actual falsity. Of course, this does not mean that no claim that accords with a self-serving intuition can possibly be true or justified. It just means that pointing to a self-serving intuition on its own does not amount to a satisfactory justification. For example, I certainly share the intuition that men do not have higher moral status than women, and it would benefit me for the intuition to be true. However, the claim that all people have the same moral status regardless of their gender is justified, not by my intuition, but by an argument to the effect that gender is not morally relevant.

I also do not think that self-serving intuitions that persist "upon reflection" escape the worry about their questionable evidentiary weight, contrary to what Bob suggests in his first reply. Bob hedges a bit when it comes to explaining what it takes for a claim to intuitively seem true to us upon reflection. But, as far as I can tell, in the end it takes no more than that, after pausing to question ourselves whether the claim *really* seems true and non-negotiable or foundational to us, we answer the question in the affirmative. But why would that make the intuition more reliable as a piece of evidence? Upon questioning himself about it, a sexist will readily affirm that it really seems true, non-negotiable, and foundational to him that men have higher moral status than women. So, even if Bob is correct that the moral judgments expressing human exceptionalist commitments with which some of the concrete practical consequences of my view conflict seem intuitively true to most people *upon reflection*, I still do not regard this as a problem for my view. Most people grow up in a human exceptionalist environment and are concerned first and foremost with their self-interest. It is thus natural for most people to find themselves with human exceptionalist intuitions that seem very compelling, even upon reflection.

Second, I do not agree with Bob that for a view to be radical in the relevant sense is necessarily a bad thing. It seems safe to say that we have not reached a state of moral perfection yet. There still is a lot of room for moral progress. But there would not be any moral progress if nobody ever challenged people's moral convictions that seem intuitively true to them upon reflection. Accordingly, it is a useful and healthy policy, for each one of us individually and for our society, to welcome views that are radical in the relevant sense and be open to engage with them. For a moral view to be radical can be a good thing. All views that are on the vanguard of moral progress will count as radical when they are first proposed. More specifically, since I believe that moral progress with respect to our thinking about and treatment of animals is urgently needed and long overdue—a view with which Bob claims to agree—I proudly and gladly accept the badge of being a radical on their behalf. My contributions to this debate in the foregoing pages may not have fully convinced you yet that you ought to adopt a benign vegan diet or to hold off from driving to the supermarket until the defenseless worms have had a chance to clear off the street. I could live with that—provided I got you sufficiently rattled so that you start re-examining your culturally conditioned moral convictions about the privileged moral status of human beings with an open mind. And if, as a result, you were to take a first tentative step in my direction, for example, by refraining from purchasing factory-farmed products or toiletries that have been tested on animals, I would consider my mission a success. Any help counts and is greatly appreciated, even if you are not ready yet to embrace the claim that all animals, human and non-human alike, are equal in the sense of morally mattering equally. But, to say it with John Lennon, I hope someday you'll join us, and the world will live as one.

Chapter 6

Second Reply to Anja Jauernig

Bob Fischer

Contents

Anja makes two main points in her reply to my opening statement. The first is about the burden of proof: I argued that she has it, whereas she thinks that I have it. The second is about the Anti-Complicity Argument for Veganism: I argued that it fails; she thinks that a refined version is successful. In what follows, I'll explain why I'm not convinced on either front. However, as we'll see, there isn't much new here. At bottom, Anja and I disagree very deeply about the demandingness of morality. That disagreement is probably driven by a yet more fundamental one about the point of moral theorizing. We aren't going to resolve those issues here, or even make much headway on them. Still, we can recognize them, which will give us some perspective on this book as a whole.

I Anja's Objections, My Replies

Let's begin, though, by tackling Anja's criticisms. Again, the first is about who has the burden of proof; the second is about whether it's wrong to be complicit in factory farming.

DOI: 10.4324/9781003441823-10

1.1 The Burden of Proof

My view is that the burden of proof is on the person who claims that you have an obligation. The default assumption is that your actions are morally okay. That is, absent an argument to the contrary, you get to presume that you're acting permissibly.

Anja disagrees. She writes:

> The crucial question that underlies the determination of which position is the default in this debate is which outcome is better from the moral point of view: (A-i) for us to regard it as morally obligatory to abstain even though it is morally permissible not to abstain, or (A-ii) for us to regard it as morally permissible not to abstain even though it is morally obligatory to abstain, all else being equal. In order to answer this question, we must compare the morally relevant costs and benefits of the two outcomes.

In other words, she doesn't think there's a general answer to the question, "Who has the burden of proof?" She thinks you have to answer that question on a case-by-case basis. And how do you answer it? By trying to sort out the relative costs and benefits of a false positive (believing that you have an obligation when you don't; the "A-i" case) and a false negative (believing that you don't have an obligation when you do; the "A-ii" case). In our particular debate, she thinks that I have the burden of proof because she thinks that a false negative is more costly. On her view, "there are no morally relevant benefits [to consuming factory-farm-derived products] but there is at least one morally relevant cost, namely, a moral-wrongness cost"—since it could be wrong to purchase such products.

On one level, anyway, I agree with Anja. She's saying that we shouldn't risk acting wrongly when there aren't any moral benefits of doing so—which seems right to me. We disagree, though, about how to apply this point.

First, while there aren't *always* morally relevant benefits to consuming factory-farm-derived products, there *can* be such benefits. Sometimes, people eat such products out of genuine concern for their health. Sometimes, they eat such products to preserve valuable traditions. Sometimes, they eat them to connect with their parents or children or friends. Sometimes, they eat them because other morally important projects—such as serving in communities where vegan options are scarce, for instance—make such foods very difficult to avoid. Granted, people often eat products from factory farms unreflectively and thoughtlessly, without the least regard for the animals behind their meals. But I'm not trying to defend every instance of eating products from factory farms; I'm only trying to defend some.

Second, when we consider any particular moral problem in isolation—whether to eat meat, whether to drive a car when we could take public transportation, whether to buy just about any consumer product where we don't know its back story—we can run the same argument and conclude that we ought to abstain. But now this very reasonable-sounding principle about not risking wrongdoing has become a more radical principle in practice. It's going to tell us to opt-out of all sorts of things.

Moreover, the advice isn't always going to align. Consider, for instance, the following line of reasoning. Beef cattle probably have lives that are worth living, even if those lives aren't good enough. If people didn't raise and slaughter them, those animals would never live at all. So, the practice of raising and slaughtering beef cattle is a net benefit to those animals. And, someone might argue, it's wrong to boycott a product where the demand for it provides such net benefits.

Now, do I accept this line of argument? No, I don't. But the point is not that this kind of reasoning is correct. Instead, the point is that if we apply the "Don't run the risk of wrongdoing" principle at the outset of inquiry—that is, before we've tried to evaluate the argument—then that principle tells us that it would be wrong to boycott beef. And if a principle gives us contradictory advice, then there's a problem somewhere.

My own view, you won't be surprised to learn, is that if we want to avoid decision paralysis, then we should stick with the idea that the burden of proof is on the person who says you've got an obligation. There are too many arguments out there for too many conflicting conclusions. If we look at each one in isolation, we end up having to give up everything before moral inquiry has even begun—or, worse, we end up with contradictory advice. So, while I agree, in the abstract, that it's morally wise to avoid running the risk of wrongdoing when there are no moral benefits to doing so, I suppose I think there's always a benefit to running such risks: namely, the benefit of being able to live our lives in the face of massive moral and empirical uncertainty.

Anja thinks that this is an objectionable way to approach our moral obligations:

> It is an attitude of seeing moral obligations as an inconvenient burden and an obstacle to living one's life as one would like to live it, and of complacently presuming that the way one is accustomed to live is just fine. But with that kind of mindset, it will be rather difficult to live up to the demands of morality, and moral progress will be very hard to come by. It seems more conducive to these ends to incorporate the goal of fulfilling as many of one's moral obligations as possible in one's conception of the life that one would like to live and presume that the way one is accustomed to live is probably not morally ideal yet.

By way of reply, part of me is inclined to say that moral obligations *are* an inconvenient burden and an obstacle to living your life as you'd like to live it. *Of course* they are! Morality tells us that we ought to do all sorts of things that it would be very nice not to have to do. It would be great to get things without paying for them! It would be great to tell lies whenever it's convenient! It would be great to get revenge after being slighted! Indeed, that's part of why it's so upsetting when people do these things and get away with them. Those people really are better off for acting wrongly; quite understandably, we resent that they've gotten ahead via wrongful means. So, there's no mistake in recognizing the tension between self-interest and morality; it's just the way things are. Morality limits us—albeit for good reason. But justified limits are still limits.

The other part of me, though, is inclined to push back in a different way. Anja seems to think that moral seriousness involves being ready and willing to submit to as many purported moral obligations as possible. I agree that that's a way of being morally serious, and lest anyone think otherwise, it's a way I respect quite deeply. But it isn't the only one. After all, arguments are everywhere; there are seemingly-endless pieces of creative reasoning you haven't considered. It's easy to be blown this way and that by the many persuasive things you hear. You can resist that, however, by thinking long and hard about what you can truly believe, what you can entertain not just in a classroom but in the day-to-day business of life. And if some arguments lead you to conclusions that you find unbelievable, at the end of sincere deliberations, then I can't see how you're failing to give morality the respect it deserves. You're trying to get things right. What's more important than that?

Let's now turn to Anja's second main criticism.

1.2 Complicity

After challenging my approach to the burden of proof, Anja criticizes what I say about (what I call) the Anti-Complicity Argument for Veganism—which is basically equivalent to her Refined Anti-Complicity Argument:

1. We are morally obligated not to be complicit in an action or practice that is morally wrong. (Moral premise.)
2. Not abstaining makes us complicit in factory farming. (Empirical premise.)
3. Factory farming is morally wrong. (Additional premise.)
4. We are morally obligated to abstain. (Abstinence; from 1, 2, and 3.)

The debate is about the first premise, which I reject and she accepts. While there's a lot to say here, I want to focus on her Spineless Steve case.

I claimed that there are factors that can mitigate complicity, including the degree of causal influence, the person's intentions, whether the person engages in offsetting, and so on. I also said that when these factors are present, it isn't obviously wrong to be complicit in factory farming—that was the point of my Sad Sally case (see p. 96). Anja replies to this by offering a structurally similar case, which goes as follows:

> Suppose there is a club devoted to perfecting the art of puppy torturing, called the Puppy Nazis. Steve's friends and family are all enthusiastic supporters of the Puppy Nazis. Steve himself does not want to encourage puppy torture; in fact, he hates it. But because it is important to him not to lose the respect of his family and friends, he joins them in paying a monthly membership fee to the club. If Steve thought that individual membership fees did make a difference to the torturing activities of the club, he would stop his payments immediately. But since

he believes—correctly, we may assume—that his payments do not make a difference, he continues to send the Puppy Nazis his monthly contributions. (The club has a large endowment and a lot of members so that individual membership fees do not influence the club's programming.) In order to make up for his complicity in puppy torturing, Steve occasionally donates money to an animal welfare organization devoted to helping dogs.

We're supposed to have the intuition that it's wrong for Steve to make monthly contributions to the Puppy Nazis. Then, we're supposed to infer that it's wrong for Sally to buy meat.

I'm inclined to agree that it's wrong for Steve to make monthly contributions to the Puppy Nazis; however, I'm not inclined to think that this case tells us much about Sally. Here's why.

First, Steve gives his money *directly* to the Puppy Nazis; he's paying the puppy torturers. Sally isn't doing that. Instead, she's directly supporting a grocery store that, I presume, it's generally permissible to support.

As soon as I say that, though, I should mention that Anja might not agree. The grocery store, after all, is complicit in factory farming. Is it wrong to support a business that's complicit in serious wrongdoing? Anja might think so. If she does, then this is yet another example of how radical her view ends up being. If it's wrong to shop at the grocery store for *anything*—including vegan food—then wrongdoing is extremely difficult to avoid!

In any case, the point is that *if* we think it's permissible to shop at the grocery store in general—as I do—then there's a moral difference between shopping at the grocery store and sending money to the Puppy Nazis.

Second, when we imagine the Puppy Nazis, we probably imagine one group acting in relative isolation. Even if we stipulate that Steve doesn't make a difference, the size and uniqueness of the group makes it *feel* like Steve's support matters; it's harder to believe that his monthly contribution is completely irrelevant to how many puppies are tortured. Moreover, since puppy torturing isn't that common, it feels much less plausible that there's the relevant gap between Steve's behavior and intentions. Those are very important points. If the arguments I made in my opening statement are correct, Sally's purchasing makes no difference to the farmers. I readily grant that if purchasing meat is likely to cause harm, even just in expectation, it's wrong to do it.

(Not incidentally, that's why I don't have much to say about Anja's Ultimate Anti-Complicity Argument. If she's correct that purchasing makes a difference, then I agree with her that purchasing is wrong. I don't think she's correct that individual purchases make a difference, either directly or indirectly, but I agree that difference-making is central to how we answer the central moral question here. Why don't I think individual purchases make a direct difference? See my opening statement. Why don't I think it makes an indirect difference? That is, why don't I think that others are going to be influenced by your choices? Because most of the time, no one notices what you buy—or if they do, they don't care.)

In any case, the point is that we need to focus squarely on cases where it's plausible that consumer choices don't have any impact on the amount of harm. Otherwise, our intuitions might mislead us. And if we condemn Steve because we think he makes a difference, then our intuition about that case isn't relevant to our assessment of Sally, who doesn't make a difference. On my view, her purchases may be less than ideal, but they aren't wrong.

For essentially the same reason, we need to focus on cases where it's plausible that people's behavior and intentions can come apart, which is easier to believe when we're dealing with enormous, entrenched parts of the economy and harder to believe when we're dealing with tiny groups that you'd have to seek out to support. And when we do focus on enormous, entrenched parts of the economy, this kind of gap between behavior and intention is perfectly ordinary, as shown by the fact that people vote for changes that don't match their purchasing habits. Some people object to the minimum wage because it isn't a living wage; they think it's unjust to pay people so little relative to their needs. Still, they buy fast food from places that pay the minimum wage. Are they acting wrongly? I don't think so. Even if it's unjust to pay people such low wages, *you personally* can't change people's income by not getting fries at McDonald's. (It might be *good* to join a boycott against McDonald's, but that doesn't mean it's wrong *not* to join the boycott.) Similarly, many meat eaters actually support a ban on factory farms; their values and their behavior come apart.[1] The value/behavior gap might be surprising, but it shouldn't be on reflection.

---

1. https://www.sentienceinstitute.org/aft-survey-2020.

How people *want* things to be, and how they act given the way things actually are, are different.

Let's take stock. I argued that Anja has the burden of proof; she argued the opposite. My take is that her case for my having the burden of proof depends largely on (a) her view about just how demanding morality is and (b) her understanding of what it means to take our moral obligations seriously. I disagree with her about how demanding morality is and I think there are other ways to be serious about our duties. So, I'm not changing my mind on this one.

I also argued that the Anti-Complicity Argument for Veganism isn't successful. Anja defended it. There again, our disagreement comes down to our views about how demanding morality is. I think that even though we participate in an economic order that harms many beings, human and non-human, we usually act permissibly when we engage in ordinary consumer activities—buying groceries, filling our cars with gas, picking up new clothes from big box retailers. Yes: things should be different; yes, people act wrongly when they directly harm or exploit others. But if you don't make a difference to whether those things happen, then *you* don't necessarily act wrongly.

2 Doing Better

All that said, you very well *might* be acting wrongly. Some of us are like Sad Sally, but many of us aren't. Many of us don't think about the harms at the ends of the many supply chains that deliver products to us. So, let's be real with ourselves about how well—or how poorly—we're doing.

In my opening statement, I argued that there are three factors that can mitigate complicity:

1. How much influence you've got
2. The degree to which you intend for the objectionable outcome to occur
3. Whether you do anything to offset or somehow "make up" for your complicity

If I'm right, then we're all roughly equal on the first point. Each individual's actions have an extraordinarily low chance of making a difference, which means that the vast majority of the time, they don't make a difference. Recall, though, the case of Meathead Mike—the one who doesn't make a difference, but would happily eat animal products even if he did. I think he might be doing something wrong. Or at least bad. In any event, Mike isn't winning any moral awards.

So, even if we're roughly equal on our degree of influence as individual consumers, we aren't roughly equal with respect to our intentions and whether we engage in offsetting. For instance, many of us don't care that much about animals, or at least we don't care that much about farmed animals. We'd prefer not to think about them, not to know what their lives are like, not to dwell on the experience of having a beak trimmed, a tail docked, or intensive confinement. We don't just enjoy animal products: we want them cheap and abundant, which means that they're going to be produced by methods we won't contemplate. We may not *like* factory farming, but we aren't exactly *opposed* to it either. We say things that make it seem like we wouldn't change our behavior even if we thought it made a difference: "I mean, farming provides a lot of jobs." "Chickens are pretty dumb, after all; they probably don't mind being in those facilities as much you think." "They're only pigs." "I just can't imagine living without cheese."

Likewise, many of us aren't doing much for animals. We aren't donating to groups like Mercy for Animals (mercyforanimals.org), which does undercover investigations to expose the conditions on factory farms; The Humane League (thehumaneleague.org), which works to improve animal welfare standards; or New Harvest (new-harvest.org), which funds research on alternatives to conventional meat. We aren't volunteering our time to do advocacy work. We aren't factoring animals into the way we vote. We aren't looking for opportunities to affect the way large organizations act—by, say, lobbying for "Meatless Mondays" (mondaycampaigns.org/meatless-monday) at schools or workplaces—which have a better chance of making an impact on production.

It follows that many of us are acting in ways that may be wrong—or, at least, are bad. And we could do better.

It might surprise you to learn that, on my view, one way to do better is to eat fewer animal products. I readily grant that people have good reasons to eat some animal products: they're tasty; they're nutritious; they're culturally valuable; they're cheap and convenient. However, we don't have to eat them all the time. You can eat an Impossible Whopper instead of the conventional kind; you can try some tofu in your stir fry; you can have lentil soup instead of chicken noodle. You can recognize that even if your actions don't make a difference to *production levels*, which is what ultimately matters, they can make a difference to *your attitudes toward animals*. They can help you adjust your sense of animals' moral importance, which can affect your judgments about the strength of your reasons, in any given situation, to make sacrifices for them. As you well know, Anja and I disagree about how extensive those sacrifices should be, but we certainly agree that it would be good for many of us to sacrifice more.

That's why I stopped eating animals a long time ago. I don't think it's always wrong to eat animal products, but I don't need them, and I feel better leaving them off my plate. But I don't feel better because I think I'm helping animals by the way I eat. I'm just trying to signal— mostly to myself—that animals matter. It feels a little silly sometimes, a bit self-righteous and sanctimonious. At the same time, it would feel strange to know everything I know and carry on as normal. The world is awful for many animals, and even if I don't have to acknowledge that with my actions, I want to acknowledge it. So I do.

Clearly, then, there's a sense in which I take it to be a "personal choice" whether to go vegan. I don't think there's a duty here, which just means that there's some liberty to make a call based on your personal circumstances. But I don't think it's a "personal choice" in another sense, where that expression is taken to mean that eating is one of those things that we shouldn't evaluate morally, in the way we shouldn't evaluate preferences regarding flavors. It's bad to learn about the plight of animals and then dismiss them. We ought to be doing *something* in response to their suffering, even if we have some latitude on what, exactly, that is.

3   Conclusion: Fitting Animals into Ethics

As we come to the end of this book, let's stand back and get some perspective. How should you understand the debate between Anja and me? What's the TL;DR version of this book?

Here's the way I see it. Some people tell the following story about our obligations to animals:

Once upon a time, people only cared about themselves and their kin. They slowly learned to expand their concern beyond the tribe, steadily building larger political communities. But those communities were still hierarchical: the leaders thought they mattered more than the followers, the men thought they mattered more than the women. Moreover, those communities broke along ethnic lines: those who looked and acted similarly were insiders; those who looked and acted differently were outsiders. As the years wore on, though, these hierarchies and divisions were steadily challenged. People stopped worshipping their leaders as gods. They questioned racial and ethnic segregation, then ended it. Women became equals. People came to recognize that the borders of their communities held no special moral significance. In other words, the circle of moral concern kept expanding—from self to kin, from kin to tribe, from tribe to country, from country to globe—and became more egalitarian at the same time. And eventually, the circle should expand to include animals. Yes, there will be resistance to including them; yes, there will be resistance to acknowledging their equality. But humans have learned to reject so many other arbitrary, prejudiced, self-serving, unjustified divisions and hierarchies. Humans have slowly become better at recognizing what is and isn't morally relevant. And the species boundary is irrelevant. Once we admit that, we'll see that our neighbors are no more important than distant strangers; and those strangers, no more important than animals.

I tell a different story. It goes like this:

Once upon a time, people lived in small tribal groups. Each person's actions had some impact on everyone else; everyone's loyalty to the tribe was a matter of survival. So, they developed norms that reflected that. Over time, though, tribes were conquered by other tribes, forming larger political orders, and other groups banded together to resist hostile takeovers. As communities grew and became more complicated, many of the old norms survived, though people were constantly refining and supplementing them as they faced new circumstances and challenges. Eventually, societies were rich enough to have a leisure class, including some people who spent their time theorizing about their communities' norms. By that point, the norms had taken on lives of their own: they'd been shaped by the accidents of history, a range of religious traditions, and an untold number of political and economic factors. But along the way, they'd shaped those things too. As a result, most theorizers, most of the time, couldn't disentangle all the arrows of influence. So, very few of those theorizers came to think of morality as a tool for solving the problems that come up when we live together. Moreover, most theorizers talked to other theorizers—people who value systematicity, consistency, comprehensiveness, and so on. Accordingly, most theorizers came up with ahistorical ways of understanding morality, building abstract and intricate systems that weren't tethered to the everyday realities of people's lives. If we insist on finishing their project in the present, making their systems maximally systematic, consistent, and comprehensive, we'll find that they have radical implications about animals. But while we *could* finish their project, whether we *should* depends on how much we value systematicity, consistency, and comprehensiveness.

If Anja had an opportunity to object at this juncture, she'd have a lot to say. What I've just written is wildly controversial; you should *not* think that she believes everything in the first story, nor should you think that it's easy or obvious to spell out the details of the second. But I'm not arguing for either story here. I'm simply sketching them to give you some perspective on the debate between Anja and me.

Anja accepts *something roughly like* the first story; I accept *something roughly like* the second. And our exchange looks very different depending on which of these stories you accept. These stories lurk behind so many dimensions of our conversation.

Seen from the vantage point of the first story, I look like a staunch moral conservative, doing his best to preserve his prejudices in the face of powerful arguments to the contrary. Consistency is dragging me in an obvious direction, but instead of giving in, I'm flailing against it, doing my best to preserve a status quo that—by my own admission—is one we should change. I'm backward; I'm confused; I'm on the wrong side of history. If this first story is correct, Anja is absolutely right in her criticisms of the way I approach the burden of proof and the demandingness of morality. She's holding my feet to the fire in exactly the way she should.

Seen from the vantage point of the second story, though, the contrast couldn't be more stark. I think we've inherited a tangle of moral intuitions and principles from the people who have come before us, but now live in a world quite different from the one that gave rise to them. The way forward isn't to perfect the systems that those intuitions and principles inspired, as our lives are built on top of

and around the inconsistencies we've inherited. Given all the conflicts between our most deeply-held values, the price of perfection is
too high. Instead, we need to be honest with ourselves about what
principles we can accept—and I mean *really* accept, in the sense that
we actually hold ourselves to the relevant standards—when we're
making real decisions about how to act. Sure: all our intuitions are
suspect; they can all be challenged. But some we can't abandon, and
because we can't abandon them, they serve as anchors for thought.
What's more, we need to be honest with ourselves about what we
can expect of ourselves and others. Not: "What standards *could*
we hold ourselves to?" but "What standards *will* we hold ourselves
to?" After all, morality can't solve any problems if we can't take it
seriously.

If we *can* take it seriously, though, then we can think long and
hard about how to make things better. Animals matter, and while
you *personally* don't have to rearrange your life for them, we
collectively need to do better. I hope we will.

Further Reading

General Introductions to and Overviews of Animal Ethics

DeGrazia, David. *Animal Rights: A Very Short Introduction* (Lanham: Rowman & Littlefield, 2001).

Fischer, Bob. *Animal Ethics—A Contemporary Introduction* (New York: Routledge, 2021).

Franklin, Julian H. *Animal Rights and Moral Philosophy* (New York: Columbia University Press, 2005).

Rowlands, Mark. *Animal Rights: Theory and Practice* (New York: Palgrave Macmillan, 2009).

Moral Standing and Moral Status

Bernstein, Mark H. *On Moral Considerability: An Essay on Who Morally Matters* (New York: Oxford University Press, 1998).

DeGrazia, David. 'Moral Status as a Matter of Degree?', *Southern Journal of Philosophy* 46 (2009): 181–198.

Horta, Oscar. 'Why the Concept of Moral Status Should Be Abandoned', *Ethical Theory and Moral Practice* 20 (2017): 899–910.

Kamm, Francis. 'Moral Status'. In *Intricate Ethics: Rights, Responsibilities, and Permissible Harm* (New York: Oxford University Press, 2006).

Rachels, James. 'Drawing Lines'. In Cass R. Sunstein and Martha Nussbaum (eds.), *Animal Rights: Current Debates and New Directions* (Oxford/New York: Oxford University Press, 2004), 162–174.

The Speciesism Objection and Replies

Horta, Oscar. 'What Is Speciesism?', *Journal of Agricultural and Environmental Ethics* 23 (2010): 243–266.

Kagan, Shelly. 'What's Wrong with Speciesism?', *Journal of Applied Philosophy* 33 (1) (2016): 1–21.

Singer, Peter. 'All Animals Are Equal'. In Hugh LaFolette (ed.), *Ethics in Practice* (Oxford: Blackwell, 2007, 3rd edition), 172–180.

Singer, Peter. 'Speciesism and Moral Status', *Metaphilosophy* 40 (2009): 567–581.

Singer, Peter. 'Reply to Williams'. In Jeffrey A. Schaler (ed.), *Peter Singer under Fire: The Moral Iconoclast Faces His Critics* (Chicago: Open Court, 2009), 97–101.

Singer, Peter. 'Why Speciesism Is Wrong: A Reply to Kagan', *Journal of Applied Philosophy* 33 (1) (2016): 31–35.

Williams, Bernard. 'The Human Prejudice'. In *Philosophy as a Humanistic Discipline* (Princeton: Princeton University Press, 2006), 135–152.

Potential and Typical Capacities and Moral Standing

Harman, Elizabeth. 'The Potentiality Problem', *Philosophical Studies* 114 (2003): 173–198.

Kagan, Shelly. *How to Count Animals, More or Less* (Oxford: Oxford University Press, 2019), esp. chapters 5–6.

McMahan, Jeff. *The Ethics of Killing* (Oxford/New York: Oxford University Press, 2002), esp. section 3.2.

Sumner, L. Wayne. *Abortion and Moral Theory* (Princeton: Princeton University Press, 2002), esp. 96–101.

Social Relations and Moral Obligations

Callicott, J. Baird. 'Animal Liberation and Environmental Ethics: Back Together Again'. In *In Defense of the Land Ethic: Essays in Environmental Philosophy* (Albany: State University of New York Press, 1989), 49–62.

Midgley, Mary. *Animals and Why They Matter* (Athens: University of Georgia Press, 1984).

Noddings, Nel. *Caring: A Relational Approach to Ethics and Moral Education* (Berkeley: University of California Press, 2013).

The Psychological Capacities of Animals

Andrews, Kristin. *The Animal Mind: An Introduction to the Philosophy of Animal Cognition* (New York: Routledge, 2020, 2nd edition).

Bekoff, Marc. *The Emotional Lives of Animals* (Novato: New World Library, 2007).

Bekoff, Marc, Allen, Collin, and Burghardt, Gordon M. (eds.). *The Cognitive Animal: Empirical and Theoretical Perspectives on Animal Cognition* (Cambridge, MA: MIT Press, 2002).

Griffin, Donald R. *Animal Minds* (Chicago: University of Chicago Press, 1992).

Rollin, Bernard E. *The Unheeded Cry: Animal Consciousness, Animal Pain, and Science* (Ames: Iowa State University Press, 1998).

Contractarianism and Animal Ethics

Carruthers, Peter. *The Animals Issue: Moral Theory in Practice* (New York: Cambridge University Press, 1992).

Cohen, Andrew I. 'Contractarianism, Other-Regarding Attitudes, and the Moral Standing of Nonhuman Animals', *Journal of Applied Philosophy* 24 (2) (2007): 188–200.

Rowlands, Mark. 'Contractarianism and Animal Rights', *Journal of Applied Philosophy* 14 (1997): 235–247.

Utilitarianism and Animal Ethics

Frey, Raymond G. 'Utilitarianism and Animals'. In Tom L. Beauchamp and R. G. Frey (eds.), *The Oxford Handbook of Animal Ethics* (Oxford/New York: Oxford University Press, 2011).

Matheny, Gaverick. 'Utilitarianism and Animals'. In Peter Singer (ed.), *In Defense of Animals: The Second Wave* (Oxford: Blackwell, 2006).

Singer, Peter. *Animal Liberation* (New York, HarperCollins, 2002, 3rd edition).

Accounts of Moral Standing Inspired by Both Aristotle and Kant

Korsgaard, Christine. *Fellow Creatures* (Oxford/New York: Oxford University Press, 2018).

Nussbaum, Martha. *Frontiers of Justice: Disability, Nationality, Species Membership* (Cambridge, MA: Harvard University Press, 2006).

Rights-Based Accounts of Animal Ethics

Abbate, Cheryl. 'Animal Rights and the Duty to Harm', *ZEMO* 3 (2020): 5–26.

Regan, Tom. *Defending Animal Rights* (Urbana: University of Illinois Press, 2001).

Regan, Tom. *The Case for Animal Rights* (Berkeley/Los Angeles: University of California Press, 2004, revised edition).

Wise, Stephen. *Rattling the Cage: Toward Legal Rights for Animals* (Cambridge: Perseus Books, 2000).

Compassion-Centered Moral Theories

Gruen, Lori. *Entangled Empathy: An Alternative Ethic for Our Relationships with Animals* (New York: Lantern Books, 2015).

Schopenhauer, Arthur. *On the Basis of Morals*. In Christopher Janaway (trans. and ed.), *The Two Fundamental Problems of Ethics* (Cambridge/New York: Cambridge University Press, *1841/2009), 113–258.

Slote, Michael. *The Ethics of Care and Empathy* (London/New York: Routledge, 2007).

Slote, Michael. *Moral Sentimentalism* (Oxford/New York: Oxford University Press, 2011).

The Ethics of Killing and the Value of (Different Kinds of) Lives

Frey, R. G. 'Moral Standing, the Value of Lives, and Speciesism.' In Hugh LaFolette (ed.), *Ethics in Practice* (Oxford: Blackwell, 2007, 3rd edition), 181–191.

McMahan, Jeff. *The Ethics of Killing: Problems at the Margins of Life* (Oxford/New York: Oxford University Press, 2002), esp. chapter 3.

Singer, Peter. *Practical Ethics* (Cambridge: Cambridge University Press, 2011, 3rd edition), chapters 4–7.

Visak, Tatjana, Garner, Robert, and Singer, Peter. *The Ethics of Killing Animals* (Oxford/New York: Oxford University Press, 2016).

The Causal Inefficacy Problem

Budolfson, Mark Bryant. 'The Inefficacy Objection to Consequentialism and the Problem with the Expected Consequences Response', *Philosophical Studies* 176 (7) (2019): 1711–1724.

Fischer, Bob. *The Ethics of Eating Animals: Usually Bad, Sometimes Wrong, Often Permissible* (New York: Routledge, 2020).

McMullen, Steven, and Matthew C. Halteman. 'Against Inefficacy Objections: The Real Economic Impact of Individual Consumer Choices on Animal Agriculture', *Food Ethics* 2 (2) (2019): 93–110.

Nefsky, Julia. 'How You Can Help, Without Making a Difference', *Philosophical Studies* 174 (11) (2017): 2743–2767.

Complicity Arguments

Brennan, Jason, and Peter Martin Jaworski. 'Markets Without Symbolic Limits', *Ethics* 125 (4) (2015): 1053–1077.

Kutz, Christopher. *Complicity: Ethics and Law for a Collective Age* (New York: Cambridge University Press, 2000).

Shahar, Dan C. *Why It's OK to Eat Meat* (New York: Routledge, 2021).

Glossary

Abstain Refrain from purchasing factory-farmed animal products.

(Not-)Abstinence We are (not) morally obligated to abstain.

Atrocities against animals Factory farming, frivolous invasive experimentation on animals without any medical benefits, and species-inappropriate treatment and confinement as well as trauma-inducing training for purposes of human entertainment.

Autonomy Autonomy is a sophisticated form of practical rationality, which centrally includes the capacity to set ends for oneself and act on the basis of reasons.

Autonomy criterion for moral standing X has moral standing if, and only if, X is autonomous.

Basic interests The basic interests of a being are those interests that must be satisfied for it to be able to live what amounts to a minimally decent life for a creature of its kind, interests such as access to adequate nutrition, not experiencing pain, living in a species-appropriate habitat, being able to properly exercise its capacities, staying alive, etc.

Benign vegan diet A kind of diet that consists of synthetically produced foods or plant-parts that have been harvested without causing more than a minimal amount of harm, possibly supplemented with parts from animals who died of natural causes or through an accident.

Burden of proof In a debate, the person with the burden of proof is the one who has to establish something. In contrast, the other person assumes the default position.

Categorical imperative The fundamental principle in Kant's ethics in terms of which the moral law is expressed. There are different formulas of the categorical imperative. The third formula is especially popular. It says to never treat autonomous beings as mere means but always at the same time as ends.

Characteristic function   The characteristic function of X is its essential activity; it determines X's good and interests.

Comparable   A and B are comparable just in case they can be ordinally ranked relative to one another, such as "first, second, third" and "better and worse."

Compassion   Compassion is empathic concern for another's flourishing.

Complicity   X is complicit in a certain practice or action W if, and only if, (a) X voluntarily does an action S that supports W, and (b) X has no legitimate excuse for not knowing that S supports W or what W is.

Complicity, influential   X is influentially complicit in a certain practice or action W if, and only if, X is complicit in W and X's support of W makes a difference to the degree of moral badness or goodness of W.

Contractarianism   Contractarianism is a meta-ethical position on which moral laws are understood to be jointly legislated by free rational agents through a mutual agreement, convention, or contract in such a way that they thereby bind themselves to these laws.

Empathy   Empathy is a capacity that enables one to recognize others as beings with a good and to emotionally identify with them in such a way that what is good and bad for them affects one in the same kind of way as what is good and bad for oneself.

Equal Consideration Principle   Similar interests deserve equal consideration in our moral deliberations regardless of whose interests they are.

Expected utility calculation   A calculation in which the utility of all possible outcomes is weighted according to the probability that each outcome will occur.

Experience machine   An experience machine is a machine to which we can "plug in" that stimulates our brain to generate experiences, previously chosen by us, that are phenomenally indistinguishable from ordinary experiences.

Flourishing (wellbeing, welfare, or happiness)   Flourishing is wellbeing that can be positively or negatively impacted by external influences and corresponds to the degree to which one's interests are realized overall.

Flourishing criterion   X has moral standing if, and only if, X is capable of flourishing.

Good of a being   The good of a being consists in performing its characteristic function well; when that happens, the being flourishes.

Good/bad for a being   α is good/bad for X if, and only if, α realizes/frustrates an interest of X.

Good/bad, absolute   A good/bad is absolute if, and only if, it is good/bad *simpliciter*.

Good/bad, relational   A good/bad is relational if, and only if, it is good/bad for a particular being or a particular group of beings.

Good criterion for moral standing   X has moral standing if, and only if, X is capable of flourishing, which, in turn, is the case if, and only if, X has a good for which it strives.

Harming and helping   X harms/helps Y if, and only if, X acts in a way such that Y flourishes less/more than they would have flourished if X had not acted in this way.

Having an interest   X has an interest in α if, and only if, X has a stake in α such that X stands to gain or lose depending on what happens with respect to α.

Higher moral status   (1) A has higher moral status$_1$ than B if, and only if, there is at least one interest of A that has more weight than a similar interest of B, and there is no interest of B that has more weight than a similar interest of A. (2) A has higher moral status$_2$ than B if, and only if, A's intrinsic value is greater than B's intrinsic value.

Human centrism   X has moral standing if, and only if, X is a member of the human species.

Human exceptionalism   There is a hierarchy of moral considerability among beings with moral standing, and human beings are at the very top in that they have higher moral status, or morally matter more, than all other beings.

Human prioritism   There is a hierarchy of beings with moral standing, and human beings are at the very top in that their interests generally have greater magnitude than the interests of all other beings, even if the interests in question are of the same type.

Impermissible action/practice   an action/practice that is morally wrong.

Incommensurable   A and B are incommensurable just in case they cannot be ranked on a cardinal scale. That is, there are no specific units in which A's being better or worse than B could be measured.

Interest-profile conception of higher moral status A has higher moral status than B if, and only if, A has a richer interest profile than B.

Intrinsic value X is intrinsically valuable if, and only if, it is valuable on its own, or in its own right. X is extrinsically valuable if, and only if, X is valuable in virtue of its relation to other things.

Kantian respect Respect for autonomous beings consists in recognizing their status as ends in themselves and thus never treating them as mere means but always at the same time as ends, that is, roughly, never treating them in ways to which they would not consent if they expressed a view.

Moral agent X is a moral agent if, and only if, X is morally responsible for her actions.

Moral debate A moral debate is a debate about whether a purported moral obligation actually is a moral obligation.

Moral standing (moral considerability) X has moral standing (is morally considerable) if, and only if, all moral agents (a) have moral obligations to X, or (b) are morally obligated to take X's interests into consideration in their moral deliberations.

Morally obligatory (morally required) Morally obligatory (morally required) actions are demanded of us by the laws of morality; they are our moral duties and ought to be done. An action is morally obligatory if, and only if, it is morally impermissible not to do the action.

Morally permissible An action is morally permissible if, and only if, it is not morally obligatory not to do the action.

Morally wrong An action is morally wrong if, and only if, it is morally impermissible, that is, if, and only if, not doing the action is morally obligatory.

Moral-wrongness cost A moral-wrongness cost is a morally relevant cost that is derived from the cost of a moral violation.

No-harm obligation Except in special circumstances, we are obligated not to harm any living being.

Order threshold This is a spot where the difference of one sale is going to be the thing that leads a store to reduce their order for some animal product by a case, or pallet, or whatever their ordering unit is.

Ought to An action ought to be done if, and only if, it is morally obligatory.

Ought-implies-can principle X is morally obligated to do something only if it is possible for X to do it.

Pro tanto reason A pro tanto reason is a reason that speaks for/against doing something and indicates the extent to which doing it would be a good/bad thing but can be outweighed by other relevant reasons.

Reciprocity condition of morality (i) A has moral obligations to B if, and only if, B has moral obligations to A; and (ii) A is morally obligated to take B's interests into consideration in her moral deliberations if, and only if, B is obligated to take A's interests into consideration in his moral deliberations.

Revolutionary scenario A revolutionary scenario is a situation in which abstaining from an individual purchase of a factory-farmed animal product would make a difference to the production quantity of a factory farm by being a partial or indirect cause for an adjustment of its production quantity.

Sentience X is sentient if, and only if, it is capable of experiencing pleasure and pain, understood broadly as positively or negatively valenced states of consciousness.

Sentience criterion for moral standing X has moral standing if, and only if, X is sentient.

Similar interests Interest I_A and interest I_B are similar if, and only if, I_A and I_B are of the same type and equal in magnitude.

Speciesism Speciesism is discrimination directed against a being or group of beings based on their species.

Status egalitarianism There is no hierarchy of moral considerability among beings with moral standing.

Threshold scenario A threshold scenario is a situation in which an individual purchase of a factory-farmed animal product would make a difference to the production quantity of some factory farm by triggering an adjustment in the supply chain.

Utility Utility is a measure of something that's valuable. If, for instance, wellbeing is valuable, then more utility = greater wellbeing and less utility = lower wellbeing.

(Not-)Veganism We are (not) morally obligated to adopt a vegan diet.

Welfare utilitarianism's main tenet An action is morally right if, and only if, it maximizes the total amount of flourishing in the world.

Bibliography

Anderson, Elizabeth. 2004. 'Animal Rights and the Values of Nonhuman Life'. In Cas Sunstein and Martha Nussbaum (eds.), *Animal Rights: Current Debates and New Directions*. Oxford/New York: Oxford University Press, 277–298.

Aristotle. 340 BCE/*2019. *Nicomachean Ethics*, trans. and ed. by Terence Irwin. Indianapolis: Hackett Publishing Company.

Bentham, Jeremy. 1780/1789. *An Introduction to the Principles of Morals and Legislation*. London: T. Payne and Sons.

Bramble, Ben. 2021. 'Painlessly Killing Predators', *Journal of Applied Philosophy* 38 (2): 217–225.

Dawkins, Richard. 1995. *River Out of Eden*. New York: Basic Books.

DeGrazia, David. 1996. *Taking Animals Seriously: Mental Life and Moral Status*. Cambridge: Cambridge University Press.

Diamond, Cora. 1978. 'Eating Meat and Eating People', *Philosophy* 53: 465–479.

Donaldson, Sue, and Will Kymlicka. 2011. *Zoopolis*. New York: Oxford University Press.

Feinberg, Joel. 1984. *Harm to Others*, vol. 1 of *The Moral Limits of the Criminal Law*. Oxford/New York: Oxford University Press.

Fischer, Bob. 2020. *The Ethics of Eating Animals: Usually Bad, Sometimes Wrong, Often Permissible*. New York: Routledge.

Foot, Philippa. 2001. *Natural Goodness*. Oxford: Oxford University Press.

Hobbes, Thomas. *1651/1996. *Leviathan*, ed. by Richard Tuck. Cambridge/New York: Cambridge University Press.

Horta, Oscar. 2017. 'Animal Suffering in Nature: The Case for Intervention', *Environmental Ethics* 39 (3): 261–279.

Huemer, Michael. 2019. *Dialogues on Ethical Vegetarianism*. New York: Routledge.

Hursthouse, Rosalind. 1999. *On Virtue Ethics*. Oxford: Oxford University Press.

James, William. *1896/2010. 'The Will to Believe'. In *The Will to Believe, And Other Essays in Popular Philosophy*. Auckland: Floating Press, 13–45.

Kagan, Shelly. 2019. *How to Count Animals, More or Less.* Oxford/New York: Oxford University Press.

Kant, Immanuel. *1785/2012. *Groundwork for the Metaphysics of Moral*, trans. and ed. by Mary Gregor and Jens Timmermann. Cambridge/New York: Cambridge University Press. Cited according to the pagination of vol. 4 of the Academy Edition of Kant's works.

Kant, Immanuel. *1797/1996. *The Metaphysics of Morals*, trans. and ed. by Mary Gregor. Cambridge/New York: Cambridge University Press. Cited according to the pagination of vol. 6 of the Academy Edition of Kant's works.

Kant, Immanuel. 1900–. *Gesammelte Schriften*, ed. by the Academy of Sciences at Berlin. Berlin: de Gruyter.

Kant, Immanuel. 2012. *Lectures on Ethics*, trans. and ed. by Peter L. Heath, and ed. by Jerome B. Schneewind. Cambridge: Cambridge University Press. Cited as 'Lectures on Ethics,' according to the pagination of vol. 27 of the Academy Edition of Kant's works.

Kittay, Eva Federer. 2005. 'At the Margins of Moral Personhood', *Ethics* 116: 100–131.

Korsgaard, Christine. 2018. *Fellow Creatures.* Oxford/New York: Oxford University Press.

Leibniz, Gottfried Wilhelm. 1710. *Theodicy; Essays on the Goodness of God, the Freedom of Man, and the Origin of Evil*, trans. by E. M. Huggard.

Marquis, Don. 1989. 'Why Abortion Is Immoral', *Journal of Philosophy* 68: 183–202.

McMahan, Jeff. 2002. *The Ethics of Killing: Problems at the Margins of Life.* Oxford/New York: Oxford University Press.

McMahan, Jeff. 2010. 'The Meat Eaters'. *The New York Times*, September 19, 2010. https://archive.nytimes.com/opinionator.blogs.nytimes.com/2010/09/19/the-meat-eaters/

Midgley, Mary. 1984. *Animals and Why They Matter.* Athens: University of Georgia Press.

Mill, John Stuart. 1863. *Utilitarianism.* London: Parker, Son, and Bourn.

Norcross, Alastair. 2004. 'Puppies, Pigs, and People: Eating Meat and Marginal Cases', *Philosophical Perspectives* 18: 229–245.

Nozick, Robert. 1974. *Anarchy, State, and Utopia.* New York: Basic Books.

Nussbaum, Martha. 2006. *Frontiers of Justice: Disability, Nationality, Species Membership.* Cambridge, MA: Harvard University Press.

Plant, Michael. 2019. 'Doing Good Badly: Philosophical Issues Related to Effective Altruism'. Dissertation, Oxford University.

Rawls, John. 1971. *A Theory of Justice.* Cambridge, MA: Harvard University Press.

Regan, Tom. 2004. *The Case for Animal Rights.* Berkeley/Los Angeles: University of California Press.

Scanlon, Tim. 1998. *What We Owe to Each Other*. Cambridge, MA: Belknap Press.

Schopenhauer, Arthur. *1841/2009. *On the Basis of Morals*. In Christopher Janaway (trans. and ed.), *The Two Fundamental Problems of Ethics*. Cambridge/New York: Cambridge University Press, 113–258.

Sebo, Jeff. 2018. 'The Moral Problem of Other Minds', *The Harvard Review of Philosophy* 25: 51–70.

Singer, Peter. 1975. *Animal Liberation*. New York: HarperCollins.

Turkel, Studs. 2005. *American Dreams: Lost and Found*. New York: The New Press.

Voltaire. 1759/2006. *Candide, Or Optimism*. In Roger Pearson (trans. and ed.), *Candide and Other Stories*. Oxford/New York: Oxford University Press.

Williams, Bernard. 2006. 'The Human Prejudice'. In *Philosophy as a Humanistic Discipline*. Princeton: Princeton University Press, 135–152.

Wood, Allen. 1998. 'Kant on Duties Regarding Nonrational Nature', *Proceedings of the Aristotelian Society Supplement* 72: 189–210.

Index

For Product Safety Concerns and Information please contact our EU
representative GPSR@taylorandfrancis.com
Taylor & Francis Verlag GmbH, Kaufingerstraße 24, 80331 München, Germany

www.ingramcontent.com/pod-product-compliance
Lightning Source LLC
Chambersburg PA
CBHW050414280326
41932CB00013BA/1862

* 9 7 8 1 0 3 2 5 7 9 5 7 3 *